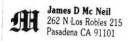

D0359898

The Seattle School of Theology & Psychology
2501 Elliott Ave.
Seattle, WA 98121
theseattleschool.edu

COUPLES
IN
COLLUSION

COUPLES IN COLLUSION

by
Jürg Willi

Jason Aronson/New York and London
In collaboration with Hunter House Inc.

CONTENTS

PREFACE TO THE U.S. EDITION................................. xi

INTRODUCTION xiii

1. COLLUSION AND THE BATTLE OF THE SEXES...................... 1
   The Behavior of Females in Therapy....................... 2
   The Behavior of Males in Therapy......................... 4
   Behavioral Differences between Men and Women
      Determined by Partner Orientation..................... 7
   Implications for Contemporary Society.................... 11
   Perspective on the Future............................... 14

2. DYNAMIC PRINCIPLES OF PARTNER RELATIONSHIPS................ 17
   The Demarcation Principle............................... 18
   Progressive and Regressive Defense Behavior............. 21
   The Balance of Self-Esteem.............................. 24

3. THE PHASES OF MARRIAGE AND THEIR TYPICAL CRISES........... 31
   The Formation of the Stable Couple...................... 32
   Construction and Creativity............................. 35
   Mid-Life Crisis... 37
   Marriage in Old Age..................................... 43

4. THE CONCEPT OF COLLUSION. AN EXAMPLE...................... 45

5. PATTERNS OF COLLUSION.................................... 57
   Love as Oneness in Narcissistic Collusion............... 60
   Love as Caring and Nourishing in Oral Collusion......... 80
   Love as Security through Dependence in
      Anal-Sadistic Collusion............................... 95
   Love as Confirmation of Masculinity in
      Phallic-Oedipal Collusion............................120
   Collusion Patterns are not Marriage Categories..........139

6. COLLUSION: THE UNCONSCIOUS INTERPLAY OF PARTNERS........141
   Intraindividual Balance................................141
   Interindividual Balance................................144

Conjunction of Intraindividual and
Interindividual Balances...................................... 146
Partners' Common Unconscious............................... 147
From Partner Choice to Marital Conflict...................... 148
Collusive Stalemate... 152
Divorce and Resolution of Collusion......................... 153

7. COLLUSION AND PARTNER CHOICE................................ 157
A Key-in-Lock Operation or a Process of
Mutual Adjustment?... 158
Is Every Marital Conflict Collusive?........................... 163
Bibliographical References to Collusion and
Collusive Group Processes.................................... 167

8. TRIANGULATION OF COUPLE CONFLICT............................ 171
Alliance Against a Threatening Third Person................. 172
The Third Person as a Buffer and Mediator.................. 174
The Third Person as a Partner in a
Unilateral Alliance.. 176
Distribution of Roles in the Marital Triangle................. 177
The Role of Children in Marital Conflict..................... 187

9. PSYCHOSOMATIC ILLNESS OF THE COUPLE......................... 193
Psychosomatic Symptoms as Neutralizers.................... 193
Psychosomatic Illness as a Joint Defense Syndrome........ 199
Psychosomatic Communication................................ 202
Dialectics of Debit and Credit................................. 205
Help-Rejection as a Symptom of Illness...................... 207
Forms of Psychosomatic Illness of the Couple.............. 211
Psychosomatic Collusion in the Doctor-Patient
Relationship.. 216

10. CHANGING THERAPEUTIC PERSPECTIVES.......................... 219
Difficulties for the Psychoanalyst in
Couples Therapy.. 219
The Effect of Individual Psychoanalysis on
Partner Conflict... 223
The Therapist in Collusion with his Client—
as Analogy to the Client's Marriage......................... 229
Goals of Joint Therapy... 230
Applying the Concept of Collusion to
Marriage Therapy... 232

APPENDIX. A CASE MODEL: Ingmar Bergman's
  Scenes from a Marriage... 237

BRIEF GLOSSARY OF TERMS.. 255

BIBLIOGRAPHY 257

INDEX 263

PREFACE TO THE U.S. EDITION

Are there cultural differences in the application of psychotherapy? I believe there are. Psychoanalysis probably could not have originated in the United States. The American contribution to psychotherapy reflects the pioneer spirit of a young culture convinced that everything can be produced, that everything can be changed. When confronted with a problem in therapy, an American will ask: "What can we do about it?"—whereas a European prefers the question: "How can we understand this?" I consider both questions relevant since they can be complementary.

In this book I wish to synthesize the systemic perspective on couple conflicts—one of the essential paradigms of American family therapy—with the analytical approach. I believe that the relationship between a couple is a system in which the behavioral pattern of one is determined by the other and vice versa. The choice of partner has generally not come about by chance; rather it is based upon an inner affinity between the partners. The collusion principle is seen as the unconscious interplay of two partners who are looking for each other in the hope of coming to terms *together* with those conflicts and frustrations in their lives which they have not yet managed to resolve. The crisis is connected to the disillusionment which results when this common defense syndrome necessarily collapses.

Zurich, August 1980

INTRODUCTION

This book is concerned with disturbed relationships between two people. It focuses upon the difficulties which they encounter once they have made the decision to form a lasting bond. Whatever legal status they assume, partners who make a commitment to each other establish a division of roles between them. They assist, complement or replace each other in specific tasks, taking responsibility for certain aspects of their joint life according to their inclinations and abilities. In this way the couple becomes more efficient as a unit, each partner is personally more satisfied and has a feeling of inter-dependence and solidarity, and the relationship becomes more meaningful. As the partners grow increasingly attuned to each other a 'mutual self' is created, such that the inner life of one cannot develop independently from that of the other.

This mutual self may ultimately prove dangerous however, binding the couple in a destructive loop.

My experience in marriage therapy over the years has shown me that marital conflicts revolve around similar themes and are carried out according to specific, recurring dynamic patterns. The couple become a polarized unit held together only by a common theme of conflict. They see themselves as irreconcilable opposites; when in fact they complement each other and create a whole. This passionate interplay between partners, or intradyadic dynamic, is the subject of this book. Other aspects of marital conflict are beyond its scope and will be mentioned only very briefly: for example the question of marriage as an institution, the marital conflicts resulting from unsatisfactory social conditions, etc.

Marital dysfunctions or ailing marriages, as they are generally understood, appear to me to result from nothing other than the same problems that one finds in all marriages—only in a more intensified form. This book is therefore written not only for specialists, but for all those who are interested in gaining a deeper insight into marital conflicts.

Although marriage is taken as the main example of the dynamics of a dyad, I choose the title *Couples in Collusion* because the unconscious interplay of partners which is described is true of any two person relationship. It is in marriage, the very closest of partnerships, that this interplay can most clearly be observed.

1

COLLUSION AND THE
BATTLE OF THE SEXES

The Behavior of Females in Therapy:
A Value-Based Interpretation

The Behavior of Males in Therapy:
A Value-Based Interpretation

Behavioral Differences between Men and
Women Determined by Partner Orientation

Implications for Contemporary Society

Perspective on the Future: The Concepts of
'Masculine' and 'Feminine' Replaced by 'Human'

My name is Jurg Willi, I am a psychiatrist and psychotherapist. I am male. I assume that this sort of introduction does not contain any unusual information; however, it is designed to define my position. That is, I wish to point to my limitations in contributing to this particular topic. One of my most important experiences in couples therapy has been the recognition of the high degree of sexual bias in my therapeutic interpretations of the conflicts among couples. This experience—which was barely mentioned during my education—has been a shock, and it has led me to doubt seriously whether I am capable of practicing as a couples therapist. The knowledge that other psychotherapist authors have the same difficulty is not sufficient consolation.

I am writing about the battle of the sexes as a *male* psychotherapist. I am making an honest attempt to understand women and I am aware that I am in the process of learning, but I confess that the women's movement has opened my eyes to the hypocrisy of men and to discriminations of which we men have not been aware. I shall not enter much into the details of the social background to this battle and neither shall I say much about the functional division of roles in the household, in childrearing, and in the job responsibilities of the future (although there is much to be achieved here). I do not intend to ignore the significance of these problems, but I would rather prefer to restrict myself to *one* aspect of them, namely, the dimension which I call 'the partner relationship'.

I write as a *psychotherapist*; that is, my departure point is the experience which I have gained with couples who have asked for therapeutic help in dealing with their problems. I am here concerned less with the sociological and psychological background (which has been the usual approach to this topic) than with the behavior through which this battle of the sexes is carried out.

To begin with, there is a difference in the way in which a woman and a man present themselves during couples therapy. In this chapter I shall attempt to describe the *contemporary situation in therapy*. In doing so, I am not saying that it is divine, designed by nature and impermeable for all time. Being aware that I am a male therapist, I would merely like to describe how I perceive the man and the woman in my practice, and in the therapy practices of those female colleagues of mine whom I have had the chance of observing. Given individual deviations, I believe that I have been able to observe the typical behavior of men and women during therapy.

The Behavior of Females in Therapy: A Value-Based Interpretation

In most cases, it is the woman who takes the initiative and goes to the psychotherapist or marriage counselor. It is also far more often she who seeks help outside of the partner relationship during a crisis, usually amongst relatives or friends. During the couple session the woman is generally in the position of plaintiff. She accuses the man of indifference towards her, of avoidance, of lack of understanding, of oppression, and unfaithfulness. Far more than the man, she complains of a variety of physical and mental symptoms such as nervousness, exhaustion, headaches, dizziness, constipation, insomnia, etc. She also feels depression, moodiness, lack of interest in life, and suicidal impulses. She either appears fragile, weak and in need of help or threatens divorce. She complains that she has to raise the children alone and does not have the opportunity for self-realization. The model relationship which she has in mind is based upon more absolute standards. She is looking for intimacy, togetherness, openness, mutual commitment and compassion, and absolute faithfulness. To her mind, a deviation from these ideals would mean the end of the relationship or the death of her lovelife. Most of the time she is convinced that it is better to have high and unfulfillable expectations of a relationship than to reduce those expectations to a practical level. She persists in them and reinforces them through support from her allies—children, friends or relatives—or by becoming ill. She is afraid that her expectations may not be taken seriously and thinks that they might be recognized if she used emotional behavior to reinforce her wishes. She is disillusioned about the relationship more often than the man; she feels betrayed and believes that she has invested more in the relationship than he. She expects the man to actively support her personal development.

Many of these observations can be statistically supported (*D. Beckmann* 1976, 1977, *Duss, Fuller* 1963). However, the woman's behavior can be interpreted in a variety of ways, even if one attempts to adopt a value-free and scientific approach. *Psychiatric nomenclature* might label her *hysterical*. There is a tendency in the woman towards pretentious, theatrical and highly emotionally-charged behavior. She uses her relationships with third parties—including that with her therapist—to manipulate her partner and intrigue against him. Her suffering and complaining are attempts at blackmail and her feeble call for help is veiled tyranny. Her excessive complaining is considered irrational and unrealistic, devoid of any logic or objectivity and evidence of regressive and infantile behavior. She is considered immature; expecting assistance from others without the willingness to accept responsibility for her own failure.

The very same behavior can also be interpreted in a positive light. Because of the more developed emotional openness and capacity to be vulnerable (*Richter* 1974), the woman is much more motivated to seek assistance when in an unsatisfactory partner relationship and is not satisfied with half-truths. She puts more effort than the man into the maintenance of the relationship and into trying to find mutual fulfillment together. To be sure, she suffers more as a result of her more highly developed emotional openness, yet she is apparently healthier than the man (*Richter* 1974, *Beckmann* 1976). The capacity to admit her own weaknesses and to ask for help, turns out to be her strength. Because she is able to make use of regressive behavior under stress she can regain her balance much more easily and is therefore able to survive more difficult crises. Her tendency to regression and somatization definitely furthers the interests of the ego. *Beckmann* (1976) questions, quite correctly, whether encouraging women to move towards the 'masculine ideal' is indeed desirable.

The emotionally exaggerated, 'plaintiff' behavior of the woman can be seen as the only adequate reaction to the emotional imperviousness of the man. Desperate, and feeling that she is not being taken seriously by him, she concludes that the only way to penetrate his world is to use powerful weapons.

Depending on personal bias, a scientific observer will interpret the same behavior differently. Whenever one assumes that one is capable of making value-free observations, one risks making very biased observations.

The Behavior of Males in Therapy: A Value-Based Interpretation

Men generally resist coming to couples therapy. They tend towards the opinion that marital conflicts should be resolved within the relationship and not be opened up to third parties. They feel uneasy in a therapy situation. They don't admit to the need for therapy, but do wish to make a good impression, however, and so agree to go along just once in order to discuss with the therapist how the woman could best be helped. Usually, they expect no more than some brief advice. When this does not happen they question the competence of the therapist. They believe that voicing disputes during therapy would only make things worse. They react defensively to the woman's complaints, control their reactions, evade attacks, trivialize reproaches and try to reduce points of contention to objective practical problems. Despite the woman's dissatisfaction and the dramatic domestic scenes, they are apparently content with the marriage and do not wish to make any basic changes. The woman's apparently exaggerated reproaches allow them to present her to the therapist as a patient: "Why don't you go ahead and see how you get along with such an irrational woman. As you can obviously see, I can't possibly respond to such arguments."

It is difficult for the man to admit to his insecurity and weaknesses during therapy; there is a fear that this will transfer power to the woman who will then turn the confession against him. Men do not like to show their hand, and they are convinced that they can manage their own problems. Moreover, they believe that a man's capacity to handle stress must be unlimited. They will tolerate the woman's reproaches for a long time without batting an eyelid. They believe that they should be able to offer their heads as punching balls to women. It is very uncommon for a man to lose control of his reactions during therapy, or to show anger or make threatening gestures.

It is man's overcompensating control in suppressing his own feelings of anxiety, guilt and weakness which prevent him from perceiving the woman's feelings and reacting to them. He prides himself on his adroitness at countering the woman's attacks without losing control. She, however, experiences this imperviousness as arrogance, mental cruelty and sadism.

Depending on personal bias, this behavior can also be interpreted in a variety of ways. In conventional *psychiatry*, this typically male behavior has *no psychopathological labels*. It is rarely diagnosed as pathological, even though shorter life expectancy amongst men, the higher incidence of serious psychosomatic illnesses, of suicide, of alcoholism and criminality should be evidence that men are sick more often than women. This male behavior corresponds to pathogenic defense behavior. *Men are known for their strong identification with societal norms*. It would be a contradiciton if psychiatry diagnosed as abnormal a behavior which corresponded completely with society's existing values and norms. After all, where would we end if we were to label the abnormal as normal and the 'well adjusted' as abnormal? Men fear that they will not meet their standards of performance and efficiency because of the destabilizing effects of therapy. And in their work relationships they fear the loss of some of their control and the ridicule resulting from a higher degree of emotional openness. Men have difficulty revealing their personal problems and the threat of an emotional breakdown. Under such circumstances they tend to cling more ardently to the masculine role model in the hope of finding renewed strength. They are afraid that if they show stress they will be lost forever, because the partner may misuse this weakness and take advantage of a chance to destroy them. I have observed physical violence in marriage—a much discussed topic today—with these types of men:

—Alcoholics;

—Men who have impotency problems and feel ridiculed by their women;

—Elderly men who feel anxiety over their reduced energy level and who fear that their younger wives no longer take them seriously;

—Blue collar workers who sense disrespect from their wives because of their low earning power.

Strauss (1974) proved statistically that there was no correlation between strength and physical brutality among husbands of the working class whose social respectability (admired characteristics, job performance, material flow of goods) was high. Among working class husbands whose social resources were poor, however, the correlation between masculine strength and brutality was 0.49. This phenomenon can also be interpreted differently: it could be said that men use any means to maintain their superior position, including physical force when other means fail. It could also be said that men are under such strong pressure to adopt standardized roles that they seek refuge in physical brutality rather than lose face.

The overcompensating efforts of men to maintain their poise and self-control and to meet society's performance standards, drive many to suppress their complaints until they suffer a breakdown, overextend themselves and ruin their health. The discrepancy in the life expectancies of men and women is increasing every year. One might be moved to compassion for the men in view of their self-inflicted isolation, their imprisonment in a standardized façade of joviality, superiority and brazen ambition. None of these enables them to experience deep contact and liveliness, and indeed it results in considerable danger to their health. But one might also take the position that they alone are to blame for the ruinous consequences of the mania to dominate. If they would renounce their illegitimate claims to superiority over women they would be less vulnerable to stress and overexertion. Men are in a double bind in relation to women, in this situation. They will be punished no matter which position they take. If they live up to society's performance standards, if they are competent, career conscious and earn enough money, they will arouse envy and jealousy amongst women and be accused of the 'privilege of masculine superiority.' But if, on the other hand, they reveal their anxieties and weaknesses, demand maternal compassion from women and deny themselves a career, they will be told that they are unmanly and unable to properly provide for a family.

According to *Boszormenyi-Nagy* (1973), women participate more in their existential obligation to society than men when they reproduce. Men are fated to a status of 'debtor', which women can exploit through regressive behavior. Further, the existential physical significance of men—again according to *Boszormenyi-Nagy*—is far less, especially today when they can no longer risk their lives as great warriors or legitimize their significance as professional pioneers. Men suffer because of their relatively insignificant participation in the important function of reproduction, and therefore have a tendency to atone for their guilt in a self-destructive manner. It is essential that men play a more responsible role in the process of reproduction and the care of the new generation.

In sum:

1. Men and women have typical and distinctly different behavioral patterns in therapy, which can be statistically verified.

2. The interpretation of these different behavioral patterns is value-based to a large degree.
3. The behavioral patterns of both men and women can be interpreted positively or negatively (as immature, infantile or neurotic), depending upon the value-based perception.
4. The particular values of the interpreter (in our case the therapist) are of importance. The perception is strongly colored by their sex. I consider one of the most difficult and also the most important problems in couples therapy to be the awareness that one's perception is colored by a sexual bias. How do I handle the fact that in every therapy session with a couple there is a therapeutic relationship between three; that there are twice as many men as women present, or, to put it another way, there is a 2:1 ratio in the distribution of the sexes? And how do I personally, as a male therapist, handle the conflict when I discover that I cannot be sexually neutral as a therapist, but instead elicit a sexually biased response from the partners and find myself involved in therapeutic collusions? How can we psychotherapists participate in the process of couple conflicts in an unbiased or 'allbiased' manner (*Stierlin*), as we ourselves are still caught in our own unresolved partner conflicts?

Behavioral Differences between Men and Women Determined by Partner Orientation

The professional literature generally speaks of 'man' and 'woman'. However, I believe it is important that I have discovered in couples therapy and couples research that men and women present different personalities depending on whether they are together with their partner or alone. *C. Manika* (1978) substantiated this observation through statistical research of the 87 marriage partners whom I tested in Individual and Common Rorschach experiments between 1966 and 1970. The essential results could be summarized as follows:

1. The Individual Rorschach test gives no indication of a typical male or female form of perception and interpretation.
2. The Common Rorschach experiment (meaning that the partners take the Rorschach test together and must agree on an interpretation of each inkblot) shows essential differences between male and female response and interpretation. A man together with a woman tends to maintain the overall view, while a woman abdicates this function to him. In this situation a man will also show a stronger tendency to emotional control and realism.

If we compare men in the individual tests and in the common tests, we observe that in the presence of their women they suppress their responses to images which suggest emotion, sexual impulses, inner conflicts, sensitivity, anxiety and depressing moods. In the Common Rorschach experiment men become more conventional and tolerant, and show less of their emotional make-up.

If we compare women in individual tests and in the common tests, we notice that they show significant changes of interpretation in the two situations. During the Common Rorschach experiment they inhibit their overall view, become less productive and withhold themselves more, emotionally.

Men demonstrate more overview, a greater sense of reality, more self-control and more emotional control in a couple situation. They become ego-enforced in the presence of the woman.

Women, on the other hand, relinquish their overview and sense of reality in the common experiment. They become unproductive and show a tendency to ego inhibition.

These differences between Individual Rorschach tests and Common Rorschach tests are significant to a factor of between 1 and 5 percent.

The Common Rorschach experiment is not only a clue to the emotional experience underlying the interpretation of inkblots, it also reveals the behavior of the partners during this problem-solving task; e.g. who props up the pictures, who is making suggestions, how the suggestions are being evaluated, and whose suggestions finally win out. The differences between men and women during the Common Rorschach experiment are much more a consequence of their social behavior than of their perceptions and interpretations of the inkblots. Men show themselves to be significantly more active, more decisive and more persistent than the women; while women hold themselves back and wait for the approval of the men. There is a much greater difference in social behavior than in emotional experience. This indicates that social role play seems to be much more the determining factor than the emotional experience, and therefore also the primary focus for 'putting things right.'

This may be expressed more simply.

1. Women become more 'feminine' and men more 'masculine' when they react to one another in a couple situation than when they are alone.

2. Men and women show far more significant differences in their social behavior than in their emotional experiences.

The result of this experiment substantiates what we hear in each couple therapy session. Women, especially, emphasize again and again how much more independent and self-assured they were before the marriage and can simply not understand how they could have become so dependent and helpless. Whenever a man is a patient in both single and couple therapy sessions we notice that where, in the single therapy session, he had just spoken openly about his weaknesses, in the couple therapy session he will hold himself back and assume a much more controlled, balanced pose. We can also observe a woman, who in the single therapy session demonstrated a constructive approach to a working relationship, behave much more regressively and passively in the common therapy session.

Whenever we speak of 'man' and 'woman' we should take note of the setting. We should define whether we are observing them in a partner relationship or in a situation where their sole reference is themselves. I call the personality which interacts with a partner the *interactional personality*, and it can differ significantly from the personality which stands alone. The interactional personalities of two partners are interdependent and are very strongly defined by the unconscious interplay of both partners; by their collusion.

U. Scheu calls her book '*We are not born as women—we are conditioned to become women*', *Scheu* (1977). One might say the same of men, 'We are not born to be men—we are conditioned to be men.' The fact that men are more active and more aggressive is probably not so much the result of their biological disposition (*Macoby & Jacklin*, 1974) as it is of appropriate social conditioning. On the one hand this conditioning process corresponds to a masculine need for domination, while on the other it is supported and encouraged by women and can be exploited by them (*Beckmann* [1977] speaks of the prostitution of the aggressive willingness of the male).

One of the goals of couples therapy is to loosen up and de-emphasize very rigid interactional personalities. Partners should learn to react less strongly to the personality of the other partner (which introduces collusions) and should develop instead a 'relative individuation' (*Stierlin*), meaning that they ought to experience themselves as separate from and relative to one another. In every couple relationship—whether it is homosexual or heterosexual—there is a tendency towards role division which will inevitably lead to the polarization of modes of behavior.

Our experience with the Common Rorschach test as well as in couples therapy has shown us again and again that women have a tendency to live below their potential and to relinquish their self-realization in a couple relationship. *Jean Baker Miller* discusses women in her psychotherapy practice who have developed phobias as a result of their marriages: fears of being locked in, the feeling of being trapped, the loss of control over their own personalities, the fear of going out without the man, the fear of being in the car alone, or the fear of making a decision. In general, these very same women were relatively independent, self-sufficient and energetic before marriage and had good

educations. With marriage they either gave up their profession or modified it. According to these women, their men were quite considerate and
understanding—which in turn caused the women to feel guilty about
their anxieties and depressions. *Baker Miller*, who is a female therapist,
interpreted these observations as "a result of subtle oppression by these
husbands." I too have treated many women who were suffering from
these symptoms. What I, as a male therapist, noted was the regressive
tendencies of these women; an attitude of "Well, now I have a man who
can take care of me, therefore I do not have to be responsible for my
own development."

The fact that women often tend to relinquish their self-realization in
favor of their partners not only has both a physical and mental effect on
them, but it also endangers others. The degree to which a woman holds
herself back and inhibits her self-realization puts a corresponding
burden on the people around her. In order to make her self-denial meaningful, she devotes herself to living only for her partner and her children
and seeks self-realization through service to others. The members of her
family consequently develop in accordance with the model which she has
designed for them, and in return are to provide for her satisfaction,
from which she nourishes herself. This may be dangerous for children,
who have to substitute for the lack of ego and self-image (*Richter*, 1967)
of the mother. If a woman denies herself her own development, her son
must develop into the man whom she has 'designed'. The son must 'reward' the mother for her self-denial. This may instill in him a feeling of
importance and drive him to pursue ambitious goals in order to prove to
his mother that her dedication has been worthwhile. The result is that
the mother has produced the particular type of man whom the feminists
call the product of a patriarchal society.

The woman's self-denial is also dangerous for her male partner. He
will initially be grateful that he has someone who is entirely his own,
someone who believes in him and is supportive of him. But this can lead
to a serious identity crisis in middle age when he begins to sense that,
with the woman's support, he has developed in a direction which has
nothing to do with his self-realization. Suddenly he feels a self-
alienation, a feeling which is not unlike the self-denial of the woman,
even though on the surface professional success and prestige have been
his compensation. This self-alienation finds expression in escape from
the confines of the marriage, meaningless spending of money, alcoholism, and psychosomatic, abrasive illnesses.

In summary we might say: An intensive couple relationship of long
standing results in a considerable change in the personalities of both
partners. It can produce rigid interactional personalities. That is, this
personality which is the product of a couple relationship and of the influence of the partner in particular will differ greatly in appearance from

the personality outside the couple relationship. A partner can become healthy or ill under the influence of his or her mate. One partner can also maintain his health at the price of the health of the other. Interactional personalities are interdependent, or relative to one another, and are defined by their mutual influence upon one another. Given this definition, it is entirely correct if partners accuse each other of 'having become this way' through the influence of the other. One of the goals of therapy is to synthesize the interactional personality with the independent personality; this is imperative for the health of both partners.

Statistics show that the death rate of divorced men is three times higher per year than that of divorced women. The death rate among widowers six months after the death of their wives is 40% higher than one would expect; the cause of death is in most cases coronary failure ("a broken heart," according to *Parkes et al*, 1969). Hospitalization for psychiatric reasons occurs 20% more often amongst divorced men than amongst divorced women. After the divorce or the death of the woman, men are more prone to alcoholism than women are after the death of their men. (German national statistics on alcoholism, 1977). These statistics might suggest that a man profits considerably by living with a woman, which suggests that he evidently leans on her and exploits her. But one might also say that the man becomes more self-alienated under the influence of the woman, that he becomes dependent on her and therefore has greater difficulty in regaining his 'self' when he is alone again. One of the most amazing experiences for a woman in couples therapy is to hear how dependent the man is upon her and how lost he would be without her. The problem is further compounded because the man often loses his home and his children as a result of the divorce. One of the central goals in couples therapy is that the man and woman overcome this self-alienation, 'retrieve their selves' and develop two separate yet mutually relating personalities—but not personalities which are determined through mutual influence. Because the woman generally tends to deny herself for the man, he becomes inflated out of all proportion—and literally lives beyond his means—so that when he suddenly finds that he must fend for himself he inevitably collapses. The woman's tendency to put the man's development first endangers not only herself but is also of questionable advantage to him.

Implications for Contemporary Society

The battle between man and woman in couples therapy is a microcosm of the battle of the sexes in contemporary society. Feminists are overwhelming men with their reproaches and accusations. They label them as tyrants, exploiters and scare-crows. The accusations are fueled by an underlying frustration, which is expressed as follows: "We simply can't throw enough anger their way because the reactions we provoke in them are not good enough." Just as in couples therapy, the reaction of men as a group is to appear impenetrable. They react defensively, trying to 'console' the women and ignore their attacks. They either adopt a hypocritical approach of openness or try to reduce the women's demands to more practical attempts at problem solving under the guise of rational argument. In reality, a direct confrontation of the sexes does not seem to come about because men do not want to be provoked. They prefer to think that the feminist storm will cease if they simply tolerate all the theatrics and let them die their own deaths. Men seem to believe that if they were to react to this noise women would only become more unreasonable. But of course what men consider to be a courageous withstanding of invective, women perceive as an arrogant refusal to take them seriously. As we see in the hysterical marriage (Chapter 5), the danger is that the women's accusations become progressively more provocative, irrational and impertinent until men, within the framework of their 'logic', can finally say that it is simply impossible to react to such nonsense.

Is a fair and constructive solution possible in this battle of the sexes? I believe that there is an aspect to feminism which may promise such a solution. Women have fought for equal rights for a long time now, yet the measure of all things has still been the man insofar as women have wanted to prove that they were equal to men in all respects. In doing so they have only proven the opposite to themselves. The quest for equality brought to the surface their own feelings of inequality. Existing differences between men and women were reduced to the insignificant differences of anatomy, and all others were seen as being the result of repressive social conditioning of women. The question "What makes the emancipated woman?" could be answered: "The man!" This was probably a necessary phase in the movement, but it left women without the possibility of developing their own identities.

There has recently been a new development. Women no longer want to fight against men, they want to fight for themselves. They retreat into their own areas and exclude men from them. They are supportive of each other in the process of self-realization, they are supportive in exploring their own bodies and they are trying to build a counter-culture within a world which is dominated by one-dimensional masculine values. This new aspect to the women's movement no longer lays claim to a male platform, but rather questions that platform. It is looking for alternatives, for a better future for their children and for the emergence of maternal compassion as a political force. In this counter-culture designed by women, competitive striving, the hunger for power, the cult of genius and false objectivity are to be de-emphasized. Indeed, there is a growing awareness that the destruction of nature can be stopped only by ending the masculine domination of nature. "Take the globe away from the reign of men—and give it back to humanity tomorrow" (*Françoise D'Eubonne*). Women are forming exclusive groups, where they practice community and solidarity, where they discover their own values in an atmosphere which is friendly, free of stress, and creative. Nothing makes men more insecure than this type of exclusion. Women are demonstrating that they can be self-sufficient and able to do without them. There is, undoubtedly, still a provocative tone to this rigid exclusion, and the solidarity of these women is further strengthened by an image of 'man as the enemy.' I believe, however, that this development points to a possibility which is also the central concern of couples therapy; that is, emancipation from sexual role-playing. This emancipation must lead not only to the modification of external realities but also to a change in our inner processes. Partners have to diminish their interactional personalities, reduce their dependence upon one another. A relationship should not be a vehicle for denying oneself in favor of a partner. On the contrary, it should enable both partners to better experience and realize themselves through the other. The first step towards such a development is a stronger self-definition with respect to the partner, an awareness of oneself, an internal separation and internal divorce. Therefore it is necessary for women, initially, to exclude men in their search for the self.

It is equally important that this change takes place within men in a calm manner. *Beckmann et al* (1977) concluded from the updating of the Giessentest in 1975 that the psychological changes amongst West Germans since 1968 had affected men more than women. In the 1975 survey, both men and women describe themselves as more loving, more capable of contact, more imaginative and more dependent. The statistics show that men now have a greater trust of other people, are more willing to reveal themselves, and are more willing to admit their emotional needs. Surprisingly, it is the older men (35 to 60 years of age) rather than the younger men (18 to 34 years) who show the greater statistical deviation since 1968. If we were to use the traditional cliches of 'masculine' and 'feminine' role play, we would conclude that there is a clear overall trend in the direction of greater 'femaleness'. Generally speaking, women have not become harder and more aggressive, but men have become more gentle and emotional. The survey by *Beckmann et al* also shows that the change in men and women is interdependent. "Wherever men have chosen greater relaxation and comfort, women have compensated (according to their own reports) by increasing their efforts, by being more orderly and more responsible than the men."

This change in the social arena is parallel to the process which couples therapy seeks to stimulate. Women and men are beginning to overcome, through different means, their interdependent role-playing cliches. They are searching for sexual identities which match external behavior with inner experience. This process develops through crisis to be sure, and is by no means finished. As in couples therapy, a change in one partner produces a resistance in the other, which at the same time triggers the necessary change for the return to a new balance. Looking at it in this way, one can interpret the rejection of women's emancipation by men as a phenomenon of resistance which corresponds to the dynamics underlying a couple relationship. It is perhaps more difficult to understand why some women feel irritated and unhappy when men play a fuller role in the logistics of the household and the rearing of children. In doing so, men are entering into an arena which formerly belonged exclusively to women and are enlarging it to include not only their physical cooperation, but also their participation in decision-making. According to *Beckmann et al*, women feel threatened by men "breaking into their traditional monopoly of the emotional sphere." This seems paradoxical. After all, men are merely reacting to a demand which women have been making for a long time. Yet these are reactions which can be observed in any couples therapy session as 'phenomena of resistance.'

Perspective on the Future: The Concepts of 'Masculine' and 'Feminine' Replaced by 'Human'

Changing social conditions must be met by a thorough restructuring of the areas of work and family. The available work will have to be redistributed. It is better for the health of society that fewer people do less work than that some do it all. If women were to be excluded from the work force because of a recession, they would feel that they were being forced into the ranks of the unemployed and would experience all the accompanying perceptions of worthlessness. Exclusion from active participation in society would create a sense of apathy and meaninglessness. The industrial nations would have to face the long-term consequences of a drastic reduction in the birthrate. It would prove very difficult to provide the appropriate conditions for the survival of families with children. This is barely possible even today. Less capable families are already giving up. In my opinion there should be in the future a shortening of the work week and a general emphasis on increased self-help in the social area. Parents with small children will have to be able to find better conditions for living, for vacationing, for financial assistance, for extending education, for favorable re-entry into the job market, and for easy access to day care centers. All of these are political concerns.

In the psychological realm, I believe that during this period of re-structuring of our sex-specific stereotypes it would be best not to rely on the concepts 'man' and 'woman', but to replace them with the more general concept 'human'. I am sure that there are statistical differences between men and women which are of biological as well as socio-cultural origin. However, the characteristics of men and women differ only in terms of the statistical mean. There is such an overlap in the nature of men and women that it would be better to talk only in terms of 'human' characteristics, and do away with the normative concepts of 'masculine' and 'feminine'. In doing so, it would be possible to avoid equating a behavioral deviation from the average with a deviation from the norm.

In this book I shall generally speak only of *progressive* and *regressive* partners, and very seldom of 'men' and 'women'. I am convinced that the problems presented here may be applied to every kind of committed partner relationship. Changing socio-cultural norms and ideals will probably produce a shift in the earning capacities of men and women in certain positions; however, the resulting conflicts will in principle remain the same. We see more and more couples today in which the woman is older and professionally more capable than the man. There is nothing wrong with this, assuming that the goal is the fulfillment of each human being according to his or her own capabilities. The situation becomes problematic only for those couples where the progressive partner now takes over the position that was traditionally ascribed to men. Now the woman feels compelled to maintain her leadership through a fear of regression and weakness, while the man strives with all his might to regressively limit his self-realization in an effort to undermine any possibility of masculine superiority.

2

DYNAMIC PRINCIPLES
OF PARTNER RELATIONSHIPS

The Demarcation Principle

Progressive and Regressive Defense Behavior

The Balance of Self-Esteem

The origins of marital conflicts are complex and diverse. The socio-cultural context is of primary importance. Intense conflicts can arise between partners if they have grown up in different cultures or social strata and have been influenced by differing concepts of what a marriage should be. In contemporary western society the declining image of marriage has added to the couple's insecurity about which image is valid for them, thus creating a further source of conflict.

In my therapeutic practice three dynamic principles necessary for the success of partner relationships have proved to be important. The first I call the demarcation principle, a term used in the structuralist approach to family therapy by *Minuchin* (1974). To function well, a dyad must define its inner and outer boundaries clearly. The second dynamic principle is flexibility of progressive and regressive patterns of behavior. In marriage, regressive or 'childish' behavior and progressive or 'adult' behavior should not be divided between the partners in a rigidly polarized way. The third principle concerns the balance of self-esteem. In a healthy marriage the partners should face each other on a basis of equal worth.

I have not investigated whether these empirically-based principles have general validity outside our culture and would prefer to forego anthropological or psychological corroboration. Adherance to principles does not in itself guarantee a good marriage, but merely constructs a framework on which a satisfactory marriage for both partners can be built. Most couples have an intuitive insight into these principles. Failure to observe them is due less to a lack of understanding than to more deeply-rooted problems which prevent the couple from putting them into practice. In the collusion model, it is these deeper problems of partner interaction that I shall be addressing.

The Demarcation Principle

We are here concerned with the problem of defining the inner and outer boundaries of the dyad. How close to each other can the partners become before they will lose their individuality? To what extent should a couple separate itself from the outside world? I think that each couple should find an appropriate position on a continuum between total fusion and rigid separation. It is in the middle range between these two extremes that they may function normally.

Demarcation: Inner and Outer Boundaries of the Couple

	pathological range	*normal range*	*pathological range*
intradyadic boundaries	rigid	clear & permeable	diffuse
extradyadic boundaries	diffuse	clear & permeable	rigid
	⟨A ┊ B⟩	⟨A ┊ B⟩	⟨A ┊ B⟩

On the right of the diagram we have dyadic fusion; the partners form a symbiotic unit or mutual self. In most cases these couples close themselves off tightly from outsiders. The extradyadic boundary remains impermeable. This is the extreme which the couple usually takes as their ideal during the early phase of falling in love. They long for absolute unity, they must belong completely to each other and share everything in total harmony. However, this may very easily lead to excessive intimacy and loss of ego boundaries, dissolution of the self (see narcissistic collusion, p. 60) and suppression of all aggressive, and often sexual, drives. At the same time the partners believe that their relationship is so unique and ideal that its mystique should be shielded from the onlooker. An image of inviolable seclusion is presented to the outside world.

The left of the diagram represents those couples who, through anxiety about loss of self, are afraid of intimacy and maintain a rigid separation within the relationship. Intradyadically, a protective barrier exists between the partners while, extradyadically, the boundaries are often diffuse. Intimacy with a third person serves to limit the extent of close contact with the partner. By using children, friends or relatives as allies the couple may ensure that the boundary between them is preserved.

I believe that in a healthy marriage the following demarcations are observed:

1. the marital relationship is clearly differentiated from any other two-person relationship. The outer boundaries are clearly delineated, the partners are conscious of themselves as a couple, they take time to be together, and they have a married life of their own.

2. within the dyad, partners retain their unique identities and respect the other's individuality. The intradyadic and extradyadic boundaries are clearly apparent both to the partners and to the outsider, but they do not become rigid and impermeable.

There is widespread experimentation with these demarcation principles at present and to assert such rules is to invite controversy. However, in therapeutic practice I frequently encounter couples who have found that the tensions and pressures within their relationship—often caused by an unrestrained quest for freedom—may be reduced simply by observing these principles. As society abandons one extreme ideal in favor of another, the principles are no longer respected. It is my belief that many healthy marriages have been undermined by anxiety and stress as a result. For decades western industrial society has aspired to the romantic ideal that 'togetherness' may be found only in love and, overburdened by this expectation, marriage has led to disappointment. The current criticism of marriage can be seen as a partical consequence of the collapse of this ideal. But as always one of the greatest difficulties is the acceptance of separation in love; the respecting of another's individuality without sacrificing one's own. Separation in love frustrates the longing to rediscover—at least with *one* person—the lost mother-child symbiosis and to return to an undifferentiated, primal harmony. Many marital crises are fruitless attempts to somehow reach this elusive goal and arise out of a defiant protest against separateness. "The partner having caused the disappointment should now at least be made to suffer for it." This mystification of marriage becomes dangerous when it leads the couple to detach themselves from social norms or, more seriously, to adopt pathological forms of interpersonal behavior.

However, in recent years the danger of the other (no less

pathological) extreme has arisen, namely careless extramarital intimacy. Marriage comes to be seen as a prison from which to escape, with the couple now anxious that their bond does not chain them together. At best they place no expectations on each other and try to satisfy a greater proportion of their needs outside the marriage. But although this might in itself be a welcome attempt to lighten the burden of expectation on a marriage, it will create confusion if the marriage is valued no more highly than any other relationship. I think it is of secondary importance how intimate an extramarital relation is, as long as it remains clear to all concerned that the relationship with the marriage partner is fundamentally different from any other. Nowadays this too is seriously questioned: by political ideologists who see in it an expression of capitalist power and possessiveness, and by the proponents of a new marital ideology who proclaim freedom and independence through partner swapping, group sex etc.

According to Denfield (1974) those psychologists who have seen partner-swapping as "one of the greatest achievements for marriage since the invention of the canopy bed," have approached the problem "with missionary zeal rather than scientific accuracy."

It is not uncommon today for therapists to treat women who are jealous of their husband's extramarital affairs. These women demand too much of themselves in trying to allow their spouses a form of independence which negates the very character of the marriage relationship. In contrast to other dyads, marriage is based on a binding and long-term commitment between both partners. It goes beyond the momentary satisfaction of a need or a short-term human encounter and shapes the couple's life destiny together.

In my own experience this contractual-type commitment is still a valid model, although it should not be overlooked that certain couples are unable to realize it because of unresolved psychological problems. These will be illustrated in subsequent chapters. A contract remains valid until it is cancelled. It should not be dissolved as a result of a momentary upset, but only after fundamental and thorough examination.

Minuchin (1974) and other prominent family therapists see the re-establishment of clear boundaries in family sub-systems as one of the primary goals of family therapy. They consider the symptoms of family disorders to be diffuse boundaries between parents and children or rigid exclusion of certain family members. It is this approach to family disorders which I would like to apply to marriage disorders: a primary goal of marriage therapy is the re-establishment of clear but permeable intradyadic and extradyadic boundaries.

The couple should establish clear boundaries not only between themselves and extramarital lovers and friends, but also between themselves and their parents and children. Parents often have difficulty in accepting a child's independence, it should be made apparent to them that these bonds must be relaxed when the child marries. The relationship with the marriage partner is separate, it excludes parents and has priority over the relationship to them. Parents should realize that in the event of a quarrel their son or daughter will side with the partner and not with them. If this is understood, the relationship between parents and a married couple will be far more harmonious than if it is allowed to develop through pressures and intrigues.

Children should also be aware that their parents' marriage is a relationship in its own right, clearly differentiable from the parent-child relationship. This rule is frequently violated, as will be described more fully in Chapter 8.

The outer boundaries of the dyadic system should also not be too rigid, however. Couples today show a greater awareness of the dangers of isolating themselves from others. They are more willing to reveal their conflicts and difficulties to the outside world and to discuss their problems with other couples and friends. This is positive. Young couples increasingly feel the need to give up the isolation of the nuclear family and expand their social contacts, which gives a greater richness and flexibility to their relationship. The traditional concept that togetherness within a partner relationship is the ultimate determinant of happiness and fulfillment in life has led to an ideal of marriage which confines the couple in mutual dependence and self-preservation. They tend to watch everything happening around them with anxiety, rejecting it as hostile or threatening, and limiting contact with it as much as possible. This ideology is symbolized in the design of the ideal home: drawn curtains to protect it from prying glances, a small garden hidden from view by walls or thick hedges and a tiny peep-hole in the front door.

A sense of proportion is the key. Rigid boundaries are barriers to communication constricting and devitalizing the couple's life together. Diffuse boundaries allow greater dynamism but also create fear and an unhealthy level of tension, because of the lack of structure.

Progressive and Regressive Defense Behavior

Marriage has many psychological parallels with early parent-child relationships and is greatly influenced by them. During the first months and years of its life, a child is introduced to the basic elements of intimate human relationships. In the family it interacts with a comparatively small and easily recognizable circle of fellow human beings. Through marriage it re-enters a similar relationship system, but now in a different role: no longer as a child and yet not quite as a mature adult. In the marriage relationship this ambivalence is reflected in regressive and unfulfilled infantile needs on the one hand and failure to develop progressive or adult behavior on the other.

An intimate couple relationship offers a range of regressive and progressive behavioral alternatives. No other interpersonal relationship comes as close to parent-child intimacy as marriage. No other relationship offers such complete satisfaction of the elementary need for oneness, for belonging to another, for caring and being looked after and for protection, safety and dependence. The behavior of two people in love is also very similar to that of mother and child: they hold each other in their arms, caress each other, encourage physical contact, look deeply into each other's eyes, smile, squeeze and hug each other, joke and kiss. Their language very often reverts to preverbal sounds and other modes of expression of early childhood.

On the other hand, hardly any other interpersonal relationship requires such a high level of identity (cf. glossary), stability, autonomy and maturity as that of the intimate, complete and committed couple. Each partner expects deep, human understanding from the other and achievement of real personal fulfillment. To find solutions to the multitude of problems facing them requires ability and insight, and in the event of personal difficulties and stresses the partner will be the first to be approached for help and advice.

Couples who have a healthy relationship benefit from being able to alternate freely between progressive and regressive roles. Each partner can in turn be helpless, crying on the other's shoulder, or comforting, giving advice and support as a mother. Since the compensatory behavior of the partner can be relied upon, it is possible to behave regressively without fear of embarassment. Correspondingly, success in the role of helper increases one's self-esteem. The reciprocal giving and receiving of support brings a high degree of satisfaction and is an important motive for forming a couple. The ability to regress partially and temporarily is an important pre-requisite to personal growth and the therapist therefore actively encourages 'regression in service of the self' in analytical treatment. *Michael Balint* (1959) has suggested that the highest levels of maturity are reached in genital love because of the opportunity to regress temporarily during orgasm. In his opinion the healthy individual is flexible enough to experience this regression without fear, secure in the belief that he will be able to come out of it. In contrast, individuals who experienced difficulty in reaching maturity feel threatened by regression and can never let themselves go during orgasm.

Although progressive and regressive tendencies are present in everyone, not everyone is able to express them both and make the smooth transition from one state to the other. A regressive fixation in a partner will be expressed in their constant rejection of demands that they behave with more maturity (more progressively). They assume that marriage will continually satisfy their needs for care, kindness, tenderness and guidance. This expectation is often rooted in unresolved conflicts of early childhood and can be a neurotic disturbance. These individuals may have been so frustrated in childhood that they now feel entitled to the satisfaction of their insatiable, unfulfilled needs; or, alternatively, they may have been so overprotected and spoiled that they now see marriage as a continuation of childhood. Frequently parents have blocked their child's every act of initiative, with the result that when these children become adults they continue to expect punishment and the withdrawal of love should they show anything but infantile dependence in their marriage. Their development may have been so discouraged that they will ask only that their partner assumes all responsibilities for both of them and tolerates their childish needs and demands.

On the other hand, some partners set too high a standard for themselves in order to seem 'adult.' They avoid any form of behavior which could be interpreted as childish, weak, helpless or dependent. They strive to exhibit the character traits associated with a strong ego: strength, maturity, superiority and control over emotion. In personal relationships, they seek self-confirmation as leader, savior, superman and unfailing benefactor. These roles are assumed not because of any real strength or maturity but because of the need to disguise childish weaknesses, for which they overcompensate by feigning maturity. Such behavior can be just as neurotic as regression. It can indicate that the individual was never allowed, as a child, to express their feelings freely or to show any sign of weakness; or alternatively that, because they were never taken seriously, they now want to make an impact on the marriage with their 'heavily' adult behavior. In contrast to regression, this false progressive behavior is often positively reinforced by society as it embodies socially approved values of competence, helpfulness, activity and masculinity. Yet progressive personalities are often socially dangerous because their overcompensatory, progressive roles can be maintained only through interaction with people who are extremely regressive, passive, dependent and in need of support, and who must be induced to remain that way.

The concept of regressive and progressive roles is of central importance to this book. Regressive and progressive positions will be understood throughout as neurotic defenses: regression as reversion to childish behavior and progression as an attempt to conceal weakness behind an 'adult facade.'

This overcompensatory behavior is termed 'reaction formation' in psychoanalytic theory. In our context, therefore, progressive behavior refers to pseudo-, rather than true, maturity.

Those who adopt the regressive role fear the challenge of responsibility or fear punishment. Those who adopt the progressive role are ashamed to reveal regressive behavior. The prevailing trend in our culture is to attribute progressive behavior to men and regressive behavior to women. A man must prove that he is superior, stronger and more experienced; a knightly protector and support for the woman. Regressive behavior, such as seeking protection and consolation or showing weakness and dependence, is still considered unmanly. Although men generally are no more mature or advanced in their development than women, they often feel obliged to play progressive roles, suppressing and denying their need for regressive contact. Similarly, regressive behavior is still considered specifically feminine, although to a lesser extent than before. Many men are particularly attracted to women who seek their attention and support; women who want to lean on them, look up to them, place a naïve trust in them and talk childish nonsense. Some women force themselves to be the weak, regressive stereotype of the ideal woman even though this does not correspond to their true nature. They accentuate their 'femininity' by suppressing all active, so-called 'masculine' modes of behavior. In this situation the woman acts as if she is weak, often using this very weakness to manipulate her 'he-man.' The interplay of 'strong' man and 'weak' woman is characterized by the *hysterical* marriage.

In the disturbed partner relationship we often observe that one partner has a need for over-compensatory progression while the other seeks satisfaction in regression. They reinforce this one-sided behavior in each other because they need each other as complements. Throughout this book we shall describe the neurotic entanglement between such progressive and regressive partners as collusion.

The Balance of Self-Esteem

In a mutually happy relationship the partners are bound by a feeling of equal worth. This implies equality not only in behavior and status within the relationship, but also in feelings of self-esteem. Either partner may take on the external leadership of the dyad—the tasks associated with social prestige such as professional status, management of finances and official representation—without violating this rule. Close investigation of actual situations may reveal that the seemingly passive wife guides the actions of her husband from the background. In fact Rorschach tests with couples (*Willi*, 1973) have shown that quite frequently it is the wife who decides and the husband who executes the decision. Even if the man is the only one with a professional career, the woman may realize a sense of equal worth as advisor in his advancement, or even as a source of 'nourishment' from which he draws the strength for his achievements. A feeling of being indispensable to her husband's professional achievements can help her identify with his success. Self-esteem can come from rearranging the traditional role patterns, with the husband taking over the 'Department of External Affairs' and the wife the 'Department of the Interior.' In many cultures, the wife as mother is the emotional center of the family. This provides her with a high level of self-confirmation.

Psychologists commonly speak of one dominant and one dominated partner in a marriage. These terms are used without due reflection however, because, even with more detailed knowledge of the situation, it is difficult if not impossible to say who is dominating whom. Following *Watzlawick, Beavin and Jackson* (1967) therefore, I find it more appropriate to refer to superior and inferior roles. The superior partner is generally more active, more verbal, more decisive and has more initiative. He or she assumes leadership functions and represents the dyad in its interaction with the outside world. The inferior partner is often more introverted, quieter and less evident, influencing decisions from the background and guiding events without claiming leadership. *This does not necessarily mean that they are inferior to or beneath the superior partner*.

Even when one partner is in fact stronger, the dynamics of the dyad prevent any abuse of power. In marital disputes a man cannot take free advantage of his superior physical strength as this is socially condemned as a sign of personal weakness. Similarly, if there is an imbalance in the personal qualities which reinforce self-esteem, these qualities may not be used in the context of marital conflicts. It is considered unfair to humiliate a partner with critical remarks about actual handicaps such as lack of education, physical disabilities and disfigurements. An unwritten rule forbids the exploitation of a one-sided advantage in battle and instead demands that one adapt one's methods of combat to the 'armament of the weaker adversary.' In duels and sporting contests, competitors are given a fair chance: a heavyweight boxer is not allowed to fight a featherweight. Grotesque marital situations may therefore sometimes arise, such as a superior tactician in politics resorting to clumsy quarreling at home, or a professional boxer trying to commit suicide after being beaten by his delicate wife.

In partner choice, equality is usually intuitively observed. Even at the first meeting, two strangers will gain extensive insight into each other from the content of their conversation. Indeed Murray *Bowen* (1972) has shown that two partners are generally of equal maturity. A sense of self-esteem can be gained through various attributes such as intelligence, strength, beauty and wealth, but also through personal maturity and the ability to empathize with a partner and give them support and affirmation. In a potential relationship all these qualities have as much importance as the partner attributes to them. A distinguished old man may marry a housemaid who, because of her warm maternal nature, means far more to him than a constantly attentive yet demanding admirer. Similarly, a dynamic executive may feel oppressed by an aristocratic but nagging wife and seek a relationship with a simple girl who appeals to those sides of his personality which were denied in the course of his constant striving for success. In general, however, a feeling of equal worth is based on a similarity of social and personal attributes. As a rule, one intuitively avoids becoming too deeply involved with someone who is more mature, because the resulting feelings of inferiority could threaten the relationship. Conversely, a relationship created with a partner less mature than oneself would necessarily remain narrow and limited. However, when partners of unequal maturity form a couple a process of mutual adjustment does begin.

The mature partner will try to avoid an image of superiority by making gestures of modesty and humility, through self-deprecation, narrowing of their interests or even through psychosomatic illness; all of which hinder potential development. Women, in particular, often deny their potential so as to avoid the appearance of superiority to men.

Case 1:

When the couple met, the man was a salesman in a department store and the woman (who was 4 years older) was a lecturer in philology with a university degree. He came from a working-class family and she from a well-to-do, established family of academics. He had grown up in an industrial part of the city, she in a villa. After knowing each other for a few weeks she became pregnant by him and insisted on getting married quickly. He thought he was too young for marriage but finally agreed because he felt responsible. Now, after twelve years of marriage, both agree that in every way, even sexually, they have lived apart. Every week the husband spends several evenings and sometimes entire nights at his tennis club where 'wine, women and song' parties take place. The woman is bitter, she feels that she has sacrificed the best years of her life for her husband and now accuses him of no longer caring for her.

He is strong, good looking, attractive and athletic, but is intellectually inferior to her and seems rather dull by comparison. He stresses that from the beginning his wife, and especially his parents-in-law, disapproved of him as a marriage partner. His father-in-law practically never speaks to him. In the tennis club he feels at home and has his fun, but his wife finds his friends too vulgar. She entered the marriage with the intention of making something of the relationship. On all sides people advised her against it, but she told herself: "It will be hard but I'll make it." She thought that things would be alright if she suppressed her views and tried to adopt his way of life. She gave up all her old friends and intellectual pursuits. She began to play tennis and wanted to adapt herself to him in every way. She enrolled him in a crash business course and encouraged him to strive for promotion, but he felt uncomfortable with her. He had the impression that she basically neither approved of nor accepted his character and was instead always trying to "improve him." She reveals with bitterness: "I have always accomodated myself to you completely and have given up everything for you. I thought you could have made more of yourself if you had wanted to and to this day I am convinced of it. If you would only show your good will in some small way, but you simply don't want to." He replies that at home his wife criticizes him constantly. He simply believes that he married too young and has had to give up too much. Angrily she responds: "Give up what? You have given up absolutely nothing. I have adapted myself to you in everything." Most of all she is hurt by his extramarital relationships with tennis partners whom she considers "complete idiots." It is evident that he feels better understood and accepted by these women.

In this case the therapeutic goal would be that the wife refrain from projecting false attributes onto her husband. This would be possible if she stopped sacrificing herself for him and tried to realize more of her own potential. Understandably both partners feel that, because of the differences in education, the mutual acceptance of their own individuality would ultimately lead to divorce. As this example shows, the balance of equal worth cannot easily be ignored.

Although the principle of equal-worth is generally observed at the time of marriage, there is no guarantee that the balance of self-esteem will remain constant during the course of many years of living together. Social conditions today allow greater opportunities for men to increase their self-esteem through professional achievement than women, who receive a lesser confirmation of their self-image in the roles of housewife and mother. There is thus the danger that envy and jealousy will lead a woman to undermine her husband. Whereas she supported and encouraged him at the beginning of the relationship, she may now try every means to criticize and hinder his development and knock him off his pedestal. The man, because of his guilt feeling, finally allows himself to be treated no better than a dog in his own house, being stepped on and pushed around with impunity. This does provide the woman with the possibility of momentary release, but ultimately it undermines still further her own self-esteem.

In the partner relationship, as in all groups, there is peer-pressure to conform, which tends to keep differences in self-image and emotional state to a minimum. Members of a group, or partners will adjust to the weakest member in order to avoid increasing that person's feeling of inferiority. The woman who makes social contact easily, suddenly holds herself back in order not to outshine her timid husband. The successful business executive gives his wife as little information as possible about his professional status so that she does not develop a feeling of inferiority. It is difficult for one partner to be happy and self-assured when the other is steeped in depression and self-pity.

As long as partners continue to engage each other as a couple it is less likely that one will become dominant and the other give up the fight and submit. The rivalry which often exists between them is carried out within narrow bounds and they adapt themselves unconsciously to balance out victories and defeats. If tensions mount the fight becomes more severe and tends towards a one-sided victory with the emergence of a new equilibrium. As *Bach and Wyden* (1969) correctly state, there are no winners or losers in marital conflicts. Actually the loser has many ways in which to re-establish the balance. While there is equality, quarrels and disputes can take place to some extent at a common, objective level. But as the balance tips to one side, one of the partners may notice that direct confrontation is causing them to lose ground. They can then resort to the great arsenal of weapons which are available to couples and which enable them—although destructively—to overcome their apparent inferiority and redress the balance. Such weapons include crying, recrimination, avoidance, spiteful silence, martyrdom and righteousness, symptoms of psychosomatic illness, suicide attempts, drinking, refusal to work, involvement of a third person, etc. Many marital conflicts end up in suffering because of disregard for the principle of equal weapons. The mobilization of destructive reserves makes an equitable solution impossible. This leads to an escalation in which each partner's sole purpose is to inflict pain on, or destroy, the other, unaware that this is equally damaging to themself. Communications therapists are correct therefore in insisting that couples carry out their conflicts equally armed. *Bach and Wyden* (1969) write: "Therefore we teach that 'victory' in a conflict with an intimate enemy can in reality prove dangerous. The loser is discouraged and prevented from being honest in future quarrels. It sounds paradoxical but if a 'victory' leads to such after-effects, then both partners are losers. . . ." They also compare their conflict-training more with learning to dance than with learning to box.

A contradiction appears to exist between the tendency towards polarization in progressive and regressive role-play mentioned previously, and the principle of equal-worth discussed here. The regressive role, however, need not lead to feelings of inferiority relative to the partner as long as it is clearly felt that the partner who is in the progessive position is dependent on the regressive attitude of the other; and as long as the regressive partner realizes that the strength of the progressive partner is only a display. The understanding that the progressive partner is equally dependent should then eliminate feelings of inferiority. This is particularly apparent in the case of hysterical women, who are able to tyrannize all around them by fainting. A seemingly inferior position can become superior and passivity can be used to the passive partner's advantage.

The solidarity of a marriage relationship will be severely tested if one partner, in order to maintain equality, adopts a consistently destructive attitude towards the other's attempts to achieve real personal development. A time may come when that partner is no longer willing to inhibit their own growth and will put themself outside the balance of equal worth. This often comes as a healthy shock to the partner who was putting on the brakes, forcing them finally to let go and come to terms with the challenge of personal growth. However, they may become even more insistent in their destructive behavior. Then with an open disruption of the balance of equal-worth, the relationship will disintegrate and divorce may appear like a release from prison, as the restriction of equal development at last falls away. In the therapeutic treatment of marital conflicts both partners should have an equal opportunity for growth. But loyalty to a partner should also imply certain limits and should not be unreasonably restricting. Ideally a constancy of equal worth can be reached openly and frankly without resort to repressive or destructive behavior.

3

THE PHASES OF MARRIAGE
AND THEIR TYPICAL CRISES

The Formation of the Stable Couple

Construction and Creativity

Mid-Life Crisis

Marriage in Old Age

Too many couples enter marriage believing that it is a static system which should remain constant throughout their married life. Fairy tales end with the sentence, "and they married and lived happily ever after. . . ." But in reality marriage is not a state but a process. Many collusive solutions to conflicts arise and persist because partners will not accept this process of development nor put at risk the happiness with which the marriage was begun. They cling to the original definition of the relationship and try to bind their partner to it. Even the slightest weakening or questioning of the relationship is seen as a serious threat. Should the original definition become less appropriate over the years, they will feel disappointment, fear, anger and defiance. In understanding the marriage relationship, it is important to recognize that each phase of development has its typical, and normal, crises. It is, moreover, precisely in the struggle for adequate solutions to these crises that a marriage is kept alive.

The avoidance of such typical conflicts takes many different forms. Idealizing the marriage is one example. In this case the partners will not accept that conflicts and differences of opinion can arise between them.

No clouds of unhappiness may appear on the horizon. Certain topics are taboo and are increasingly excluded from conversation, with the result that the marriage loses its vitality. One way of preventing an outbreak of conflict is to use social or religious codes which are imposed by outside obligations and sanctions. There is also a tendency at present for young couples to air all conflicts, no matter how small, which may be termed 'flight forward.' They have learned that conflicts are an integral part of marriage and that they should be discussed openly and not avoided. In endless 'marriage therapy' they clear away any possible conflicts before they can take root. And yet these commendable intentions may be mixed with contradictory motivations. Beneath the desire for total openness may be an unconscious desire to control the partner and to manipulate them 'with understanding.' The need for immediate resolution of all differences of opinion may thus be the result of a fear of anything which separates.

Marriage demands the courage to embrace real growth and change and to put at risk one's freedom. Couples should be willing to expose themselves to crises in an honest way. Marital crises are not in themselves symptoms of pathology. The pathological phenomena of marriage arise from the avoidance of the normal and inevitable crises of growth. Withdrawal from real conflict is an impetus to collusion, as I shall show in subsequent chapters. Before I turn to neurotic marital disturbances, therefore, I would like to briefly outline these normal crises of marriage.

Marriage can encompass, practically speaking, an entire adult life. It passes through different stages which I shall classify as: the formation of the stable couple, construction and creativity, mid-life crisis and marriage in old age. Each of these four stages has its own character, differing in intensity, intimacy and motivation. Each has its specific problems and conflicts. As the relationship progresses from one stage to the next, anxieties are created and a high degree of flexibility and adjustment is required from both partners.

The Formation of the Stable Couple

Erikson (1977) describes a phase in which young people try to acquire the personal and sexual abilities necessary for close and stable cohabitation. During this phase, which lasts many years, partners are changed frequently. Little recognition is given to the partner's autonomous individuality, and neither is this quality the reason for their being the object of love. What these young people really desire is to prove, firstly to themselves and secondly to others, that they are capable of making conquests and that their choice of partners is worthy of esteem. Partners thus serve as status symbols or prizes and the more desirable their at-

tributes the more admiration and prestige they provide. Rela
young couples are strongly narcissistic, changeable, idealiz
centered; all a natural part of the search for identity. This experimentation allows them to explore their abilities in relationships and to
experience the limits of their potential. They gain in self-esteem and
learn, through their partner's reactions, how to assess more accurately
their own character. Gradually, conquests lose their playful element.
Decisions are increasingly required which will result in final self-
definitions and irreversible roles, progressively establishing the course of
future life. The continuity between the young adult's self-image and the
impressions of others develops in them a secure feeling of inner-outer
consistency. Erikson has emphasized the importance, in this stage of
identity-formation, of social recognition of the individual and
acknowledgement of a purpose in their gradual development. They feel
a growing need to share the most intimate aspects of their personality
with a partner, seeking recognition and confirmation of identity through
them and giving the same in return.

Identity develops out of the role models of childhood and youth into an encompassing, unique and increasingly integrated whole. As with
any gestalt it is defined by positive and negative, foreground and background. When decisions are made which determine identity, they necessarily exclude the choice of other possibilities. This is as true of choosing
a partner as it is of choosing a profession. Committing oneself to a
specific, permanent relationship inevitably implies rejecting others. The
choice of a single partner may therefore create difficulties. In Erikson's
opinion, young people are not ready to make this judgement before they
have made certain basic decisions about themselves.

The choice of a partner signals the end of the search for momentary
satisfaction and self-confirmation. This is replaced by the desire to form
a single, lasting relationship, to take up challenges together with that
person and to share a common path through life as a couple.

The first objective is to build a home together, raise a family and
create a common life style. These future tasks lend a sincerity to couple
formation which is consistent with the difficulties ahead.

The couple relationship is characterized by exclusivity, both with
respect to the families of each partner and to other possible partners.
During this stage adolescents generally become dissatisfied with life in
the parental home, where they feel that they are still being treated as
children. Their parents have the same, unchanging image of them, they
feel caged in and restricted. Separation from home is made more decisive by the belief that they will be more successful than their parents in
marriage and the raising of a family. In this sense, tension and dissatisfaction at home often provide the necessary impetus to face the un-
certainties and problems inherent in entering marriage. In pioneer spirit,

the young adult moves away from the unsatisfactory conditions of home to make a start elsewhere. The feeling of being exposed to the oppressive 'understanding' of one's family, of being shaped and confined by their attitudes and expectations, creates a longing for the freedom to be oneself with an unbiased and supportive partner.

The couple-formation phase can be a time of great strain, often dominated by doubts and fears such as separation from home, surrender to a partner, sexual inadequacy, obligation and responsibility, being bound, suppression of individuality, and failure. Depression often sets in before a wedding, together with panic flight-reactions, neurasthenic complaints, fear, identity-confusion and even psychosis.

Erikson has observed that latent weaknesses in identity often become manifest only in the sexual intimacy of a love relationship.

"The meeting with the 'du' (you familiar) is the result and at the same time the proof of a definite, embracing feeling of identity. While the young person, experimentally at least, looks for playful intimacy in friendship and rivalry, in flirting and love, in verbal quarrels and self-expression, from time to time he experiences strange feelings of tension as if these trial encounters, transformed into a bond, could lead to a loss of identity. A cramped inner withdrawal and a careful avoidance of commitment results. If the youth does not overcome these tensions, he may isolate himself and at best engage only in very stereotyped and formalized relationships."

Construction and Creativity

This stage spans the first years of married life and is generally the most active of the relationship. It is a time of consolidation of the couple's identity. They need to establish their place in society and to take the numerous decisions which will give their marriage a definite form. The dreams of youth must now become concrete. They set up their own home, which is both an expression of their life-style and an influence on it. They begin the struggle for professional achievement, which not only shapes the identity of each partner but also determines to a large extent the social status and identity of the family.

Life together brings about internal division of functions, the establishment of which is a continuing process. Thus while the dyad now has a definite external form, the respective roles and positions of the partners are not yet fixed. The creation and discovery of a life-style is an intense process of discussion and experimentation. The struggle to achieve shared norms and values is no longer an abstract or theoretical exercise, but involves such realities of everyday life as the division of tasks and responsibilities, work and free time, friendships and relations with society, management of finances and the setting of concrete goals for the partnership. The couple must be ready and resolved to make joint decisions in many areas of life. The common search for solutions reaches a unique intensity during this phase and can be very productive in identity formation. The range of concrete challenges, problems and tests stimulates the development of both partners.

Theodore Lidz (1968) writes of marital adjustment: "A successful marriage will generally both lead to and require a profound reorganization of the personality structure of each partner that will influence the further personality development of each. The marriage necessitates forming a union in which certain functions are shared, others undertaken by one spouse and in which some aspects of individuality are renounced. Certain facets and traits of the personality will be developed further and others fade . . . the ego must expand at marriage to consider the spouse as well as the self and also the marriage as an entity. Optimally, the spouse becomes an *alter* ego whose desires, needs and well-being are considered on a par with one's own. . . .The change involves small matters as well as major decisions, and indeed becomes an inherent part of a way of life."

This process of adjustment leads to a loosening of the personality structure before it has fully overcome the identity crisis of adolescence. The personality is restructured through interaction with the partner. When certain aspects of the personality do not elicit a response they are inhibited. Through lack of reinforcement therefore, much of what was acquired during adolescence is re-evaluated or rejected. Certain responsibilities are either overtly or tacitly conceded to the partner, which may result in partial regression or mutual dependence. But personal growth is also enriched in many ways through the experience of living together. It develops maturity not only because of the common task the partners undertake, but also because of the expectations each has towards the other.

In adolescence there is vast potential for personality formation. This potential now takes a definite form. An identity is created in which the experience of self matches the perceptions—and assimilates the responses—of the environment and in particular the partner. The process of mutual adjustment between partners is difficult and hazardous and often cannot be accomplished because of individual psychological problems. Disturbed forms of relationship can quite easily develop, which I shall describe as collusion in the following chapters.

One example is the conflict between intimacy and independence. The difficulty arises because of uncertainty about the degree of adjustment which is possible without loss of self. Close intimacy can be destructive when it leads to undifferentiated fusion. Separation in love is particularly painful when one realizes that one is not all and everything

(*Mandel*) to the partner. Often one partner will try to establish a balance of greater intimacy only to be hurt by a lack of responsiveness in the other. Ideally they both come to see that their partner's individuality broadens their own experience and that separateness too is a part of love (*Caruso*). A common fear in early married life is that if one loses an argument one will then always lose all arguments. To give in is to appear weak and one should therefore never yield or submit. This fear can be the basis for a power struggle. Nevertheless, it can be equally dangerous to capitulate too hastily whenever the threat of separation arises.

These fundamental problems demand from the couple an ability to deal fairly with differences of opinion and to bargain for solutions without self-sacrifice and without demanding that sacrifice from the partner. This is an art which is practiced today in partner counseling sessions. But the effectiveness of counseling is often limited by deeply-rooted, neurotic disturbances in the relationship which stand in the way of real solutions to conflicts.

An important problem area is the need to restructure relationships with the family, and especially the parents, of each partner. Fear and guilt often hinder the establishment of clear boundaries between the couple and their parents, permitting the parents to interfere in the development of the marriage. A battle may then ensue in which parents compete for ownership of their child with the other partner; a fight caused by the conflict between dependence and separation. Another problem situation arises when the couple decides to have children. This is especially difficult for the woman because, despite current trends, she must assume that by raising children she will deny herself some professional opportunities. The young mother will probably not be able to attain the same occupational status as her husband, a disadvantage which is felt more deeply as values have changed. The absence of these male privileges may arouse deep resentment in women experiencing pregnancy and motherhood.

When a couple have children their relationship undergoes a major transformation. They no longer have as much time alone together, they can no longer direct their attention uniquely towards each other and the period of exclusive intimacy comes to an end. Typically it is the husband who is jealous of the attention which the children receive, but wives too may feel cheated of the tenderness, attention and security they expect from their partner. Where there is a fear of intimacy, the children may provide a welcome channel for deeper contact, although serious problems later arise when they leave the family. Children may also strengthen a couple's mutual attachment as fears of separation recede into the background. These too will re-emerge, however, when the children are no longer present to bind their parents together.

Mid-Life Crisis

During the stage of construction and creativity the need to overcome numerous external difficulties produced a high degree of dyadic cohesion. The scale and seriousness of the common task maintained the stability of the relationship despite possibly critical marital frictions and problems. As the couple enters middle age the situation changes dramatically. Their life is no longer directed towards concrete goals to be realized in the near future. These have now either been reached or their probability of attainment has been realistically assessed. The man's professional career is now firmly established and its future course can be predicted with relative certainty. The family's social status and financial position is thus determined. All the furniture has been installed, the TV altar erected and the family has made its home or is planning one. Hardly any relevant external goals remain which could, of themselves, hold the couple together. The children are no longer at the age where the presence of both partners is absolutely necessary for their development. In contrast to the preceding stage, in which the couple's capacities were continually put to the test and they longed for more peace and free time, a great emptiness now enters their lives. Mutual consolidation has been achieved and is no longer a focus for welding the couple together.

Where previously both partners established their identities in discussion and joint problem-solving, they now find that these images may no longer be appropriate. They revert to a kind of second adolescence and a second identity crisis. As the amount of freedom increases, the obligation to identify themselves with the marriage disappears and eventually they come to resent it. It is no longer acceptable to subordinate personal interests to marriage and family. Indeed they want to catch up with the opportunities which were put aside because of the commitment to their partner. The balance of equal worth is no longer respected and the need to make up lost ground is considerably intensified by the approach of old age. Despite a basic similarity in experience, men and women react differently at this point.

For some men the crisis arises because they have failed to achieve what they expected out of life and must now live with the burden of this fact for another 30 to 40 years. There has not been any real acknowledgement of either their lives or themselves and they blame the marriage for hindering their personal and professional development. They are irritable and argumentative at home and any attempt by their wife to console them makes them feel even more trapped by their lack of fulfillment. If she resists being made a scapegoat, he feels misunderstood and looks for a lover who will be more sympathetic to his tragic lot.

Although one might expect the contrary, the successful man's experience at this stage is not very different. After he has fought for and achieved all his professional ambitions, an uneasy feeling of emptiness and depression often sets in. Success, prestige and material wealth all seem trite. He asks himself whether life has turned out to be as he had hoped. In the great effort to achieve his goals, did other totally different opportunities slip by unnoticed? Although he admits that he has been aided by the guidance of his wife in realizing his potential, it seems now that she has placed him instead in a straightjacket. If he could renounce success and the obligation to achieve, he could enjoy life more and pursue his interests. On the other hand, he finds it difficult to give up the comfort, security and prestige for which he has fought so hard. Some men now face an occupational crisis, and may change their jobs or even professions and set about learning new skills.

The first wrinkles appear on his wife's face. This is disturbing not only because she seems to be losing her youth and beauty, but also because the effects of ageing are far more noticeable on her than on himself. These wrinkles eventually seem to represent the scars of their many conflicts over the years; conflicts which wounded deeply and were never completely healed. A younger woman would not only be more attractive, she would also allow him to feel young again. Making a fresh and more confident start he could leave behind the tensions accumulated over the years, the unsatisfactory compromises, mutual violations and accusations. During this phase he may enter an extramarital relationship or initiate a divorce, hoping to break free from the static identity imposed upon him by his partner. Another partner offers new opportunities in life. Initially, an extramarital relationship makes him feel younger, full of vitality and inspired by a new purpose in life. This process is often very similar to a trip to a foreign country. At first he is overwhelmed by new impressions and idealizes them, feeling reborn. But after a time he sees the other side of the change and welcomes the return to the familiar homeland. He finds a greater appreciation of the things he always had, having learned to see them differently. He renews and broadens his perspective and discovers something continuous and enduring about himself, which confirms a meaning to his existence. When one travels to a foreign country there is always a risk that one will not return home, a risk which is reduced if the return is not made unnecessarily difficult.

The woman now needs to exercise considerable discretion. It will be to her advantage if she can accept this voyage as a necessary and valuable period of transition. However, she should also insist forcefully on maintaining or re-establishing a clearly defined marital structure. Although she may offer compassion and forgiveness, it should be understood that the marriage cannot continue on any other basis. Attempts at coexistence with an extramarital relationship generally result in confusion, tension, suppressed jealousy, insecurity and the decline of the marriage. Such relationships violate the demarcation principle and are incompatible with a reasonably happy relationship. I shall later describe cases of marital triangles in which the inclusion of a mistress is an acceptable solution for all concerned.

Mutual ambivalence about staying together or breaking apart establishes a collusion of jealousy and infidelity, in which each partner provokes reactions from the other that simultaneously bind and separate them.

In many ways this phase is more difficult for the woman. Her children have now grown up and she no longer looks forward to an equally rich and rewarding future. If she returns to her former occupation she will probably not be able to achieve the same status as her husband, who has been establishing a career over a period of 20–30 years. And if she chooses to prepare for a new profession, she will take introductory courses where her fellow students may be no older than her children. In addition she is generally considered less attractive than her husband at this point. The physical changes of menopause, especially loss of menstruation, give her a feeling of wilting. She may become bitter, realizing that the best years of her life have been sacrificed for a family which is now dissolved. Her children abandon her, her husband no longer respects her and she feels alone. However, some women may now experience a new lease on life, being free at last to do the things which were sacrificed in order to raise their children.

The balance of equal worth is disrupted. While the man is at the peak of his success, the woman is left standing empty-handed, feeling robbed of everything which formerly provided her with purpose and status. The marital relationship becomes dangerously lop-sided because the woman is no longer able to participate as an equal partner in the dynamics of the dyad. In her disadvantaged position she cannot confirm her husband's dazzling success without a feeling of envy. And yet much as she may wish to give vent to her anger and disappointment she cannot do so. This might drive her husband into the arms of a mistress who will take pity on him because of his ill-natured and unsympathetic wife.

The significance of the mutual self diminishes. Friendships with members of the same sex again become important. Men are drawn together by the common bond of their unhappy marriages. They complain to each other about the 'sour old bitch' at home, rave about the mistress who brings fresh breath into their lives, indulge in self-pity, nostalgia and tragic disillusionment and play boyish but cynical pranks on each other. They do seem to show a certain detached wisdom, however—having experienced something of the complexity of life—and question the straight path that they have followed in search of their goals. In melancholy indifference they take to drinking, and may ultimately even lose their professional positions. Suicidal tendencies become more common at this age.

Women also get together much more frequently to talk out their problems. They suffer more from the marital friction because of their outward dependence on the impending social decline of the man and many of them become bitter and subject to acute anxiety. Moreover, they may have to tolerate their husband's disrespect because they dare not risk the consequences of retaliating.

In this situation it is often the woman who takes the initiative in contacting a marriage counselor or psychotherapist. She hopes that this may convince her husband to give up his mistress and come back into the marital fold. But he will be reluctant to attend therapy sessions, knowing that he will have to make concessions in order to re-establish the balance of equal worth between them.

I believe it is extremely important in this situation to set realistic expectations in therapy. If one of the partners no longer wants to continue the marriage, the therapist should respect their freedom to make this choice. As the children have now grown up, there can be no urgent necessity nor moral obligation for prolonging the marriage. The partners must decide whether or not it is worthwhile to continue. The marriage therapist generally should not introduce new motives for marriage, but should concern himself with clarifying the true nature of the marital disturbances. Where there is an extramarital liaison, the mistress has importance only in as far as she represents something which the man is unable to find in his wife, but which might be rediscovered in more favorable circumstances. The essential question is whether the mistress can be made superfluous, given a better marital relationship. A sustained effort is usually required from both partners to achieve this therapeutic goal, but they may be unwilling to make it, as it is easier to compromise with existing conditions than to restructure a relationship that has become habitual. During 20 to 30 years of married life husband and wife may have grown apart and the mistress may elicit behavior from the man which corresponds more closely to his actual self-image. This is often a cause of great anxiety for the wife because the mistress often has considerably less experience of life than herself, and her husband's new relationship will appear more a decline into primitiveness than a step towards greater maturity. He may nevertheless be happier and more satisfied in this new relationship, even if it develops into a second marriage. He feels that his wife has been too demanding and that he was emotionally frustrated by her. But the mistress, whose role has previously been defined only by her complete and unconditional confirmation of the man, will often experience great difficulties in the marriage relationship that follows.

Although both partners find the marriage painful they may still lack sufficient motivation to make a sincere commitment to therapy; that is, to undertake the serious effort required to change the situation. Their desperate predicament does elicit a certain social responsiveness and all-round sympathy. Some would fear being thought naïve if they declared themselves happily and faithfully married at their age. There is a special attraction to living ambivalently in a love-hate bond, half-married half-divorced. In marriage therapy one must therefore determine whether there is a real desire to change the situation or whether the partners have basically come to terms with the misery of their marriage.

Even without the problem of an extramarital affair, the woman must realistically assess the opportunities open to her for weathering this difficult period. Her most positive attitude would be to really stand on her own two feet, become involved in her interests and create her own circle of friends. She thus frees herself of dependence on her husband's good will and the marriage continues, although in a less intense form. It now assumes less importance, and equality is restored between the partners who need not suffer any further unhappiness.

Many women cannot make this adjustment, however. Some try to work with their husbands professionally, but only a few achieve success. Most often they enter into employee relationships with their husbands which only exacerbates the problems of equality. Many women now recall the satisfaction of the intense construction phase of their marriage and try to salvage what they can from it. One consequence of this is the attempt to keep the children young and dependent. But the couple may cause great harm by exploiting and abusing their adolescent children in order to bind the marriage together and deflect the crises in their own relationship. Family therapists are therefore correct in warning parents against redirecting marital problems through their children, although they may often fail to understand the specific difficulties caused to parents, and mothers in particular, by each of the different stages of marriage. The parents most commonly referred for therapy are in this precarious mid-life stage. This provides some insight into their reluctance to part from their children, whom they see as the only means of mediation between them. Persuading parents to contain marital conflicts and deal with them themselves can be both difficult and arduous. Yet the many problems which they experience at this stage in their lives may be partly alleviated if they can be made to feel less anxious about their marriage and family bonds.

The mid-life crisis may be of crucial importance to further personal growth. The façade of life together becomes apparent, but if the props can be torn down everything is not destroyed. Instead one discovers the real and enduring qualities of the relationship, and a process of reacquaintance with the partner may take place. One may recognize the mistakes which were made both jointly and individually and accept that some of the consequences may never totally be reversed. One may also learn to reach a deeper understanding of the partner and achieve a re-conciliation with them. This process brings with it tolerance, maturity and wisdom, giving new value to the many years which have been shared.

Fidelity ultimately depends on whether the couple will remain loyal to the path they have travelled together and see it as something that has grown and been shaped by destiny, something which now represents their own, unique history.

Marriage in Old Age

For many, old age implies the man's retirement and his withdrawal into a ghetto of the aged, of widowers and pensioners. It means frailty, illness and the approach of death. Old friends and acquaintances are dying and familiar surroundings change. One is no longer directly con-cerned with current events and it becomes increasingly difficult to keep abreast of them. The couple move closer together again, and now the balance frequently tips in favor of the woman. The man stays at home in her realm where she can claim him totally for herself and even use him like a helpless and dependent servant. Looking back over their long life together the partners re-establish their attachment to each other. They again find themselves facing a joint task, sharing a common enemy in sickness, death and a threatening environment.

They are companions in destiny. Their increased interdependence appears blissful, but it also creates new problems. Each partner tries to encourage the other to be dependent while at the same time maintaining their own independence. This may finally result in an endless round of quarrels, power struggles and exchanges of pettiness as they fight to gain the upper hand. Trivial frictions may indeed become their only purpose in living, keeping them fit and alert and giving them the assurance of some remaining personal strength. It is not uncommon for the couple to close themselves off from a seemingly alien world, taking shelter in their home and thriving on the disappointments and offences of their children.

The death of one partner is extremely painful. 50% of women and 20% of men are widowed when they enter the twilight of their lives. The mutual dependence and familiarity with the partner had lightened the burden of old age and now, left alone, they must not only overcome the loss of one who was a part of their life, but also accept dependence on others who are probably strangers. The woman is usually in a more favorable position to weather this loss, being more used to managing the household.

This is a brief outline of the usual course of a marriage. Obviously there are many variations. In particular it should not be forgotten that a high proportion of marriages end in divorce at a relatively early stage and that a significant proportion of the remainder are childless, and therefore do not fit the description I have given. Further, I have dealt with marital infidelity as if it applied only to men and not to women. The diversity of life cannot be covered in a few pages. This description should simply show that marriage is a play of several acts, a drama full of tension, happiness and unhappiness, hope and disappointment. In other words, marriage is life and therefore inevitably bound up with conflicts, tension, crises and disagreements. Each phase of life, and therefore of marriage, presents new external and internal conditions to which adjustment is difficult. For some, these crises are enriching experiences, for others they are overwhelming.

It may be that these conflicts are not confronted because of disturbances originating in childhood. In this case they will develop into serious marital crises which the couple will be unable to resolve. In the following chapters I shall be discussing this type of marital crisis.

4

THE CONCEPT OF COLLUSION.

AN EXAMPLE

Marital and partner conflicts are among the most frequent reasons for psychotherapeutic treatment. It is surprising therefore that specialists were not actively researching and treating these conflicts until the mid-sixties in North America and Britain, and even later in German-speaking countries. Some therapists believe that marriage therapy simply is too demanding; that delving into the unconscious of not one but two individuals is too exacting. But this need not be so, particularly if one observes that couples usually carry out their conflicts in continuing variations on a constant theme. The daily incidents leading to disagreement always echo the refrain of a similar 'song'. Looking beyond the specific circumstances of a conflict, one discovers a narrowly defined basic theme which disturbs the couple. This constitutes their *common unconscious*. Marriage therapists may simplify their task by concentrating on this common denominator and disregarding the many areas of the unconscious which are not of direct concern to the marital conflict. In agreement with *Henry Dicks* (1967), I define the interplay of partners based on this common unconscious as *collusion*. Collusion is the central theme of this book.

No single concept can claim to embrace all aspects of a complex marital conflict, yet concepts are necessary if one is to draw meaningful conclusions from the wealth of information which couples disclose in their disputes. What is at issue is not only whether a particular concept is right or wrong, but also how appropriate it is to therapeutic work. What insight does a concept of marital conflict provide and what does it cause to be overlooked or omitted? To what extent does a concept give the partners in a conflict the reassurance that they are being understood? There are many different therapeutic approaches to marital conflict. I shall describe, in a somewhat simplistic manner, what may be deduced from a marital problem by applying three of them: contemporary psychoanalysis, early family therapy and modern communications therapy. I shall then describe the insights which may be gained by employing the concept of collusion.

Until quite recently, psychoanalytic investigation concentrated almost exclusively on the individual. Unconscious processes were examined in detail. External conflicts, such as those between partners, were considered relevant only in so far as they might activate an existing, internalized conflict. An actual partner relationship was examined as an interaction between inner objects; that is, from the perspective of the individual's attitudes towards relationships created by early memories and experiences. The subject or individual was assumed to have come into conflict with external objects, in this case the partner, because of traumatic childhood experiences. The psychoanalyst was little concerned with who that particular partner was. The actual relationship to the environment was not seen as a determinant in the case. In general, object relationships were investigated on the level of fantasy since it was assumed that fantasies determine the perception of the real and responses to it.

The psychological one-way street of the subject-object relationship was then put in question by family therapy. It became clear that certain individual disorders could not be treated without confronting the pathogenic milieu.

Therapies sometimes failed because patients could not be separated from the pathological influences of their parents or because acts of sabotage by relatives rendered therapy impossible. In other situations, patients who had been removed from their former environment were still unable to cope with the new one because they could not free themselves from the inner conflict with their relatives. External objects, in this case the relatives, rapidly became the focus of scientific investigation and therapeutic work—although the therapist's attitude was often distinctly critical. The concept of family therapy developed initially out of the study of families of schizophrenics. It was held that schizophrenia is the child's only possible reaction to the untenable interpersonal contact offered by its parents. The child becomes schizophrenic because it is exposed to behavior which inexorably undermines its sanity (*Searles*). The parents create situations causing psychosis in their children while they themselves remain free of manifest symptoms. The psychosis is externalized or 'acted-out.' In order to protect themselves from it, they create psychosis in their child, whom they send for treatment as a 'front' patient. The child is the symbolic patient of the parents and family, a victim of their attempts to act out their illness through it. The child fulfils certain roles assigned to it by its parents, becoming the surrogate or substitute for those aspects of the self which the parents rejected or which were insufficiently developed.The most seriously ill are always the last to seek treatment.

Certain reports give the impression that the child was seen as a blank sheet of paper, as a formless mass or substance which was imprinted by parental influence without resistance: the child as a helpless victim with no means of opposing its overpowering parents; the child as an object through which the parents can abreact, externalizing their neurosis and stabilizing themselves; the child as a mirror and visible symptom of parental neurosis. So it was no longer the patient who was ill, but rather the clinically healthy relatives who were able to act out their illness through the patient. Some authors then transposed this observation from family therapy to marriage therapy. The dominant marriage partner was assumed to actualize their own neurotic disturbances through the patient and to cause the patient's illness. Examples of this type can be found in the literature on wives of alcoholics. *Grotjahn* (1960) describes a case of psychosomatic illness where the behavior of the wife of a coronary patient had the same effect as if she had slowly closed her hands around the coronary arteries of her husband and squeezed them together. Having been a bitter, cold and often cruel partner over the years, she became a compassionate nurse the moment her husband became ill.

The model described here is to be found in the earlier studies of family therapy, where the psychological one-way street was seen to run in the opposite direction; that is, solely in terms of the effect of the object on the subject. The field of study was limited to what the relatives did to the patient, there was almost no investigation of the patient's effects on the relatives. However, any child psychiatrist can confirm not only that parents have an effect on their child but also that the child, from birth on, has an extraordinary and decisive influence on the behavior of its parents. This same relationship is even more evident in a marriage, where one must also ask: Why has the patient chosen a partner who has such a pathogenic influence on them? It would be worthwhile to investigate the extent to which the patient themself provokes and reinforces the pathogenic behavior of the relative/partner and assigns the pathogenic role to them.

Parents often feel overwhelmed by the task of raising their children and can be very receptive to lessons drawn from the illness of their child. But the therapist should avoid accentuating their existing guilt feelings by suggesting that their behavior has been malicious. If the therapist does so, parents will strongly resist, in order to protect their own identities and to justify their existence. I have often observed, particularly with adolescents, that although the parents exploit the child as a narcissistic substitute, the child also has its own reasons for fulfilling this role.

It is now widely recognized that the individualist approach must be transcended. Communications therapy has shown that when the relationship between the partners is seen as an entity or system it is inappropriate to place the blame for a marital conflict on the maladjustment of either one. Communications and systems therapists often attempt to distance themselves from the psychoanalytic aspects of marital conflicts, however. This both restricts them and opens them to the criticism that they are merely manipulating behavior.

I shall now apply these theoretical approaches to a specific example in order to clarify the concept of collusion. By this concept, marital conflicts are described as mutual neurotic disturbances of the partners in conflict.

I should state here that in the following example the need for treatment arose out of serious conflicts in fulfilling masculine and feminine roles. These are described as neurotic disturbances without questioning their social origins. I am also aware that the psychoanalytic categories which I use to describe these disturbances may be disputed.

> A young man who had impotency problems came to me in desperation, afraid that his wife would leave him. She was in a psychiatric hospital at the time, having developed an hysterical leg paralysis during the marital tension. The couple had been married for one year and lived together for six months prior to their marriage, they had no children. He was an engineer, an only son with two older sisters. His father, who was also an engineer, had suffered all his life from recurring impotence and his wife had ridiculed him in front of the children because of it. By the time the patient reached puberty his parents had divorced. Both his sisters were now divorced as well, because of the impotence of their husbands. The younger sister then married the ex-husband of the elder sister.

> This young man lacked a model of a happy relationship. Moreover he had seen, both in the marriages of his mother and of his sisters, that impotence leads to divorce.

> His mother was an egocentric, possessive and domineering woman. She had always tried to remove difficulties from his life and solve his problems herself, thus binding him strongly to her. She openly encouraged incest fantasies, making it impossible for him to free himself from the Oedipus complex. When she took a bath the boy had to sit and read to her. Until puberty, whenever he washed himself he would have to let her inspect his penis for cleanliness. At the age of eight he underwent a traumatic operation for phimosis. His

mother took him to the hospital where he was tied to an operating table by nurses without being told what kind of operation it was to be. When the doctor and nurses started to operate he was panic stricken at the thought that they might cut off his penis. His mother, standing next to him, let out a piercing laugh. When he was a student she fantasized with him about living together on a secluded island. The young man wet the bed until the age of eighteen. As a consequence of his own marriage, he now experienced problems of impotence.

A psychoanalytic interpretation of this case would place special emphasis on the fact that the incest and castration fantasies of the subject were reactivated upon his marrying. The patient transferred the inner object, in this case the internalized experience of a demanding and castrating mother, onto a real object, a wife whom he perceived as someone just as possessive and castrating as his mother. When his parents' marriage ended in divorce, he was in puberty. In his mind, he assumed the role of substitute husband towards his mother. Guilt feelings encouraged him to identify with his impotent father because, in his fantasy, he had driven his father out. With the concrete demands of the real situation (the intimate marriage relationship) and with the demands of the object (his wife), his castration complex was reactivated. Impotence occured as if predestined, independent of the behavior of the real external object. Because of a strong sense of guilt, the incest prohibition of the superego and a weak masculine identity, phallic instincts were repressed by the ego.

Now the wife did not in any way behave as a neutral object, her role was clearly that of 'castrator'. After she had been separated from her husband for some time, he visited her and once again failed at intercourse. She criticized and abused him and sent him away.

She was a science student, approximately the same age as her husband and the eldest of three daughters. She had often been laughed at in school because of her large build and was, in comparison to her two sisters, less successful with men. Her mother also dominated the family. Her father was a rather colorless businessman who often sought sympathy from his eldest daughter. The mother tried to belittle her husband in front of the daughters and to set them against him.

Lacking an acceptable maternal or paternal model, the young woman developed a weak sense of identity both with her own female role and toward the male role of her partner. In her own marriage she was sexually capricious, always wanting the opposite of her husband's desires, making him feel insecure and belittling his masculinity. She instilled in him a fear that he would never really be able to understand a woman.

Early psychoanalytic *family therapy* would have interpreted this example of marital conflict as a failure by the woman to identify with a female role in spite of her determined attempts. Covertly, she competed with the man for the masculine role, but did not openly adopt it. She preferred to show him that he was a failure both in his masculine role and in the use of his male organ and therefore no better than herself. By causing impotence in the man, she could repress her own conflict about her sexual identity and thus avoid her own problems. Although a male therapist tends to identify with a male patient, it is clearly evident in this case that the man, in acting out the woman's castration complex, is both her victim and the vicarious bearer of her symptoms.

The one who is really ill is not the impotent man but the woman whose sexual disturbance is not manifest. It is in fact she who needs treatment, for she is the actual pathogenic focus of the couple's relationship.

I think both interpretations are valid in themselves, but neither is sufficiently comprehensive. We must ask the question: Why does this man, burdened with so many doubts about his masculinity, specifically choose a woman who because of her unresolved conflicts tends to reinforce his insecurity? On the other hand, why does this woman specifically choose a man who makes it impossible for her to resolve the conflicts in her own sexual role? (His failure in the masculine role makes it difficult for her to identify with her own sexuality.)

Communications therapy helps us to progress further in answering this question. It leads us out of the individualistic orientation of psychoanalysis towards the concept of the partner relationship as a complete system and whole organism. When partners are in conflict their behavior interacts like a feedback circuit or a circle having neither a beginning nor an end. It is no longer possible to say that the behavior of one is caused by that of the other. Cause and effect, stimulus and response are impossible to separate. Referring to our example, we cannot say that the man's impotence is the result of the woman's castrating. Similarly, we cannot say that the woman's castrating is caused by the man's impotence, although each of them will express these opinions and be partially correct from their point of view. However, we come closer to the truth if we assume that the man and the woman mutually reinforce each other's behavior and that the resulting impotence of the man is a symptom of the couple's relationship. The more demanding the woman is the more impotent the man is, and the more impotent the man is the more demanding the woman is.

Communications therapy refrains from exploring the complex make-up of the individual because this would involve hypotheses about internal drives and conflicts which cannot be proven (*Watzlawick*). Communications therapists are not interested in the motivation behind specific behavior patterns, nor in explaining neurotic maladjustment in terms of early childhood development. Consequently they do not set themselves the therapeutic goal of presenting the individual or partner with an interpretation of their behavior which might help them understand the real reasons for it. Communications therapists would work on the problem of our couple through an actual communications situation, such as the following event.

When therapy began, the wife was being treated in hospital and the couple was thus physically separated. The husband visited her for the first time after several weeks had elapsed and they went on a long walk together. He wanted to make love to her in the forest, but again was impotent. She became upset and screamed at him: "I don't want to make love with you until you can give me a guarantee that it will work with you. I'd rather have nothing than be disappointed by you again." Communications therapists would point out that the man's fear and expectation of sexual failure is greatly increased by this kind of remark. Communication exercises and behavior alternatives would be prescribed which would enable the man to enjoy being with his wife in an atmosphere without fear, where he would not be under pressure to perform. Most importantly, the marital conflict would be reduced to a disturbance of sexual communication between the partners and treated as such.

It is possible that the couple would now be completely satisfied, with their sexual function restored and a better understanding in non-sexual matters as well. But the sexual disturbance may be only an image of a deeper and more widespread problem in the relationship between the two partners. Perhaps the woman is not only angry about the impotence of the man but also unconsciously driven to cause his impotence. She may fear sexual surrender, or be unable to identify with her female role. She may see in the potency of her mate an expression of masculine superiority and privilege which she refuses to accept, or even wants to destroy! Although the sexual function can be restored, there is no guarantee that the couple will also enjoy their sexual relationship. For this to happen, it would be necessary to analyse the causes of the sexual disturbance itself.

Each of these three theoretical approaches—psychoanalysis, family therapy and communications therapy—can provide important insights into the conflict of this couple. With the concept of collusion we can integrate the more significant aspects of these three approaches into a coherent whole.

According to the concept of *collusion therapy*, the marital behavior of the individual is to a large extent determined by personal prehistory (the genetic aspect of psychoanalysis). But in its manifest form marital behavior is also greatly intensified or diminished depending on the behavior of the partner (communications therapy), whose intensified or diminished behavior is likewise reinforced by personal background (aspects of early family therapy). In the above example, we observe that in an unresolved couple conflict there is an equivalence of neurotic structures. *Both partners display similar basic disturbances in relation to marriage, but they play them out through contrasting roles.* Similarly-disturbed partners encourage each other's pathological behavior and develop an unconscious arrangement or *collusion*. They both do this even though, in choosing the partner, they had consciously intended to come to terms with their existing disturbances. In order to understand the actual marital conflict in our example, I think it is necessary to go back to partner choice since the bitterness of this quarrel has its real roots in the failure to achieve the expectations and ideals that both partners shared when they married. Let us first analyse the *collusive partner choice* of this couple.

They met in a student restaurant. The man, who had always been very shy and hesitant towards women, saw his future wife talking with a friend at the next table. He found her gentle and very feminine and plucked up enough courage to stand up and invite her to have a cup of coffee with him. She was surprised at his boldness and saw it as an expression of 'masculine' self-assurance. Impressed by the dashing manner of the young man, she naturally accepted the invitation. They rapidly fell in love.

He had consciously chosen a seemingly gentle female in need of support whom he felt would strengthen his masculinity.

She had chosen the seemingly self-assured male in whom she hoped to find strength and support.

As mentioned earlier, the man had entered into this relationship without having resolved his attachment to his overprotective, domineering and 'castrating' mother. His strongest desire was to find a woman with whom he could prove his masculinity, one who would not mother him, but whom he could mother. His fear of marriage was that it would become a repetition of his parents' marriage and that he would become just as weak and just as much of a failure as his father. His wife seemed to offer him a safeguard against this danger as her helplessness and desire to lean on him for support reinforced his masculinity; she made no attempts to mother him but rather expected him to mother her. She made it possible for him to have a defense against his threatening mother by enabling him to identify with the aggressor (the caring mother). He neutralized the threat from his mother by placing himself in her position.

The woman entered into the marriage with an unresolved problem of sexual identity. She tried very hard to behave in a 'feminine way' in counter-identification to her domineering mother. She had felt very frustrated at home and now that she was married she longed for protection, tenderness and support. She was also afraid that her marriage would closely follow that of her parents and that she would become as domineering and insensitive as her mother. Her husband seemed to provide protection against this danger because he took an interested, maternal and considerate attitude towards her and spoiled her right from the beginning. In choosing a partner her conscious intention had been to transfer her own masculine tendencies to her husband and now, in marriage, she wanted to play a passive role and let herself be mothered.

The personal motives for partner choice corresponded very well on both sides. What went wrong?

In conscious counter-identification to her mother, the woman had done everything possible to appear weak and helpless, adopting a passive, feminine role which was not at all in keeping with her character. Her physique was muscular and boney. She had masculine facial features which she had tried to hide by growing her hair long, holding her head to one side and talking in a soft whisper. She attempted to assign her suppressed masculine characteristics to the man, but during the course of the marriage these resurfaced. With great effort she kept repeating to her husband: "After all, you're the man," and tried even harder to suppress her desire to be active. Consequently she regressed still further and affected such helplessness that she eventually developed hysterical leg paralysis as a symbol of her weakness. Her increasingly persistent demands evolved into 'castration behavior' as the man came to see himself as an impotent failure. He felt overwhelmed by her expectations and began to experience problems of impotence. At the same time the tendencies which he had suppressed returned. He had entered marriage intending to prove his manhood, but the longer the couple lived together the greater became his fear that he would suffer the same problems of impotence as his father. To overcome these fears he sought to prove himself through acts of chivalry, which served to keep his wife in a weak and dependent position.

He internalized his wife's excessive expectations until they led him to a break-down and a pattern of helpless childishness. By being awkward he ensured that she would adopt the maternal role and criticize him just as much as his mother had done. The couple regressed more and more, competing with each other in illness, helplessness and desperation until they finally came for treatment. Instead of active rivalry, they now tried to outdo each other in infirmity.

The first step in therapy was the reversal of roles. As the man had originally taken the role of care-taker and the woman had been helpless, she now made herself more independent of her husband and stood on her own two feet. She became pregnant by him. She made him feel that a symbiotic, mother-child entity would be created and that he would no longer be needed. Initially he regressed further. Shortly before the birth he was in bed with a mid-summer cold being nursed by his wife and came to a therapy session wearing a thick woolen shawl. At work, he became childishly defiant and would run home in the middle of the day to be calmed down by his wife. Whereas he had been a bed-wetter up until the age of eighteen, he now had dreams in which he urinated on the whole world. After the birth of the child he wanted to be nursed every day as though he were the child seeking its mother's breast. But his wife refused to give him any motherly attention, expressing her contempt of his behavior.

Gradually the man began to resume his paternal duties and accept his responsibilities at work. He regained his sexual ability. The relationship became more balanced as the autonomy of each partner increased and they lowered their expectations of each other. The woman was happy as a mother and gave birth a second time one year later, this time to twins. Through coping with her children she found her identity as a woman and learned to accept her husband, despite the fact that he remained somewhat childish. He overcame his jealousy of the children and became more aware of his masculine potential. He could also express his masculine weaknesses more without needing to overcompensate for them.

This example shows how marital conflicts can originate in a similar basic disturbance in both partners. Both partners had comparable experiences with respect to the marriages of their parents and, as a result, a similarly distorted image of their own sexual role as well as that of their partner. Both had a domineering mother and a weak father. The man had consciously chosen a woman who seemed the antithesis of his mother and the woman had chosen a man who seemed the antithesis of her father, but unconsciously each had chosen a partner who was very much like that parent. By overcompensating, both sought to avoid a repetition of the parental marriage, but both slipped into quite similar patterns of relationship because of their exaggerated defenses. We thus see how similar neurotic attitudes form the basis of the marriage conflict. In psychoanalytic terminology, both suffered from a castration complex with a tendency to regress to oral object relationships. The woman sublimated her masculine instincts by transferring them onto the man and behaving in an extremely feminine and helpless way, whereas the man repressed his obvious passive-feminine tendencies and assigned them completely to his wife in order to fulfil the desired male role with less fear. As their marriage continued, the false female identity of the woman collapsed. Her desperate attempts to suppress her own masculine instincts by regressing more and more placed too great a burden on the man's male identity. He could not maintain this false identity because his earlier fears of impotence and his rather feminine tendencies were externalized by living with a woman who was very much like his mother.

To conclude:

1. *Collusion refers to an unconscious interplay of two or more partners which is concealed from both of them and which is based on similar, unresolved central conflicts.*

2. *The common, unresolved central conflict is acted out through*

different roles which give one the impression that each partner is the exact opposite of the other, when in reality we are dealing with polar variants of the same theme.

3. The bond of the similar, central conflict causes one partner to seek a resolution through progressive (overcompensatory) behavior and the other through regressive behavior.

4. This progressive and regressive behavior is a major reason for the mutual attraction and the resulting bond. Each hopes that the other will release them from their central conflict. Both believe themselves now to be protected against the things they fear most and expect that their needs will be met more than ever before.

5. In the long run, this collusive attempt to solve the problem fails because the repressed elements in both partners return. What was transferred onto the partner (projected or externalized) re-emerges in one's self.

At this point these compact definitions may be a little difficult to understand. Hopefully they will become clearer and more meaningful to the reader in the following chapters.

— THINGS CHANGE WHEN PEOPLE TAKE RESPONSIBILITY for them

5

PATTERNS OF COLLUSION

Love as Oneness in Narcissistic Collusion

Love as Caring and Nourishing in Oral Collusion

Love as Security Through Dependence
in Anal-Sadistic Collusion

Love as Confirmation of Masculinity
in Phallic-Oedipal Collusion

Collusion Patterns Are Not Marriage Categories

In describing conflict as a normal part of each phase of marriage, I attempted to show that every marriage goes through a process of development with continual crises. In addition, I specified three psychodynamic principles (between couples) which should be observed for the couple to function. Now serious difficulties in the relationship itself may disturb the couple's attempt to comply with these structural principles and to deal with the typical crises of a particular stage in marriage. In the example in Chapter 4 the partners were affected by the same unresolved problems of masculine-feminine identity and concentrated their attention increasingly on their problem because of its common basis. A couple may become so entangled in a common basic theme that a normal stage of maturing becomes paralysed, inhibiting the individual development of both partners. In therapeutic practice, I have observed four main themes which I would like to introduce as patterns of collusion. These themes fall entirely in line with those of the early stages of childhood development as described by psychoanalysis and will therefore be described in those terms. In short, we are concerned with the following themes: PATTERNS OF RelATIONShip

1. *the narcissistic relationship*, which centers on the question: How much does love and marriage demand that I sacrifice myself for my partner and how much can I be myself? To what extent do we need to set limits for each other and to what degree can we become one with each other? How much should my partner identify with me, live only for me and confirm my self-concept, and to what extent can I assume a better self under the influence of my partner?

2. *the oral relationship*, focussing on the question: How far should one be concerned with helping and supporting the partner in love and marriage? How much right do I have to expect that my partner will care for me like a mother without expecting the same treatment in return? How much can and should I be a guardian and helper, a tireless and generous mother for my partner?

3. *the anal-sadistic relationship*, or the theme relating to autonomy, which centers on the question: How much can I be the autonomous leader in love and marriage, to whom my passive partner submits? How passively dependent on my partner can I become without fear of manipulation? Do I have the right to possess my partner completely and to control all their thoughts and actions or do I have to allocate autonomous areas to them?

4. *the phallic-oedipal relationship*, which is concerned with love and marriage as a confirmation of masculinity in terms of phallic admiration. As a woman, how much should I deny the development of 'masculine' characteristics for the sake of my partner, be passive, and lean on him in weakness? As a man am I always obliged to show male strength or can I also sometimes give in to passive tendencies?

These four themes pose real problems for every couple. Every couple is affected by them and must find a solution in each case which is acceptable to both partners. If a couple cannot master the difficulties associated with these themes the problem is usually the result of much deeper conflicts of relationship originating in early childhood. The stages of development of the first years of life place the child in analogous conflicts. Even then the child must find solutions to problems of relating to their parents in terms of the themes: 'love as oneness,' 'love as caring and nourishing,' 'love as completely belonging to each other' and 'love as confirmation of masculinity.' If the child cannot learn through interaction with their parents, brothers and sisters how to resolve these conflicts in a fair and acceptable way and if these conflicts remain linked with feelings of fear, shame and guilt, it is understandable that they would hope to find refuge in marriage. However, this expectation frequently fails to materialize since they will encounter conflicts in the partner-relationship which correspond to those which blocked them in their relationship to their parents. In disturbed marriages we find that the couple regresses because of purely emotional reactions to the problem which is blocking them. All psychic energies are spent on these problems. In living together they focus so exclusively on them that they are hardly capable of functioning and the process of mutual development is hindered. Therapy should attempt to enable the couple to break free of this paralyzing fixation, making it possible for them to grow again.

The interplay of partners in a mutual theme of disturbance in relationship will be shown through the four patterns of collusion. The experiences on which this presentation is based are for the most part derived from treatments of seriously disturbed neurotic marriages. What will be described here, partially in a dramatic form, exists in potential in any marriage, however.

Psychoanalytic theory distinguishes three pregenital stages of development of the libido:

—*the oral stage* (approximately the first year of life) in which the child is totally dependent upon the care of the person it relates to and during which the primary experiences are the need to be satisfied and to be in the world, to be fed and taken care of. Touch and eye contact are of central importance.

—*the anal-sadistic stage* (2–4 years), also called the autonomy or separation phase, during which the ego develops and asserts itself and motor and speech skills are gained. The child learns to create distance between itself and the environment; it develops self-assurance through the ambivalent but joyful experience of ruling and having power on the one hand and the submission of self on the other.

—*the phallic-oedipal stage* (approximately 4–7 years) in which the sexual difference between male and female takes on special importance; boys enjoy showing their penis, values and standards are formed, conscience unfolds and the super-ego and ego-ideal enter into a decisive phase of development.

The narcissistic aspect concerns the development of self in relation to objects and while not corresponding exactly to the outline of the stages of libido development, runs parallel to it as another side of the process of early childhood development. Freud differentiates between primary and secondary narcissism. Primary narcissism corresponds to the circumstances of the first months of life when the child cannot distinguish between himself and his surroundings; he feels at one with the

world around him and the world around him feels at one with him. This
condition exists before any subject-object differentiation, or any
delineation of the self and non-self. Adults with a primary narcissistic
disturbance have a fragile self-configuration; they are threatened by
disintegration of the ego-function and the consequent danger of dissolving into their surroundings, ontological security is lacking. They are
distrustful and can be subject to primal anxiety. In interpersonal relationships, they find it difficult to differentiate between their own self
and that of the other. There is always a risk that they will relapse into
the original, undefined primal state where they felt at one with their surroundings and the world around them existed only as a function of
themselves. In their fantasies, they tend to see themselves as grandiose
and omnipotent.

We speak of secondary narcissism when previously established
object-relationships are given up. The fixation on objects is put aside
because it becomes too painful and the libido is totally directed towards
itself. In this case self-love is a reaction to an alien and frustrating environment. Adults with a secondary narcissistic disturbance are insecure
and feel their self-confidence easily wounded. They are strongly dependent on narcissistic confirmation; however, their ego-functions are established and their self-image is developed in such a way that it remains
intact despite the break-down of self-worth. In this respect, unlike
primary narcissistic psychotics, they are not threatened by chaotic disintegration of the ego. During the phallic stage, the child often experiences illnesses which are factors in forming secondary narcissistic
disturbances in later life.

Love as Oneness in Narcissistic Collusion

*The narcissistic character; mother-child experiences of the narcissist;
forms of narcissistic partner-relationships, the complementary narcissist
as partner of the narcissist. The narcissistic marriage; the narcissistic
partner choice; the narcissistic couple conflict. The principal aspects of
narcissistic collusion.*

The theme which disturbs the couple in narcissistic collusion is the question: How much does love demand self-sacrifice and how far is it
possible to remain oneself? An additional question is: Can the wife be
perceived as a being with her own autonomy or should she simply be an
extension of her husband?

In the narcissistic stage of the development of the psyche, during the first six months of life, the boundary between the self and the environment is not clearly defined and the child experiences complete oneness with the love object.

Clinically speaking, illnesses which can be considered extreme forms of narcissistic disturbance are: schizophrenia, manic depression and personality disorders including demoralization patterns, asociality and hysterical psychopathy. In psychotic states the patient may fantasize a fusion of self and object, a loss of personality and alienation from self as well as from the environment (depersonalization, derealization). The ego is unable to exist as a distinct perceptual structure towards the outside world, and a loss of ego-boundaries results.

Milder forms of narcissistic disturbance play a particular role in problems of marital relationship. Before introducing the narcissistic marital collusion, I would like to describe the narcissistic character structure, the disturbance of the maternal relationship in early childhood and the forms of the adult partner relationships which follow as a result.

The Narcissistic Character

There are two basic types of narcissistic characters: firstly, schizoid narcissists who experience a primary narcissistic disturbance and secondly, phallic-exhibitionist narcissists who suffer from secondary narcissistic disturbance.

Phallic-exhibitionist narcissists are found mainly in the business world where the prevailing ideology conforms to their personality structure—dynamic, ruthless, selfish and successful. The female of this character is generally found in professions such as show-business, fashion and cuisine. Their social relations are geared towards raising their self worth.

Phallic narcissists have a way of introducing elements into a conversation during the first meeting which allow them to inform the other about their attributes in a few moments: a fantastic sports car, a villa with indoor swimming pool, a girlfriend with a fur coat, an eccentric hobby or a collection which they regard as the greatest and most valuable in the country. In addition they will be friendly with the most well-known celebrities, with whom they are on intimate terms. Should they deign to inquire about the attributes of their companion, it will not be out of genuine interest but rather as a means to let them know that they are hopelessly inferior by comparison. Should the companion happen to be an unusual and interesting person, they will be appropriated like a jewel. The phallic narcissist would like to hear that you are a really crazy guy or a day-dreaming loner, a revolutionary, a superman, a pervert or a genius. At the next party they can say, "Do you know my friend Bill, you know, the famous so-and-so, he's really a weird guy. . . ." Generally, however, they will simply assign you the role of an astonished listener. Your only possibility is either to listen respectfully to all their talents or to reject their boasts and oppose them.

This example basically sums up the structure of the relationship. Phallic narcissists need social contact because they are dependent on the admiration of others. People who are accepted as friends are insignificant as individuals and characteristically lack a center of their own initiative and activity (*Kohut*). Their role is only to mirror the brilliance of these great narcissists, to offer themselves as jewels to them. If one is unable to accept any of these definitions, there is no basis for a relationship and therefore one does not exist. If the narcissist is verbally skilful and humorous, he may often succeed in breaking the ice at a party and entertaining everyone. He will get the party off the ground, giving everyone the impression that they are having a great time, and create a collective euphoria, an oceanic feeling of festivity. The audience must shriek with laughter lest the narcissist's feeling of well-being be disturbed and his good intentions spoiled. At other times the narcissist might seek an enemy or opponent to cut down by ridiculing and humiliating them in mean and shocking ways.

Narcissists lack self-confidence and cannot accept a partner as an autonomous individual but only as a 'narcissistic object.' They see the partner as an extension of their own self, something which expands, flatters and heightens their self-esteem.

Kohut (1971) writes that there is often a mistaken assumption "that the existence of an object relationship excludes the narcissist. On the contrary, some of the most intense narcissistic experiences relate to the objects, that is objects which are either used in the service of the self or in support of his instinct or where objects are experienced as part of the self."

Basically narcissists long for the primal narcissistic existence in which there was no separation between subject and object, where everything was still one in primal origin in the mother's womb. Since they now cannot succeed in uniting totally with the object, they accept only those aspects of it which accord with their imagination and expectations. By idealizing the partner in a relationship they try to maintain their illusion and react with anger when the discrepancy between reality and their idealized expectations can no longer be bridged and they are forced to recognize the divergence.

Those who cannot quite swing along with them, they find threatening. They divide people into 'black and white,' friends and enemies. Since narcissists are always disappointed in their hope for total harmony in their relationships, they will often display resignation, bitterness, cynicism and fantasies of retribution. They are in a *paranoic situation*; they are deeply mistrustful, they do not believe in love or in any values in general and they dare not embrace their deeper feelings as these contain only the danger of more deception. Often they suffer from a feeling of emptiness and meaninglessness. They try to avoid recurrent depressions through hypomanic activity or conceal them behind constant theatrical and social exertion. Many are intelligent social critics or cynical satirists who resort to conspiring with others or lying or deceit. They are totally unshockable because they have nothing to lose, having lost it all a long time ago. In their bitterness they want to destroy the other's illusions of goodness, idealism and the nobility of human empathy and love. They regard human existence as an all-out battle and see only the unscrupulous egoist in man, exploiting altruistic gestures to attain his own ends. Their desperate zeal in defending the ethics of ruthless egoism in social conduct clearly proves that they long to believe in the contrary, i.e. the primal state. The discrepancy between their verbal nihilism and reticent, hidden longing for tenderness has a strong effect on persons relating to them, who would like to restore their faith in love, envelop them in utter comprehension and support them in their frailty.

As direct and uncompromising as the narcissist is in his criticism of others, he himself reacts oversensitively to every critical remark or refusal to admire and idealize him. If a companion does not support him unconditionally, they are put on the black list and dropped; they are robbed of further existence and the break is radical and absolute. The narcissist lives according to the motto: "Either for me or against me." He will do nothing to bring about reconciliation. An honest quarrel between friends is difficult for him to conceive of. The narcissist's radical methods, his unwillingness to compromise and fearlessness in fighting and taking a stand against his enemies is experienced by many people as solidarity and independence. They see in the narcissist a strong leader, often a martyr or victim of his enemies. This provides the narcissist with unquestioning followers who, out of similar motives, try to identify with him. They take the narcissist as their idol, they are completely at his beck and call, and will willingly respond to his demands for self-sacrifice. With messianic zeal the narcissist presents an image of himself and his disciples as antagonists in a quasi-holy war. He demands unconditional faith and maintains group cohesion by creating the concept of an enemy into whom everything bad is projected. Religious, political or psychotherapeutic sects often form around him. He is idealized by his supporters who see him as an omnipotent leader or prophet, threatened by mighty opponents, guiding humanity towards paradise. The narcissist seems to consider the external enemy so threatening that no method of aggression is beneath him. He fights so mercilessly and cruelly that his followers tremble with fear at the thought of finding themselves in the enemy camp. Throughout history we find that entire nations have been, and will always become, the victims of narcissistic leader figures.

The socially inhibited, and empathetic-schizoid narcissist seems to present a clear contrast to the phallic exhibitionist. He does not impose himself upon his environment, he is introverted and waits quietly until others discover his worth. But his very shyness and profound modesty impresses his companions who wonder at what may be going on inside him, and often tend to idealize him. It is said of him: "Still waters run deep." He often is extraordinarily perceptive, is an attentive listener and rapidly becomes a trusted confidant with whom others share their innermost secrets. Although he does not offer his opinions, others feel an inner understanding with him and achieve the feeling of well-being which they desire. A certain 'mystical union' is created, an oceanic feeling of happiness, a primal condition which cannot be blurred by any subject-object split.

In this idealized harmony, as is common with all schizoid narcissists, much in the conversation is only hinted at, the spoken word being rejected as superfluous and insufficient. In his impression of harmony the narcissist assumes that the partner agrees with all his feelings, endeavors and fantasies and is often surprised and hurt if during treatment, the therapist asks questions about his past history or his present state. He feels alienated if the therapist does not already know everything about him since he is in constant internal dialogue with the therapist. But the therapist is faced with a most difficult dilemma: either to present the reality that there is no such orientation and thus destroy the only fragile relationship possible with the narcissist, namely idealized symbiosis; or not to challenge the narcissist's fantasized union and be idealized as omniscient and consequently risk uncertainty about the true meaning of his intimations. Often one will be able only to guess at what is going on inside him without ever achieving any certainty. If asked to express himself more clearly, and to be more specific in his opinions, he feels that one wants to take hold of him, force him or pin him down to a concrete image. He escapes like a dove someone wants to capture.

Given the particular nature of the therapeutic relationship, a therapist can tolerate this uncertainty. For a partner in love, this is scarcely possible to endure. They will demand the clarity which the narcissist wants to avoid. The narcissist must always keep an exit open and be assured that this exit is granted him.

The partner does not sense confirmation of themselves as an independent being, but rather must adapt their behavior to conform to the narcissist's conception of it. The relationship is so tenuous that neither partner can express their demands or expectations towards the other. This lack of demonstrativeness attenuates the relationship to such a degree that it becomes sterile and leaves the partners scarcely sure that it actually still exists.

The narcissist's lack of contact with reality also often manifests itself in unperturbed lying. During psychotherapy, he will provide a constant stream of information on events and happenings which he hopes will interest the therapist and thus consolidate the idealized relationship. It is of little concern to him whether or not the reports are based on fact. The therapist can therefore not be certain whether his patient is making real progress or whether apparent improvements are being made only to satisfy him. Similarly, in a love relationship, the narcissist often lies thoughtlessly in order to shield his partner (and also himself) from anything that could cloud the idealized relationship.

Mother-Child Experiences of the Narcissist   Psychic Needs of CHILD NOT MET

There is abundant literature on the characteristic forms of the narcissistic personality's maternal relationship. As a rule the mother cannot perceive the child as other than a part of herself. This form of relationship can no longer be maintained when the child develops physically, learns to walk and talk, develops its own initiative and wants to be separate from the mother. She reacts with anger to the personal injury ✓ and ingratitude which she senses in the child's every attempt to deviate from her own ideas and expectations. She develops strategies to prevent the child from experiencing itself as a separate being. One of these is to constantly assign to the child only those characteristics which correspond to the mother's ideal, as in this example: "You cannot think something so bad. I know it's not you. You can't know yourself as well as I do. I knew you before you were born." The mother believes she knows what the child should feel, what it should think and how it should perceive. A particularly severe experience for the child is the association of guilt feelings with every deviation from the expected image: "How ungrateful of you. Think of all I have done for you and suffered for you." It is because of the child that the mother had to get married, stay unhappily married, go through a difficult pregnancy and sacrifice her career. She now suffers from exhaustion and migraine headaches. Often the mother will maintain her hold on the children by imposing certain behavior codes upon them: "You cannot refuse your mother this wish. I knew that you would remember me." The child will then be forced into the paradox: "I am only myself when I am the image my mother creates. When I am how I feel, I am not myself." Any variation on this image will be denigrated and punished. The mother experiences the child only as an extension or function of herself and the language she uses reflects this. "We stayed in bed this morning and wouldn't go to school, would we? We wouldn't get up when it was time and we didn't have a thing for breakfast."

Under these conditions, the child cannot develop an autonomous self. Any initiative to establish an identity is disparaged. Such personalities, consequently, are characterized by self-doubt, a weak self-image, vague ego-boundaries, inferiority complexes, etc.

Above all, the child is deeply disillusioned with 'love' and hates and rejects any form of it. Love is seen as a tactic to make others dependent, to take advantage of them, to exploit and manipulate them. The child cannot develop a mature super-ego; in its experience, all values and standards are imposed by others and it is never given the freedom or opportunity to exercise responsibility and acquire and test an ethical-moral standard. Often this child will be the mother's prized possession; the son with his professional achievements, the daughter as a beautiful princess, ballet dancer or movie star. He must become all this and fulfil what the mother herself could not realize in her life. As *Richter* (1967) describes, the child becomes the substitute for the mother's self.

Separation from the narcissistic mother is extremely difficult. One imagines that she has the magical abilities of an Old Testament God. She is an invisible worker, omnipotent and omnipresent; a figure who demands complete self-sacrifice and whose rage is destructive and cruel. Since she knows one's every thought, one dare not think of criticizing her. She is the giver of life, reigning over one's very existence. Precisely because of the mystical nature of the relationship to the mother, one can never be rid of her, even if she has long been dead or one has moved to a foreign country.

Influenced by these experiences, it is very dangerous for the narcissist as adult to enter into an intimate, enduring, partner relationship. Although the partner may not behave like the narcissistic mother, they will often nonetheless be experienced as someone wanting to manipulate to serve their own needs or to shape their partner as an extension of themself.

Conversely, those narcissists who lack any moral capacity generally did not have a stable relationship in their earliest childhood. No 'false self' was imposed on them by a mother. On the contrary, their existence was never really recognized. They never experienced a relationship in which they were considered important; there was never anyone who sincerely and conscientiously cared for them and concerned themselves with their feelings. To compensate for this lack, they withdrew into a world of imaginary wish-fulfillment and fantasy which belonged only to them, and which centered only on them. The end result is that they produce the same narcissistic disturbances in partner relationships as those who have been manipulated by their mothers. And similarly the partner is seen as someone without initiative and independence who merely performs a set of functions in their fantasy world.

Forms of Narcissistic Partner Relationships

In the context of an intimate relationship, the narcissist is in an almost unresolvable situation. According to his point of view, love requires either of two things, either that you sacrifice yourself for the partner or that the partner sacrifices themself for you. He cannot conceive that love is possible without one of them having to give up their individuality, opinions and rights for the benefit of the other. It is unimaginable that there could be harsh quarrels and differences of opinion without jeopardizing the love bond. To the narcissist, an intense love relationship is a total oneness, a fusion with the other in perfect harmony. But such a fusion poses a difficult threat for someone so insecure. He feels overwhelmed by a stable relationship with a partner whereas he may perform well in groups. Many remain single, or are unable to marry or fail if they do marry.

A number of possible forms of partner relationship can be identified with Freud's concept of the narcissistic object relationship between auto-eroticism and mature love.

The first stage is the fantasized partner relationship during masturbation. The partner does not exist in reality but is realized only in the imagination; which is an extreme form of a narcissistic partner relationship. The partner is identical to the image one creates of them. One does not need to give them an independent, autonomous existence. They have rights only if we allot them some. A number of narcissists remain in this stage in their heterosexual relationships.

The next stage is generally the relationship to prostitutes. The narcissist often has sexual relationships exclusively with call girls. In her professional role the prostitute defines herself as someone who offers sexual satisfaction according to the desires of her client without demanding satisfaction for herself, except through financial reward. The 'partners' don't even know each other's names. Their encounter is impersonal. The suitor does not face the challenge of conquest, nor even the need to adjust himself to the prostitute as a person. He uses her purely in terms of her function.

The relationship of the phallic narcissist to his mistress approaches more closely a mature relationship to the love-object. But she too is frequently not acknowledged as a person. She serves his pleasure and self-esteem and complies with his wishes. She must always be radiant, happy

and full of life, showing only her Sunday face. For this she is amply
rewarded with gifts, in the narcissist's terms "spoilt." For him, an important element of the relationship is the admiration of his mistress. If
she manages to convince him that an expression of the generosity of his
love would be not only a fur coat for Christmas but also a matching
sports car, he will give her just that. The relationship has "no
problems," which means that the mistress may neither create any personal difficulties nor make any personal demands which do not correspond to her lover's expectations. Generally she is replaceable and has a
purely functional role. Often the female partner is expected to fulfil a
role similar to that of a dog: relating only to her master, existing totally
for him, being grateful for everything he gives her, happily wagging her
tail when he appears, sad when he leaves, and all without making any
demands or pretensions of her own. A famous French singer was asked
when he was 80 years old and seen with a beautiful young blonde at the
Riviera whether he thought she loved him. His answer was: "If I enjoy
eating lobster, I don't ask it to love me." The mistress is an article of
decoration which should give pleasure; no real personal encounter is
intended.

Transient love relationships may be considered a preparatory step
towards a two-person relationship. In this case, there is a partial recognition of the partner as an autonomous being. Schizoid narcissists have an
overdeveloped ability to identify with the feelings of another and are
always in danger of losing themselves in their partner. But this does
enable them temporarily to enter into a love relationship and become
very close to the partner. They are quick to understand how to make a
conquest.

Sexually, the narcissist is not an inconsiderate lover, he is often concerned about whether his partner is equally satisfied. But his concern is
less for the partner herself than for the growth in his own self-esteem
when he brings her to orgasm. He wants to hear her say that he is unique
and that sexual relations have never been so satisfying. If the sexual relationship does not work he feels this as a personal injury and becomes
angry and impatient.

The relationship is often dissolved as soon as the partner has been
won. These experiences frequently follow in quick succession. We speak
about men as Don Juans or wolves, and women as nymphs although
they do not form the female counterpart to Don Juans (see oral collusion). As a transient phase, a succession of temporary love relationships
is a normal part of development during adolescence. The conquest on
which these flirtatious relationships are focused provides an optimum of
mutual confirmation and idealization and to this degree is satisfying to

the narcissist. A quick, temporary union is formed because it protects the narcissist from anything which could affect or obscure their being at one with the love-object. Other aspects of the relationship come into play once the conquest is over, and impede continuation. The narcissistic drive diminishes when the exhilirating tension of whether or not the conquest will succeed has passed. The partner proves to be an average human being and is no longer idealized. Their negative qualities, which were previously excluded from the relationship, now become very apparent. Most importantly a bond appears which, to the narcissist, implies a duty or commitment of which he feels incapable. Initially he had succeeded in devoting himself completely to the relationship and letting his partner come close enough to form a bond with him, but this closeness now becomes a threat. He abruptly disrupts the relationship and destroys it. Suddenly the partner no longer interests him, no longer even exists for him. For the partner it is incomprehensible that the narcissist can reject her, for no apparent reason, just when she feels so close. But the reason is precisely that the two partners have come too close. The narcissist has to 'excorporate' his partner, to force her out of himself. Often the narcissist wants to put this unexpected end to the relationship in order to avoid the risk of being rejected by her. He may frequently have felt abandoned in his childhood and now enjoys being able to abandon others as revenge for past frustrations.

The sexual lives of narcissists appear to vary greatly. Often they are sexually fully functional and able to enjoy sex as long as they are not in love with the partner. They may be sexually liberated and more confident when they can distance themselves from any possibly intruding influences. But the closer the partner becomes, the more difficult it is. Narcissists may become impotent during marriage to a partner with whom they formerly enjoyed sexual intercourse. Some women are able to reach orgasm easily, have a long plateau phase with several consecutive high points, like to feel the penis inside them for a long time and feel literally "set up" and reborn after intercourse. Others are frigid because the loss of control during orgasm awakens especially strong fears of dissolving into the other. Men also can experience in orgasm the danger of dissolving the boundaries of self. Suddenly they are no longer sure whether sexual arousal is felt by them or by their partner (*Erikson* 1963), or whether the penis is a part of them or their partner. Some men fear that too much of their life force is taken from them during ejaculation.

Homosexual tendencies are often expressed and indeed are an aspect of narcissistic relationships. *Freud* (1914): "One loves in accordance with the narcissistic type that one is oneself." Perversions may also be characteristic of narcissistic relationships, depending on the nature of the motivating force or goal. However, although homosexual and perverse tendencies can play an important part in the psychopathology of marriage, they fall beyond the scope of this book.

The Complimentary Narcissist as a Partner of the Narcissist

Narcissists and their partners display certain similarities to each other. Colloquially speaking, we generally consider the narcissist to be egotistical and the partner to be altruistic. Partners are permeated with feelings of inferiority, feel worthless and undeserving of love, and have low self-esteem even to the extent of a tendency to self-destruction. They appear to be modest human beings who make no show of themselves and no demands; they adapt themselves and fit in without offering any resistance. Usually they have become used to being degraded since childhood. Rather than having a false self imposed upon them, they were denied the right to autonomy.

Upon closer acquaintance, we notice that they are not as unselfish as they appear and that they have fantasies of grandeur, which are often associated with deep feelings of guilt, and which they feel ashamed to admit. They try to suppress these fantasies because they believe they have no right to them. Often they are very competent professionally but do not feel that they are being themselves. In the majority of cases these are women who are unable to develop a positive feminine self-image. They look for a partner whom they may idealize and onto whom they may project their ideal self in order to be able to identify with him and thus appropriate an acceptable self (projective identification with the ideal self of their lover). Quite a few executive secretaries serve as examples; they identify completely with their boss, whom they adore and whose fame and glamor they glorify. They are completely at his service, feel in tune with his needs and fulfil any of his wishes. At the same time they create his infrastructure by taking care of his phone calls, making his appointments, organizing his brief-case and making his coffee. If they have held their position for several years, they know and control everything, gradually becoming indispensable to their boss, who is still as great as before but can no longer function without his secretary. She is not only his right hand but the very ground on which he stands and grows. She becomes indispensable to him, thanks to her seeming humility and service. She complements and guides his thoughts and deeds. He has become a part of her and she a part of him. Often she may really be the one who advances him to an executive position, while sitting in the antechamber, jealously guarding the entrance like a Cerberus and exaggerating his unavailability to his subordinates. The visitor seeking admittance to the holy chambers is overcome with reverence and his heart thumps as she conjures up before him the stature and importance of her boss's position. One dare not show lack of respect towards the master.

The situation is also quite analogous in love. These women are willing to give themselves for their captivating, adored and idealized man without making any demands of their own. They live for him and through him; they appear to obey their partner and be willing to idealize him without criticism or conditions, as in the saying: "Love is for me only if you are."

The complementary narcissist is also basically narcissistically constructed, but with reversed symptoms. While the narcissist seeks only to admire himself, the complementary narcissist wants to sacrifice herself to the other. While the narcissist wants to enhance his self-esteem, his partner seeks to forfeit her own self in order to elevate the self of the narcissist, with whom she identifies. While the narcissist fears engulfment in a relationship, his partner's only desire is to merge completely with the other. Both manifest the same disturbance, namely a weak definition of self and a sense of inferiority. It is only the defense mechanism or the means to come to terms with the weak self that is different: the narcissist tries to upgrade his inferior self through the partner, while the complementary narcissist tries to appropriate an idealized self from the partner.

The narcissist responds to the complementary narcissist as partner because he wants to be admired by the love object and because he values the absence of obligation to attend to the initiatives of an autonomous partner. He does not feel threatened because she subordinates herself completely to him. This type of relationship can frequently be observed in the marriages of creative men. They identify completely with their work and demand that their wives subordinate themselves to their husbands' careers, suppressing their personal demands in case these might create obstacles. This is generally successful when the woman can perceive herself as the nourishing mother earth of her husband and can project all her aggression—created by frustration towards him—onto others, more particularly onto his enemies and rivals. Such women are often the wives of professors, and their every second sentence is: "My husband, John, says . . . does. . . ." This continues sometimes even after the husband's death, becoming more grotesque. As much as 20 years later, these women may still be living with a self-image which is only borrowed from their husbands: "If my husband, John, were still alive, he would have said . . . would have done. . . ." Although in reality their husbands may have been very inconsiderate towards them, they are idealized unconditionally and continue to provide their life with meaning.

But as the couple spend more time together the confidence and free-dom of the narcissist begins to prove false for his subordinate partner. Since the partner can live only through empathy with the narcissist and is completely focused on his every move and change of feeling, she lives out every fantasy through him. She merges with the narcissist, pene-trates him and exercises strong control over him precisely because, para-doxically, she forfeits her own self-image. Finally, it is no longer clear whose self-worth is being enhanced and who is borrowing a self-image from whom. A relationship similar to that which the narcissist had with his mother begins to develop—one which he has taken great pains to avoid—in which the woman may feel she knows him better than he knows himself. Her idealized image restricts him still further. What was formerly a source of prestige or flattery now becomes a duty. Ad-miration becomes a burden, entirely drowning his demand for auton-omy. The image she has of him, which was initially his ideal and role model, now becomes his prison.

The situation becomes untenable for the narcissist. He would like to coerce or destroy the partner for succeeding in getting so close to him. He tries to put her down, to hurt and injure her; his behavior towards her becomes petty, ruthless and cold. All is to no avail. She swallows it all with the comment: "I know you too well. I know that deep down you don't really mean it." Faced with this the narcissist is completely power-less. If he behaves like a loving devil the partner will interpret this to be his false self: "That's not him. He is basically a good person, only he is very sensitive and easily hurt. It's only out of weakness that he behaves like this." The narcissist can no longer withdraw from the partner. However, he can extricate himself forcefully or get a divorce and marry another woman or commit a crime and spend years in prison, or become mentally ill, or beat up his wife or kill himself; but nothing will change. His partner will continue to live for him in almost magical ways. She is there only for him and regards the separation as no more than a tem-porary phase to which she attaches no importance, convinced of reunion in life or death.

The Narcissistic Marriage
The narcissist dreads marriage and is opposed to this institution. He can-not bear committing himself with a vow to a life-long relationship. He delays the marriage decision for as long as possible until, under pressure from the partner or other circumstances, he finally agrees—much against his own will and with great mistrust. As far as he is concerned he

would rather live together with someone. Current trends diminish his difficulties. Society develops towards narcissistic values with the concept that partner relationships should further self-development. This means, in its extreme form, that a relationship has a functional character and is considered valid only in so far as personal development is furthered or at least not impeded. Often the narcissist will prefer to remain childless in marriage because he feels that a child would take advantage of him.

If the narcissist must marry he will control the partner totally and keep her to himself, while at the same time refusing to recognize her personal needs.

The Narcissistic Partner Choice

The narcissist's intention is to find a partner who will make no demands of her own and who will adore and idealize him. He identifies with the ideal images which his partner projects onto him. She should sacrifice herself completely for him and live only for him, so there is no danger of his having to make sacrifices or restrict himself on her account. The narcissist frequently will protect himself from the danger of having to adapt to the partner by choosing someone who is inferior in character or in intelligence, education or family background; the partner might be much younger or older than he is, or have an illness, disability or outlook that prevents her from being judged on an equal basis.

The complementary narcissist interprets these expectations in terms of her own motivation. Because of her weak self-image she forfeits the right to her own self-development and wants to grow through adoration of the narcissist. She projects her imagined ideal onto her partner and identifies with it, finding in the partner an idealized substitute for self. The partners complement each other in terms of an ideal. The narcissist experiences the idealizing of the complementary narcissist as decisive self-development and can feel grandiose. The complementary narcissist is happy to be able to identify with the narcissist. Both feel sure of their defenses. The narcissist believes no threat of loss of self, engulfment, fusion or a false definition of self exists for him, since the partner idealizes him and sacrifices herself for him. For the complementary narcissist there can be an end to the feelings of inferiority caused by her fantasy of unfulfilled greatness, as the partner will now fulfil these demands in her place. Translated into interaction, the narcissist says: "I can be so grandiose because you adore me so effusively, because I am so grandiose for you." Graphically represented, the dynamic of the narcissistic partner choice looks like this:

Narcissistic Partner Choice

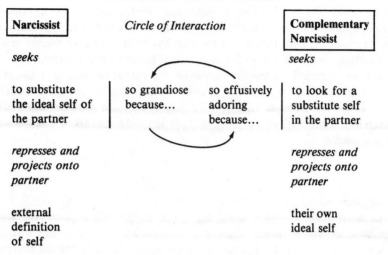

<table>
<tr><td>**Narcissist**</td><td>*Circle of Interaction*</td><td></td><td>**Complementary Narcissist**</td></tr>
<tr><td>*seeks*</td><td></td><td></td><td>*seeks*</td></tr>
<tr><td>to substitute the ideal self of the partner</td><td>so grandiose because...</td><td>so effusively adoring because...</td><td>to look for a substitute self in the partner</td></tr>
<tr><td>*represses and projects onto partner*</td><td></td><td></td><td>*represses and projects onto partner*</td></tr>
<tr><td>external definition of self</td><td></td><td></td><td>their own ideal self</td></tr>
</table>

The Narcissistic Couple Conflict

While the complementary narcissist completely sacrifices herself for her partner and lives exclusively for him through identification, she also claims the self of the narcissist as her own and steadily confines him to her idealized image of him. Since the narcissist thrives on positive projections and admiration from his partner, he allows his identity to become more defined by this superimposed ideal image. He may try to differentiate himself from the complementary narcissist but he is becoming steadily more imprisoned in his partner's imagined ideal. He may try to defend himself by degrading, rejecting or destroying her.

In existential anger and cold-bloodedness he fights to preserve his self-image, yet fails to free himself because he is completely permeated by his partner. His blows against the partner fall into the void because the latter does not retaliate as an autonomous individual. Instead she embodies, lives and breathes, as representative and advocate, that ideal of his own better self to which he wants to commit himself. The vicious circle for the narcissist now looks something like this: "I am so malicious and ruthless because you trap me and fence me in"; and for the complementary narcissist: "I trap you and fence you in because you are so malicious and ruthless."

The complementary narcissist is also truly desperate. She has sacrificed herself completely for this relationship and has lived only for her partner. She trusted him totally and now feels cheated out of her deepest hopes and dreams: "I have loved you so much, how can you disappoint me like this? I saw everything in you that I could have hoped for from life, nothing had any meaning for me without you and now you turn out to be so horrible.'' The complementary narcissist is obliged by definition to protect the embodiment of her ideal self in the partner. In an almost deluded way she hangs onto this image and no disappointments will induce her to modify the expectations which she projects onto him. She tried continually to make the partner correspond to her ideal image, without being prepared to perceive and accept him as he really is.

While only a very diluted relationship would be possible for the narcissist, the complementary narcissist will consider only an ideal and refuses all half-truths and compromises in a relationship.

The connection between partner choice and conflict between partners may be represented as follows:

It is characteristic of many narcissistic marriages that in due course the partners appear to live together coldly in complete disillusionment; each following their own interests and having his or her own lovers. Over the course of years many partners have no sexual relationship to each other. It would seem that they remain together only for the sake of the children or for material advantage. If one examines the circumstances more accurately, however, the situation is much more complex than it appears. Behind the cold façade, wild passions, jealousy and hatred are brewing. Behind their restrained behavior partners watch and control each other in all their thoughts and actions. Indifferent behavior becomes a desperate defense mechanism against the threat of too much intimacy.

Narcissistic marriages frequently end in divorce. The narcissist takes it very badly when his wife leaves him, it being much easier for him to leave his partner. Then he has the advantage of being able to cut himself off from his feelings more easily. Temporarily he may lapse into a narcissistic emptiness, feeling stunned and depressed, but he can very quickly overcome it by starting a new relationship. The former partner simply no longer exists for him or becomes the embodiment of that negativity, stupidity and insensitivity from which he must free himself.

To be deserted by the partner often means, however, a primary crisis. One of our patients suffered serious depression and locked himself up in his apartment. For weeks on end he took refuge in bed, and threatened a hunger strike when his wife unexpectedly told him of her intention to divorce. Finally he had to be hospitalized because of severe weight loss and underwent psychiatric treatment. Another patient in a similar situation developed hypochondriac fantasies and delusions. He believed himself to be suffering from a brain tumor and multiple schlerosis and saw himself fading away completely, unfit for life and dehumanized. Both had experienced difficulty in deciding whether or not they wanted to get married and had in actual fact only given in to pressure from their wives. Both had advanced their professional careers unexpectedly well during their married lives. As soon as the narcissistic impetus of their wives was withdrawn, however, they both collapsed like empty gloves.

The complementary narcissist, in contrast, often continues to remain faithful to the partner after divorce, even if the latter has remarried, has other children and maintains no further contact with her. The complementary narcissist fantasizes that she is basically indispensable to her former partner who cannot live without her and would literally collapse without her. No one could possibly love or understand her partner as she did.

Narcissistic collusion points to a problem that is currently much discussed, which is whether one should pressure someone into marriage or whether one should be free to choose cohabitation over marriage. Although personally I find that the institution of marriage offers greater possibilities in terms of long-term goals, I think it is important to distinguish between specific cases. Certain particularly narcissistic personalities undergo too much stress in marriage but are fully able to build satisfactory and meaningful relationships which may not be as exclusive, intimate, long-lasting and committed as marriage. We are concerned with the question of how much togetherness a person can tolerate with continued benefit to themself. Maximal intimacy is by no means the best for everybody.

Narcissistic Collusion

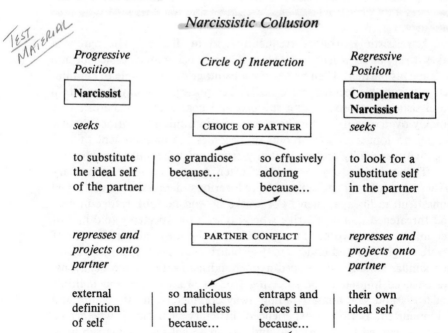

Case 2:

A 40-year-old bachelor married a woman 15 years younger. Both had jobs in the business field. Up until then he had had countless intimate relationships and relished the freedom of being able to break up the relationship at the moment when problems arose. He came from an unhappy family background and had seen almost nothing but quarrelling between his parents. He was filled with fear lest this happen to him in his own marriage. His wife seemed to him to be the ideal partner. She was a beautiful, intelligent and angelic creature and it seemed that he could risk marrying her. Because he was regarded by her as an experienced man and fatherly protector, there did not appear to be any danger of having to adapt himself to her demands. He did not plan to have any children and his wife accepted this. She was supposed to be both wife and child for him. She idealized him as a superior partner who would remove all life's problems. The couple had pre-marital sexual relations, supposedly without any problems. However, since their wedding day two years earlier, all sexual relations had ceased. This was the only cloud in an otherwise tension-free marriage. For this reason the couple sought group marriage therapy.

During treatment, it became obvious that there were not only difficulties in communication sexually, but also that similar communication problems existed in other areas. The couple had never fought through a disagreement, let alone a quarrel. Both believed that such a conflict would destroy the idealization on which their relationship was based and that the break-up would be final. In the beginning the wife was scarcely able to express herself in the group and seemed like a frightened deer that everyone had to treat gently. The husband was more active and social in his character, but was embarrassed by his wife's presence in the group because he always sought to bring his opinion into agreement with his wife's reactions and was unable to express his own convictions. Originally he had feared that his life-style might be influenced in some way by his inexperienced wife, because of what he saw as her almost super-human perfection. He now tended to feel increasingly that she kept him prisoner by her very idealization of him. In the beginning he had been happy to be able to shape her through his ideas, but he now felt that he had to live up to her image of him as a master. In group therapy they were both surprised to learn that other couples could disagree with each other without destroying their relationship; moreover they came to see how these people were capable of exchanging intense feelings of love. Gradually they began to differentiate themselves more clearly from each other and learned to tolerate dissonance in their relationship. The wife began to develop her own initiative, which was not easy for her husband to accept. He once jokingly stated that an ideal partner would really behave towards him like a lapdog.

Case 3:

The wife came for treatment depressed about an unhappy marriage. She had been married for two years to a man who at the time of their meeting had just come out of prison, having served a sentence for repeated embezzlements and petty theft. Prior to marriage he had led a loose and unstable life, playing the great gentleman and constantly living beyond his means as a successful con man. In appearance she created a grotesque contrast to him: while he was well-dressed and good-looking, she looked unattractive and drab. Before her marriage she had had little experience with men and was inhibited and shy in making contact. She had agreed that he need not adjust himself to her in any way in their marriage. He spent most of his week-ends and evenings in bars, as he had done in the past, where he flirted with other women to nurture his self-confidence. Once he infected his wife with gonorrhea. In his free time he went fishing, where he had to be alone to pursue his fantasies of grandeur. His wife accepted these frustrations for a long time without complaint and kept the house in his absence, although she had a full-time job. She lived in the elusive hope that she had made a great man out of him and saved him from an unstable life. In fact under her influence he actually had stabilized professionally and worked himself up to a position which was clearly above his educational qualifications. Thus the woman had the satisfaction of realizing herself through him. But her doubts gradually increased as to whether this form of living together was really right.

In therapy we tried to work on the contrasts between the partners. The wife fantasized that she too could have some freedom and occasionally go out alone. The husband protested vehemently: "I married you because you are my better self. If you want to go running off perhaps I don't need to be married anymore." He used his wife as a substitute for his superego, which enabled him to stabilize his self-image. He emphasized that the marriage would become meaningless for him if his wife refused to fulfil this role any longer. On the other hand the wife also used her husband as a substitute for her own motivation, and for her deeply-disturbed narcissistic self. She suffered from serious inferiority complexes and felt that, through her contribution to her husband's success, her own personality would be enhanced.

In the course of treatment the husband became increasingly disturbed. Because of his poor self-image he could not accept his wife's criticism about the unequal division of rights and duties. He became more and more anxious and unable to work effectively, and so discontinued group therapy. The marriage temporarily broke up as a result. Joint therapy had, however, allowed him to realize the necessity for psychotherapy. He began psychoanalysis, and his wife analytical group therapy.

Principal Aspects of Narcissistic Collusion

The couple mutually resist any questioning of their ideal of a love relationship; it is the attainment of a primal harmony by fusing as one. Basically both agree that they should try to reach this goal: where the complementary narcissist sacrifices herself for the good of the narcissist who in turn fulfils the idealized expectations of the complementary narcissist. The impossibility of realizing the ideal of fusion ultimately fills both partners with anger and disappointment. In therapy their basic desire is that their wishes might still become realities.

In therapy, however, the narcissist tries outwardly to hurt the complementary narcissist. He frustrates her and belittles her, maintaining his distance as a defense against his own feelings of guilt and shame for his betrayal of the mutual ideal. In reaction to this frustration the complementary narcissist pressures the narcissist with her expectations and insults. Finally she creates her own frustration voluntarily. In fact she also comes ultimately to fear symbiotic oneness. She fears that her imagined ideal of fusion could take control if she allows the partner to come closer to her and she might then be unable to tolerate the frustration of another disappointment or disharmony. She provokes her partner until he confirms anticipated disappointments, thus clearly cutting herself free of his ideals. In doing so, she hurts the narcissist and she herself becomes rejected and frustrated.

The relationship is characterized by retribution fantasies, the need to injure and hurt one another in order to avoid becoming one. In most cases, the partners expect therapy to help them attain the ideal harmony they long for. They discover a new and unexpected experience when they realize that they can become closer to each other if they differentiate themselves more clearly from one another.

The complementary narcissist should learn in therapy to express her own identity and be less dependent on the confirmation or disparagement of her partner. She should recognize her needs, feelings and fears as her own, defend them and not always react solely to the behavior of her partner. Similarly, the narcissist should learn to be less pressured by the idealized expectations of the partner. The aim would be to establish clear but more flexible boundaries between the partners and between what lies inside and what outside the dyad; as in the saying: "I am me, you are you and we are both different."

Love as Caring and Nourishing in Oral Collusion

The oral stage of development; the oral mother-child collusion; the oral character; the maternal character. Oral collusion; oral partner choice; the oral partner conflict. Principal aspects of oral collusion.

Oral collusion is centered on love as caring for, being cared for and nourishing one another. The relationship can be defined simply as one in which one partner has to care for the other as a mother would a helpless child. The implicit assumption is that, similarly, the partners will be united by a tendency to demand that gestures towards each other be reciprocated and that the one in need of help will be spared all expectation of response. Oral collusion develops from this basic assumption.

This theme symbolizes the earliest mother-child relationship, or the oral stage of development of the first years of life. Since unresolved difficulties in the earliest mother-child relationship underlie oral collusion in marriage, I shall start by describing the oral stage of development in the child and the oral mother-child collusion.

The Oral Stage of Development

As the psychoanalytical view of the developing psyche illustrates (I base my examples of early stages of development on work by George Engel and Erik Erikson), the first human relationship of the new born baby is determined primarily by his need for food. The child announces his need to be fed through restlessness, kicking and crying. The still primitive instinctual mentality responds to an increasing need by behaving in such a way that the need will be satisfied.

Need-satisfaction is, however, dependent upon the participation of the one who feeds him, generally the mother. The crying of the child stimulates an appropriate response in the mother which is strongly dependent on her own life-experience. Ideally, she exhibits a basic maternal pattern in the wish to approach the crying child, comfort him, feed him, hold him and satisfy him. A positive response gives the mother a secure feeling, a satisfaction and fulfillment of her own needs. It is a reciprocal relationship between mother and child in which the mother experiences pleasure when the child becomes quiet and the child finds contentment in that he is fed and satisfied (*G. Engel*).

During the third to sixth week of life, the child smiles for the first time. As a rule this gives the mother great joy. Wolf noticed that the length of time the mother plays with the child greatly increases as soon as the child responds with a smile. It is the first form of exchange of understanding and elicits joy in both mother and child. Gradually smiling occurs naturally when a familiar object appears, when the child is attracted to something or simply feels happy.

The next stage of development is instinctive recognition and guessing which is accompanied by the ability to wait. According to *Erikson* (1977), this ability in the child is dependent upon the internalization of a good mother image and the trust that the need will satisfactorily be met at the appropriate time. The child learns to let the mother out of his sight without becoming overly angry or anxious. The child internalizes those attributes of the mother which serve to decrease tension and the need for satisfaction. Since much happens in connection with experiences of feeding, the child associates the first form of relationship with the environment. Whatever is good, desirable and tension-reducing in the surroundings is taken into the body. This is the oral modality of relationship.

Gradually the child learns to imagine satisfaction and even imitates vicarious substitutes for those he was formerly totally dependent upon, for example, thumb sucking or rocking. The memory pathways are interlinked elements of the outer world which give partial satisfaction and an anticipation of even greater satisfaction. The internalized image of a 'good mother' is associated with feelings of need-satisfaction. Hence the mother becomes a part of the developing ego of the child.

The ego begins to fulfil its integrating function. The first defense mechanisms are formed in order to attain pleasant things and avoid unpleasant ones. The child develops the idea or opinion that what brings satisfaction has to be enclosed, grasped and taken in (introjection) and that what is unsatisfactory and associated with bad feelings must be thrown away, kept out and pushed away (projection). If the mother is not satisfying, the child tries to release its bad feelings by experiencing the mother as 'bad,' namely as the source of his bad feelings. If the mother is able to comfort the child through this, he will again introject the 'good' mother. Possibly the ideas of a 'good mother' and 'bad mother' are separated for the first time.

The functional ability of this ego-structure cannot be overtaxed, but must become strengthened by real, positive experiences that develop it. Learning how one can obtain pleasure and avoid pain takes place through the changing relationship between mother and child. The mechanisms of introjection and projection lay the groundwork for later identification. They gain relative integration only through a satisfactory relationship between a caring motherly figure and the child to be cared for. Only through experiencing this basic give-and-take does the child gain the confidence of self-esteem from which he can go to the opposite pole, the first love object.

After some months, the child begins to dissolve the mother-child symbiosis which gives rise to anxiety. However, this dissolution is necessary for the child's development and is correlated with motor development, development of speech and all the other possibilities of communication. Towards the end of the first year of life, the child learns to distinguish more clearly between self and non-self. Gradually the subject-object split establishes itself. The child notices that the same mother is satisfying and frustrating and slowly learns to perceive her as an individual who has needs of her own.

The main factor in the development of the psychic apparatus is the way in which the pleasure principle works in general, the child seeks that which brings acceptance and pleasure and avoids that which brings pain and dislike. In the course of development, the pleasure principle is gradually transformed through the demands of reality. The child has to realize that specific demands of persons in the external environment have to be satisfied so that his needs can be fulfilled. Continued functioning on the basis of the primitive pleasure principle would fail because, when attempts for satisfaction are in conflict with the needs of others on whom the child is dependent, punishment and rejection result. The child must gradually learn, even painfully, to delay some of his desires for satisfaction or give them up in order to maintain a satisfactory relationship with the environment. Pleasure and need-satisfaction are better ensured when the external reality through which satisfaction can be reached is taken into account. For this development, it is important to be able to predict what brings pleasure, what brings pain and what will result in frustration or disappointment. These efforts become a powerful motivating force for learning to understand the environment and represent an important determinant factor for intellectual growth.

The Oral Mother-Child Collusion

Even in the earliest phases of life, a conflict between mother and child can arise which will form the basis of marriage disturbance in later life.

As mentioned previously, the child initially lives in full accordance with the pleasure principle and makes known his need for food by piercing screaming and eager devouring. This behavior will arouse anxiety and defensiveness in the mother if she herself did not master the demands of the oral stage of development. She fears the child will consume her; she envies the child who can announce his need freely and thus reach immediate satisfaction. Most importantly, if she has not mastered the transition from the pleasure principle to the reality principle, she will tend to indulge the child orally and then respond just as quickly to the slightest tension in any other need if the child's demands arouse in her a corresponding tension. This frustrates the child who is unaware of the conflict in the mother. Since she has no rhythm of her own and cannot delay satisfaction of her own needs, she is plagued by guilt at having failed as a parent. As a reaction to her anger and fury towards the child, she will eventually almost suffocate him with overindulgence. The child cannot develop the ability to wait. He does not learn to allow a time to elapse between the development of hunger and the satisfaction of his need for food, and to build the trust that in time his discomfort will be followed by satisfaction. Similarly the child does not learn to let his mother out of his sight without being filled with anxiety, just as the mother cannot let the child out of her sight without feeling uneasy and afraid that something might happen to him. A vicious circle builds up: the more nervous and tense the mother is, the greater is the child's irritability and crying, and the greater the child's irritability and crying, the more nervous and tense the mother becomes. Eventually the baby refuses the breast and is lazy in drinking because he senses his mother's tension. The mother reacts to this refusal with increased tension which is again transferred to the baby. *Erikson* (1977) writes:

"The loss of mutual regulation with the maternal source of supply is exemplified by a mother's habitual withdrawal of the nipple because she has been nipped or because she feels she will be. In such cases the oral machinery, instead of relaxedly indulging in sucking, may prematurely develop a biting reflex. Our clinical material often suggests that such a situation is the model for one of the most radical disturbances of interpersonal relations. One hopes to obtain, the source is withdrawn,

whereupon one tries reflexively to hold on and to take; but the more one holds on, the more determinedly does the source remove itself."

Some mothers almost suffocate their children with love. They stuff them with food in an impulsive, hearty way, squeezing them almost to death in their arms and assume unhesitatingly that the child is a part of them and belongs to them. If the mother becomes aware of her own oral character structure, then she may desire to satisfy her oral need through the child. Her longing for comfort can then be resolved in the satisfaction of her child. Skin contact with the clinging and smiling child answers her need for tenderness. Caring for and nursing him satisfies her own unfulfilled needs for caring and being cared for.

The mother hopes for an everlasting symbiosis with this one being who belongs totally to her. She is frustrated and hurt if the small child refuses to let himself passively be manipulated like a doll and begins instead to develop his own initiative at an early age.

This can become a real crisis for the mother. Her existing insecurity and mistrust will be shaken even more by the child and her self-image still further devalued. She feels she is a worthless failure and becomes depressive, tense and easily excitable; unconsciously hating the child while at the same time exaggerating the compulsion to sacrifice herself for him. She allows herself to be drawn into a collusion which causes an oral fixation in the child, with the result that if the child becomes a mother, she too will probably pass on to her child the same oral disturbance. In this way, neurotic disturbances are often passed on by tradition from generation to generation like a curse.

In the early literature of family therapy, the child is often portrayed as the victim of his parents' neurotic intentions, as a blank sheet of paper, a malleable substance or a creature who passively accepts being sacrificed, and has no defenses with which to resist his parents. This view should be criticized as too one-sided. It is not only the parents who react neurotically to the child. The child also has neurotic effects on his parents, sometimes even before he is born, although he cannot be held responsible and does not bear the guilt for the reactions of his parents. Obviously, the child does not cause the neurosis of his parents, although he may have a neurotic influence on them simply through his presence and patterns of behavior. As helpless as the child is, he often has a powerful advantage over the mother in the ability to scream and make persistent demands. The conclusions in the early literature of family therapy need to be corrected in some way, or at least expanded so that it is no longer exclusively the child who is viewed as the mother's victim, but also the mother who is seen as the victim of the child.

The Oral Character *P.P.*

The oral character is epitomized by his greed in wanting to swallow up everything within reach, relentlessly announcing his needs and pleasures, demanding their immediate satisfaction, and always wanting more—a bottomless pit. In partner choice, he will search for someone who will give unceasingly and take care of him like a mother. The oral character may often have the charm of a small child in his unrestrained demanding. He can beg heartbreakingly, plead and flatter. He often has a low frustration-tolerance level and is not confident that his demands will regularly be satisfied by those in his environment, usually with justification. So he adopts the attitude that the present moment must be used to the utmost in the hope that it will be able to provide something. He knows how to exploit his mistrust towards the partner by arousing the partner's desire to satisfy, with unlimited care and attention, all his frustrations.

Many oral characters are slaves to their instincts, sometimes tending towards neglect and criminality. Their craving finds expression in getting high and feeling good by taking stimulating medicines, alcohol, drugs and cigarettes, etc. Women who are oral characters, may make addictive demands for sexual relations and behave like nymphomaniacs. They long for skin contact and warmth and want to be held, but they generally avoid stable relationships because their weak self-image makes them feel incapable of sustaining them. Other women, in particular hysterics, need to entice men. In order to fill their inner emptiness, they must constantly stimulate all those around them by using every means they know. Subject to waves of jealousy, they fall into a deep depression when they are no longer the constant center of attention.

Oral characters, and women in particular, are driven by a feeling of emptiness to go on binges in which they will devour everything edible until they vomit; which may give them an experience equivalent to satisfaction of their sexual drive.

Oral characters suffer from feelings of low self-esteem and lack of motivation, any effort or action to overcome their passive oral traits seems meaningless because it cannot succeed. They think they are unworthy of being loved and deprecate themselves by their passive-regressive behavior. The path to mature, active behavior may also be blocked by an unresolved Oedipus complex, which creates fear of maturity, prevents identification with the parent of the same sex and inhibits the relationship to the parent of the opposite sex. The oral need is thus a substitute for a sexual need. An inexhaustible oral need can have a 'castrating' effect on the partner. They see themselves as failures in the role of giver, which can lead to sexual impotence.

The oral character is ambivalent in his partner relationships. On the one hand he seeks partners who will give without restraint and with whom he can allow himself to be passively indulged. On the other hand, he fears becoming dependent on his partner and unable to tolerate the frustration of a refusal. Frequently, he simply hates those partners who respond to his wishes since they undermine his self-image by giving in to him.

The Maternal Character *(oral)*

The maternal character constitutes a complement to the oral character and therefore combines with it favorably.

These are people who appear unassuming and modest. Even their clothing often displays a strong attraction to warmth and security; they wear thick sweaters, woollen shawls, capes in warm colors, etc. They understand how to create security in even the most difficult circumstances, such as when camping in rain or snow. They love the warmth of candlelight, sitting by the fire, singing songs accompanied by the guitar. Their life-style, which they value highly, is of wood and wool with the emphasis on comfort and homeliness.

They seek social recognition by offering their services to others. Typical examples, among men almost as often as women, can be found in social professions, such as nursing, welfare work, medicine and psychotherapy.

They are competent and efficient in their ability to help and appear to do everything out of unselfish concern with no expectation of receiving anything in return. The way in which they deal with every problem, weakness or helplessness and their eagerness in offering assistance encourages contact with people who are looking for help. Usually the level of assistance and care proves to be the sole basis of communication that is fruitful. If no help be needed, the relationship will be threatened with disintegration. Their method of giving help creates a regressive reaction in the other. They feel that they are equal to a partner when the partner is weak and insignificant. It can be observed that nurses have more joy in treating a patient when he is lying completely helpless in bed than when he has regained his independence. Often this is an indication of the extent to which their motherly behavior is linked to their own infantile needs; which can also be seen in their choice of soft animals and teddy bears in decorating their rooms.

 Observing the oral character more closely, we notice that he has three main characteristics: an inferiority complex, mother-dependence and an inability to make his own demands.

He is frequently dependent on his mother, although he may be ambivalent towards her. In his marriage relationship he may try to liberate himself from the relationship to the mother by identifying with her or with a maternal role. In order to substitute for the loss of the mother he replaces her and tries to treat others as he himself would like to have been treated by his own mother. Rather than seek satisfaction of his own needs, he will seek to please others. He attempts to sublimate his own needs through caring for others. Defending his own need to be cared for, he searches for a love object that he can make totally dependent on him in its helplessness. Since he is unable to demand that his own needs be satisfied he suppresses his impulsive extravagance and oral greed denying them as insatiable, which engenders fear because it is associated with destructive aggression, consuming jealousy, guilt feelings and a weak self-image. He appears to feel unworthy of being acknowledged in himself and always feels obligated to earn friendship and attention through altruistic efforts. The sublimation of oral greed in caring activity has, in addition, social value and thus a narcissistic benefit. Caring persons find the narcissistic benefit primarily in the greatness of the task for which they desire to sacrifice themselves, but also through the appreciation which their partner shows towards them. Appreciation is the only form of satisfaction which someone can give them. Indeed, it is a substitute, in an acceptable form, for oral satisfaction. Taking care of helpless people and the gratitude expressed on their beaming faces often brings joyful satisfaction. However, although orally motivated, the caring personality is the opposite of the oral character. In contrast, he has built up active defenses which make him independent of a giving object and protect him from frustration of his needs.

Unlike the oral character, he rarely suffers the symptoms of illness, but is particularly adept at maintaining composure through psychosocial manipulation. His success is even further assured because his caring behavior is actively sought by society and rewarded with status and recognition; although, in its extreme form, it may be pathological by imposing oral regression upon others. However, if he becomes psychosomatically ill, his ailment will be serious; stomach ulcers or *Anorexia nervosa* for example. Treatment is difficult as he refuses psychotherapeutic help, not wanting to be a burden to anyone and emphasizing that the therapist should give his time to others who need his help more urgently. Similarly, he has a deep fear of the regression necessary for the therapeutic process.

As a lover, he offers himself for the fulfillment of his partner through care and maternal service and chooses a partner whose oral greed, the result of past frustrations, he believes he is capable of satisfying.

The Oral Collusion

The Oral Partner Choice

In partner choice, the expectations of the partner are ideally complemented.

The partner who is being cared for wants passive satisfaction of his oral needs in the relationship. He wants to be looked after and cared for by the partner. He fears that his partner's caring attitude may ultimately falter. He does not want to assume a giving maternal role of any kind since he not only insists on regressively playing out his early childhood frustrations or indulgences, but also fears behaving similarly to his 'bad mother' (mother as internalized bad object). The maternal functions which he denies himself are reassigned to the partner who comes to personify in idealized form the sacrificing mother.

The partner in the mother role tries to protect and care for the other in a relationship. She fears that he might suddenly no longer need her as a nurse, or refuse her his gratitude. Fear causes her to suppress her own oral needs and desires. Both partners experience a considerable development of their self-image through their partner choice: the 'child' because of the high degree of attention he receives and the mother through her caring task which provides her with a clearly defined self-image.

The partners' defenses complement each other. The 'child' does not worry about his constant need to be satisfied because he feels not only that 'mother' assumes this task for him, but also that her own needs are fulfilled. 'Mother' does not need to feel threatened by the 'child' because she feels that he is not simply giving in to her need for caring, but also fears losing her caring attention. Thus the danger of her own regression to oral dependence seems non-existent.

Transposed to a circle of interaction, the formula for partner choice is as follows:

Child: "I can let myself be taken care of passively because you care for me so much."

Mother: "I can care so much because you need so much."

The relationship is an attempt at self-healing in which each maintains their defense mechanisms because it appears to offer the possibility of overcoming their difficulties. The 'child' forces his partner into the role of nurse, and the 'mother' forces the 'child' into a regressive need for help.

In the mutual oral fixation, the 'child' takes the oral regressive role and the 'mother' the oral progressive role. Regression of the one and the progression of the other are interdependent.

The Oral Partner Conflict

When the needs and anxieties of two partners complement each other like a lock and key, it does not seem possible that any conflict could arise. The conflict results from a history of individual neurosis and is caused for the most part by the return of the repression.

During the course of a longer period of living together, the 'child' is gripped increasingly by former doubts of whether the partner really fulfills his expectations of an idealized mother and whether he will disappoint the partner as he did his own mother in the past. Everything that the 'mother' says or does, or doesn't do or say, is observed with a view to confirming the suspicion that his partner does not represent the idealized mother but rather the bad mother. The partner is tested and must prove herself. More and more demands are made until the partner no longer manages to satisfy them and the 'child' therefore feels justified in treating her like he did his 'bad' mother.

[margin handwritten note:] AM I GOOD ENOUGH TO KEEP MOTHER

Over a longer period of time, regressive behavior leads to an undermining of self-esteem, bringing the recipient or debtor to the conclusion that he is incapable of offering the partner any balance. However, the 'child' notices, with justification, that 'mother' does not allow him any role other than that of a helpless regressive and will not allow her own needs to be satisfied. The 'child' feels that 'mother' does not regard him as an equal partner. But since there is no question of his taking over the giving role because of his own defenses, he feels driven to seek revenge, to destroy the partner, devouring him in insatiable oral greed.

This becomes manifest socially through an exaggeration of the original behavior to the point of absurdity. The 'child' regresses steadily to oral behavior, becoming more and more demanding and unsatisfied. He refuses to acknowledge services rendered by the partner because of anger at seeing himself placed in the position of debtor and because of fear that the partner's care and attention would diminish were he to express thanks and appreciation.

Therefore in this game the progressive partner can do nothing but capitulate. The more she offers herself as 'mother', the sooner—because of the transference of earlier maternal experiences—the 'bad mother' haunts her and the stronger becomes the indignity and fear of remaining dependent on such a mother. If she wants to withdraw from the mother role, the 'child' will feel frustrated and justified in his mistrust.

Initially, 'mother' identified completely with the image of idealized mother which the child projected onto her and which corresponded to her own ideals. Through the task which she fulfils for the 'child', she hopes to liberate herself from her own mother-dependence. Her ability to maintain the role is threatened however, for several reasons. Because identification with the maternal role is a defense against her fear of becoming mother-dependent on the partner, 'mother' always feels in danger of regressing into the role of being nursed. To protect herself against this danger, she must keep the 'child' helpless and regressive so as not to yield to her own regressive desires, either internally or externally. 'Mother' will always help the 'child' in such as way as to make the latter feel even more in need of help. Since the 'child' reacts to this with offense and fear of dependence and frustration, his demands to be taken care of steadily increase, though without giving 'mother' the appreciation she needs. However, appreciation would be oral compensation for the denial of direct satisfaction of her oral needs. If appreciation is withheld, then the gratification which mediates the defenses against her oral desires diminishes. Now it is twice as difficult for 'mother' to give the 'child' exactly what she is denying herself. She feels jealous and envious of everything that the 'child' receives, resorting to recriminations and accusations about what she has assumed and sacrificed for his sake, without receiving any gratitude. She harshly castigates the 'child' for being so demanding or becomes so clumsy in her helping that the 'child' cannot receive any satisfaction. Thus the idealized mother has become the bad mother who not only frustrates the 'child', but also causes 'mother' to feel guilty and hurt.

'Mother' is just as greedy and devouring in her demand for praise and recognition as the 'child' is in his direct oral demands. Because of her fear of not being able to control the sublimation of her oral needs, she increases her demands for appreciation until the expected ingratitude comes, which she feels provides justification for refusing further oral demands.

Basically, 'mother' cannot help but vanquish the 'child'. What was originally a self-sufficient and acceptable defense mechanism fails because of the personal history of each partner, and the specific behavior which initially ensured defense ultimately undermines it. The only thing the 'child' *should not* do is fail to express grateful recognition. Through the history of their individual neuroses—to which the other partner is predisposed—each instigates the other's failure. They both react with understandable anger and disappointment, heaping accusations on each other which, from their respective points of view, are justified.

The 'child' will say: "I am so insatiable and ungrateful because you criticize and reject me." The 'mother' will say: "I criticize and reject you because you are so insatiable and ungrateful."

The entire process of partner choice and conflict may be represented graphically as follows:

Oral Collusion

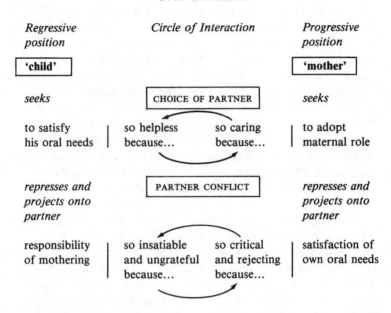

Regressive position	Circle of Interaction	Progressive position

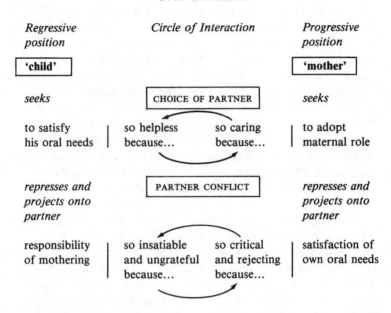

The process of self-healing must be considered a failure. The progression of one partner and the regression of the other do not in the long run, prove a valid solution to the mutual oral conflict. In the longer term, particularly, one of them will no longer be able to keep the suppressed elements of the conflict outside the relationship, and will project them onto the partner, persecuting or destroying him. The 'mother' becomes jealous of the attention the 'child' receives and demands from her. The 'child' reacts in fear and anger against his regressive mother-dependence. The mutual fantasy on which the partners base and act out the oral collusion is the mother-child symbiosis, particularly through caring and being cared for. Sometimes a symmetrical collusion may exist in which both partners assume the maternal role or the child role. However, this can by no means be taken as an example of a dyadic system. If both partners assume the mother role, they will generally need a third person—an invalid or their children—to take care of together. And if both partners regress into the child role, they can no longer function as a dyad and will need a helping, protective and caring third person. Often partners will compete with each other in the flight into illness and weakness neither being willing to assume the maternal role for the other. When the wife becomes ill, the husband will often do so too; caring for his wife would be intolerable.

Case 4:

A woman who had been married to a social worker for
three years suffered from heavy depressive moods during
which she had attempted several times to commit suicide.
The depression began at the birth of her only child, a boy.
She complained that her husband had, since then, given all
his attention to the child, taking little or no interest in her.

The couple had met at a party. The woman sat freezing
in the dark garden in front of the brightly lit house, grieving
over a love affair that had just ended. The man came into the
garden, saw the pitiful creature and like Saint Martin put his
jacket over her shoulder. In this way they started a conversation. The woman brightened up quickly under his comforting
words. From the onset they constructed a therapist-patient
relationship. The man noticed the woman's improvement as a
result of his efforts and thus gained in self-esteem.

The individual history of the partners:

The man, the youngest of ten children of a poor family, had
always felt unrecognized as an individual in his own right.
His mother was a strong, domineering woman, while his
father was timid and withdrawn. The man was very dependent on his mother and at the same time very much afraid of
her. In marriage he hoped to strengthen his confidence and
looked for a wife who would be less domineering than his
mother. The woman was the eldest of four children. Her
mother had supposedly tyrannized the family in a callous and
selfish way. When the woman was four years old, a brother
was born. She felt that this pushed her into the background
because both parents adored their son. She reacted through
bed-wetting, spitefulness and various kinds of provocation,
for which she was severely punished. But she did at least succeed in attracting attention. She entered marriage with the
conscious desire of remaining the center of attention for her
husband and avoiding becoming as tyrannical as her mother.
During marriage, she was constantly afraid that the caring
behavior of her husband would diminish. She repeatedly created new situations which forced him to rescue her, support
her, and save her and do everything for her. She assumed entirely the role of the weakling in need of help. The birth of
her first child precipitated a difficult conflict; on the one
hand she felt the need to fulfill her role as mother and thus
become a mature woman, on the other she reverted to a repetition of her sibling rivalry, fearing that her husband would

give more attention to the boy than to her. During this conflict, her behavior became steadily more regressive. She was depressive, made tearful scenes and tried to commit suicide in order to attract her husband's attention.

In contrast, the husband primarily sought confirmation of his self-image in the marriage. He believed in the ideal of sacrificing himself for his family and giving love to the utmost of his ability. He put everything into it and finally collapsed exhausted into a depression. He was grateful for the opportunity of marriage therapy because it freed him from the demands of his wife. In group marriage therapy, the man presented himself quite quickly as co-therapist and helper of the entire group. While he emphasized that he expected his wife to be independent, he immediately spoke for her whenever she tried to say anything. It became very obvious that he did not want her to speak up for herself and that he could only function in their relationship in the role of therapist. The man felt most secure when the woman looked to him for help and when he could offer himself as protector, or when he was confirmed as such in serious discussions. During the course of treatment the wife became a little less aggressive and expressed more of her autonomy, whereupon the man fell into a deep depression and appeared more tense and aggravated. He felt he was being forced out of his mother role in relation to the 'child' and became afraid of having a wife who was his equal. However, the woman feared she might become as tyrannical as her own mother if she assumed more autonomy; although she had managed to tyrannize her husband quite effectively with her scenes of weakness and helplessness. They both gradually gained insight into the inadequacies of their behavior and were able to improve considerably. A second child was born, towards whom the wife assumed the mother role from the beginning. The husband was able to accept his wife as a more mature, autonomous woman without threatening the basis of their relationship.

Case 5:

A country doctor was married to a former nurse who was a few years older than him. He was in despair about the marriage. He felt sexually frustrated by his wife, but did not dare free himself of her. He was, however, an excellent doctor and had a successful practice. He cared for his patients paternally and attended to their psychological needs. Yet he realized that at home he behaved like a deprived child, expecting care, tenderness, warmth and love. By his account, his wife was reserved and would often ignore him. They had met and married at an early age. He tended to project an ideal image onto his wife and see her as the embodiment of feminine virtue, competence and maternal sacrifice. His wife obviously identified with this ideal image although she was in reality unsure of herself. Both regarded their relationship as something absolutely unique and ideal; they were convinced that the marriage counted for everything in their lives and that all else was insignificant in comparison. They had three children and each birth had been difficult. The youngest child, five years of age, suffered heavy defects at birth and was completely dependent on care. The wife had put a great deal of attention into this child. The child demanded all her strength, could never be left alone and received excessive care and attention from her. The husband denied any feelings of jealousy toward the child and idealized his wife's caring efforts, looking upon her as a virtual saint.

Sexual relations had been difficult from the beginning because of the wife's unwillingness. The husband felt hurt and personally rejected. Finally the marriage had been shaken by his involvement in an extramarital affair with a very motherly woman a year earlier. This extramarital relationship caused the couple to talk openly with each other for the first time and also brought a temporary improvement in their sexual relationship. Suddenly the husband was in love with his wife again and for a few months very happy. Then the husband's expectations proved illusory. He lapsed into a state of depression while his wife felt just as unhappy.

He had grown up in the country, where his parents kept a store. It seems that his mother was an exceptional woman, interesting and broad-minded, but feared by most people. In expressing her feelings, she was unemotional, cold and puritannical. This caused suffering to the father who was a vital, loving person. As a child, the husband received much less attention than his elder brother whom his mother favored and who was considered a genius by all the family. The feeling that he had received too little maternal love stayed with him all his life and he was conscious of the fact that he had hoped to find a mother-substitute in his wife.

During conversations with the couple, we noticed immediately that the woman appeared older than the somewhat childish-looking man. She was thin, exhausted and already quite worn out. During the first part of the conversation she was rather reserved, but gradually became warmer and more open and ultimately revealed grievances against her husband which had been pent up for years. She felt that she was a failure in every way. She had hoped to fulfil her husband's expectations and observed that she was simply not in a position to give him more love. Everything would tremble inside her when she became aware of his desires and she would withdraw like a snail into a shell. She experienced the sexual act simply as a process in which she was supposed to give something to her husband. For her, it had no connection to her own needs. She lived solely for her husband and tried to fulfil his idealized expectations. The relationship appeared to be polarized between the husband's need for help and the wife's role as mother. However, the deeper cause underlying the similarity of their points of view became obvious even during the initial interview. Both conceived of marriage, particularly sexual relations, only in terms of giving and taking. Both were too strongly disposed towards seeing marriage as the only significant relationship in their lives and placed it under too much stress because of their idealized expectations.

Principal Aspects of Oral Collusion
Both partners agree that the real meaning of love is to take care of each other and do everything for one another.

The mutual obstacle for the couple is that they question whether caring functions should be equally distributed in the relationship. Both agree that the 'child' cannot be expected to assume a motherly role. Their thinking remains idealized; as we may infer from their concept of therapy as a means of improving the 'mother's caring capacity,' to make her efforts more efficient and to improve the 'child's reactions.' The idea that the 'patient' should now have a turn at assuming some of the tasks of the 'nurse' did not occur to them at first and, when it did, seemed initially threatening.

Love as Security Through Dependence in Anal-Sadistic Collusion — *Control*

The anal-sadistic stage of development; the anal sadistic parent-child collusion. The anal disturbance of interpersonal relationship; the active leader; the passive-anal character. The master-slave collusion. The sado-

masochistic collusion. The marital power struggle. The jealousy-infidelity collusion. Principal aspects of anal-sadistic collusion.

Anal-sadistic collusion is perhaps the most common form of marital conflict in our culture just as the anal character is the most common personality trait of the middle and upper classes. Qualities such as punctuality, diligence, cleanliness, politeness, thrift and orderliness are attributes which are highly rewarded and seen as virtues by an achieving society. Among the youth, however, there seems to be a trend towards the oral narcissistic character, which is specifically supported by the needs of a consumer society.

Anal collusion centers basically on a single problem: how much autonomy the partners will allow each other and what leadership and control methods they will employ to ensure reciprocal dependence and security without destroying the relationship.

I shall start by describing the anal-sadistic stage of childhood development—usually from the second to the fourth year of life—and the standard model of the parent-child collusion, which lays the groundwork for the later development of the anal-sadistic character and marital collusion. This will be followed by a description of the marital power struggle within the sado-masochistic partner relationship and the game of jealousy and infidelity.

The Anal-Sadistic Stage of Development
According to psychoanalytic theory, the child begins developing autonomous ego-functions between the ages of one and three which are of great significance for social behavior. He learns to discriminate, to move freely on his own, to conquer his environment and grasp hold of it. Characteristic of this development stage is the game in which the child will run away from his mother, delight in her unsuccessfully calling him back and having to run after him, and then catching him and re-establishing the symbiosis. Should the mother not run after him, the child will soon stop running and return disappointed and a little afraid.

Speech also develops now and this further strengthens the child's autonomy and enlarges and diversifies his range of expression. Communication is no longer simply giving signals to indicate needs as it was previously (crying when hungry for example), but through language becomes a binding agreement with rules. What a person says is remembered by another and takes on an irreversable quality. Domination of the external world, possessing and ruling connote something magical and give a feeling of omnipotence. It is a slow and painful experience for the child to realize that there are limits to his power and possessions and that he is often subject to the will of others; something which he rebels against by exerting his stubbornness and will.

This development is accompanied by much ambivalence. All the gains of growing up imply a loss of the pleasurable feelings of early fantasy. Winning autonomy—the discovery of the ego—and the establishment of the subject-object split lead to a loss of primal harmony and the feeling of oneness with everything.The ambivalence between separation and remaining united is represented in all the polarities which characterize this stage: independence (autonomy) and dependence (heteronomy); dominating and being dominated; activity and passivity; creating order, structure and form as opposed to loss of order, destruction and retreat into anarchic chaos. The longing to remain inseparably one with the world also emerges in masochism which is characterized by ecstasy and pain, dissolution of the ego (which is rediscovered in the surrender to oneness and subjection to the mercy of the other) and allowing oneself to be guided and supported in order to satisfy the regressive longing for unity (non-separateness).

The Anal-Sadistic Parent-Child Collusion

As in the oral stage, the normal conflicts of anal development can be particularly difficult for the child to master if he is entangled in collusions with his parents. These collusions result from the child's reactivation of the anal fixation of the parents. Some mothers feel threatened and robbed of their power when the child becomes independent, and this independence is indeed being tested out on them in a provocative way. The child does the opposite of what they want and thus destroys the symbiotic unity with them. Others fear losing contact with or being separated from their children. These conflicts can be heightened in social situations. When the child does all the things he is not supposed to do, and is dirty, noisy and restless, the mother is subjected to accusations from others. She becomes neurotic when cramped living conditions force her to teach the child the need for restraint, while preventing her from implementing her ideals of a liberal education.

The most common collusion is the power struggle in which both child and parents are equally concerned as to who subjugates whom. On the surface the parents may appear to have the advantage, but the child holds very effective trump cards just because he is physically weaker. He can scream much more; he is much freer to express his aggressive feelings and needs and he easily wins the support of other adults if the parents become too overtly aggressive. The parents are burdened with feelings of guilt should they lose their self-control with the child.

The parents are more easily drawn into a destructive collusion with the child if they have not sufficiently mastered the demands of the anal stage themselves. A power struggle usually develops during toilet-training. It is the first task that the child is required to master; the first time that he is expected to fulfil an obligation as a true partner, in that he decides for himself whether he wants to please or anger his mother. The mother will try to manipulate the child with praise and criticism in order to raise him up to her expectations. If she has not yet resolved the autonomy-heteronomy conflict, she will find having to pit her educational goals against the will of the child especially difficult. She will feel torn between the wish to passively give in to his will and the requirements of providing active leadership. If she is afraid of being dominated by him, she will become authoritarian and try to break his will, rigidly requiring that he conform. Lacking the flexibility to accept a disagreement with the child, she will strictly forbid any contradiction. For the child this becomes an early signal that disagreements cannot occur on a verbal level. He becomes conditioned to tactics of quarreling which will be important in later marital relationships, and learns that the primary figure in a relationship is the one who is stronger and has the power. He who does not want to be dominated must dominate others. In a semblance of obedience he submits to others through flattery, passivity, spite, silence or lying. He learns to infuriate them with his stupidity, forgetfulness, malingering, awkwardness, dawdling and obstinacy. A vicious circle of interaction grows up between mother and child. The mother thinks "I am so authoritarian only because he is so spiteful." The child thinks: "I am so spiteful only because she is so authoritarian."

The mother may avoid confrontation with the child because she fears jeopardizing her relationship with him, or even losing him. This danger is especially acute, of course, in situations where the mother's relationship to the child is truly threatened, as for example in a divorce. This mother will tend always to give in to the child and attach him to her primarily through fear. She will want to protect him from all dangers and unconsciously prevent him from becoming independent and freeing himself from her. She will feel hurt every time he attempts to establish his independence, as she wants to maintain the symbiotic relationship with him at any price. The circle of interaction between mother and child plays a part in this situation as well. She thinks: "I am so critical only because the child is so aggressive." The child thinks: "I am so aggressive only because mother is so critical of me."

The child will tend to repeat these patterns of conflict with his future marriage partner.

Disturbances in the Anal Relationship

The anal character exhibits ambivalence with respect to the following opposites:

activity	passivity
autonomy	heteronomy
(independence)	(dependence)
stubbornness	non-committal
	adaptation
domination	subordination
sadism	masochism
thrift	squandering
pedantry	neglect
cleanliness	squalor

The fantasies which are associated with these opposites are not mutually exclusive in the same person, although a single side may predominate in social contact. Someone with sadistic fantasies may willingly subordinate himself to authority, for example.

Generally it appears that social behavior derives from the active-passive polarity; however, there are many intermediate possibilities related to autonomy, power, possession and order.

The Active Ruler

With active anal characters such as the domineering type and sadists, one may easily overlook the extent to which they are creating defense mechanisms against the fear of being ruled or subjugated. They try to sublimate their own wishes for dependence by making others dependent on them. They believe they can develop in an autonomous way as long as they are assured of their partner's mutual dependence. They will push themselves into leadership positions, for example, and yet fail to accomplish their tasks very effectively because they would in reality prefer to be friends with their subordinates. They would like to feel completely accepted and supported by them. However, they repress these 'weak' needs by being harsh with their colleagues and expecting that their orders will be carried out without question. They demand absolute obedience from their partner and children, but the overt expression is not based on deep inner conviction. It is an unresolvable dilemma. In order to avoid facing the fear of separation, they demand absolute obedience. But since they fear, with justification, that the obedience is only a pretense, they demand even more personal commitment and conviction from their subordinates. This can be observed in adherents to religious movements who demand the strictest obedience to moral standards from their family and also that this obedience be given voluntarily. They fail to see that true allegiance can be given only in the freedom of not having to obey—autonomously and at the risk of separation—recognizing that the other's right to their own initiative and autonomy also frustrates the narcissistic need for complete unity.

Similar behavior can be seen in other characteristics of active rulers. An active ruler will demand that the partner gives up all their possessions for example, although he himself does not have to do so. In marriage this goes beyond material objects alone; he will also demand that everything which the partner thinks and feels should be experienced and controlled by himself. This is perceived as open love, but is in reality a means of domination.

Love of order, pedantry, nagging and thrift are other qualities which the active partner may exploit in his autonomous execution of power, in order to place the other in a position of dependence. It is difficult for the dependent partner to resist this form of domination because the 'superior' partner is always right, from his point of view, and because his position is legitimately established for maintaining peace and order.

The Passive-Anal Character   (Learned helplessness)

They allow everything to happen to them and offer no resistance to forces influencing their lives. Their behavior is regressive; they basically prefer not to have to worry about problems themselves and take refuge in the security and protection of allowing others to do everything. They too try to maintain their dependence above all else, but not by submitting completely to their partner. It is clearly apparent how, in seeming to let themselves be ruled, they become the dominant partner. An old German proverb states: "The man is the head and the woman the neck; she knows how to turn the head." Generally, women have played the more passive, stable role and men the more active, progressive role. History provides many examples of men being led and dominated, without their knowledge, by clever women who actually determine decisions and actions despite having conceded the formal leadership position. However, it is not always the woman who assumes the passive role. Whoever does assume it, accepts it in appearance only and creates insecurity in the active partner by opposing their right to dominate in other ways. Any direct confrontation is avoided, but submissiveness is a façade. Although there is never open disagreement between the partners they accept everything without commitment. Passivity is a means of protection. Submissive behavior lulls the partner into security, so that he runs into the net with greater confidence and may be more easily dominated. The net is spread so wide that the partner fails to notice it for a long time—sometimes not even when it has already been drawn tightly together. Should this partner suddenly feel trapped and try to defend himself, the other is able to conceal their real feelings so cleverly that he can never really be sure whether a net exists at all. Domineering behavior, brutality and aggression are frowned upon by society, but they are usually only frustrated reactions against vague boundaries which have been imposed by the partner.

The passive-anal character will not express any direct demand for the possessions of the other, but he does know how to keep his own possessions a secret. Housewives might have a hidden place or a private savings account for their housekeeping money; men might secretly invest in property or have clandestine extramarital relationships. The active partner will often suspect something, but never be able to confirm it. The passive partner gives no clues away and will not say yes or no, sometimes denying something only to take it back and then admit something else. In this way they succeed in wearing the active domineering partner down and bringing him to his knees. And should this not succeed there remains the alternate strategy of talking completely openly and appearing to give the partner truthfully all the details of an extramarital relationship so as to hurt him or make him jealous.

The passive-anal character succeeds in thwarting his domineering partner's demand for cleanliness and order by being neglectful, clumsy and forgetful. These provocations serve merely to crystallize the conflict in the relationship and to heighten the mutual dependence through the respective power positions. In no circumstance, however, does either partner intend to separate from the other because of the conflict.

The Master-Slave Collusion

This pattern of collusion results from the interaction between active-anal and passive-anal characters. The active partner demands autonomy and leadership in the relationship while the passive partner accepts a position of dependence in the role of follower, thus protecting himself against the fear of separation and abandonment. The active partner is able to repress his own fear of separation because it is embodied in the passive partner. By surrendering, the passive partner foregoes their autonomous development. In partner choice, the active partner thinks: "I can be so autonomous, active and omnipotent because you are so dependent, passive and obedient.'' The passive partner thinks: ''I can remain so dependent, passive and free from responsibility because you are so autonomous, strong and omnipotent.''

The turning point in the conflict occurs when the repressed elements are reactivated. The active partner is haunted by the regressive tendencies which he repressed. He fears the discovery of his need to be recognized and followed, and also fears giving in to his own desire for passive dependence and acceptance of his partner's guidance. In an effort to counteract these fears he will try even more to emphasize his power and subjugate his partner. The passive partner at the same time fears being exploited and tries to develop their own autonomy in order to maintain a balance within the marriage. They endure the external role of follower only as long as they feel that the domineering partner is dependent on them and can be manipulated.

By passively opposing his power demands they assert their own power and autonomy and leave the active partner hanging in the air, feeling abandoned and ridiculed.

Fear drives both partners to strengthen their original behavior *ad absurdum.* One says: ''I am so authoritarian and domineering because you withdraw from me and make no commitment.'' The other says: ''I don't commit myself because you want to tyrannize me.''

Anal-Sadistic Collusion

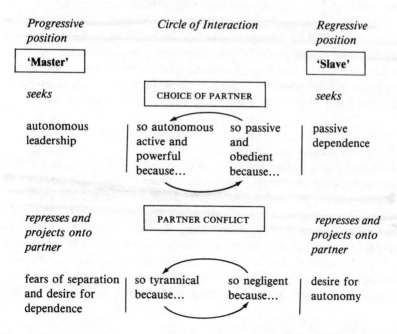

Progressive position	Circle of Interaction			Regressive position
'Master'				**'Slave'**
seeks	CHOICE OF PARTNER			*seeks*
autonomous leadership	so autonomous active and powerful because...	so passive and obedient because...		passive dependence
represses and projects onto partner	PARTNER CONFLICT			*represses and projects onto partner*
fears of separation and desire for dependence	so tyrannical because...	so negligent because...		desire for autonomy

Case 6:

A woman had tried to commit suicide because of her husband's extramarital relationship. She and her husband had a traditional, patriarchal marriage. He felt unquestionably that he as a man had rights which were not due to a woman. He limited the marital relationship to daily sexual intercourse, eating and sleeping. He spent the rest of his time at work or in pubs. He was an efficient and highly-praised craftsman. He demanded that his wife ask his permission for everything and give him absolute obedience. At home his word was law, and she had to accept his rules without discussion. In relation to him, she felt like an inferior slave. She was always frigid during their daily sexual relations, which made him feel justified in having extramarital relationships. The daily sexual relations were the husband's ritual of domination over his wife.

The man came from a poor family. His father was a lumberjack, a coarse man who never spoke a word at home and could only express himself with his fist. His mother also worked. Before the man met his wife, he had a longer relationship with a doctor's assistant who was more intelligent than he was, however, and the relationship was terminated. He wanted a wife who would serve him unconditionally and confirm his role as master. The woman grew up in traumatic circumstances. Her father was a patriarch of many contrasts. On the one hand he was a member of a fanatical religious sect, while on the other he was a pompous self-important actor, petty criminal and recent member of a nudist colony, which caused a shocked reaction in the country where they were living. The mother was a silent martyr who had completely subjugated herself to her husband, even allowing herself to be forced into participating in the nudist colony. At home, the woman was in the position of a Cinderella. Often the father treated his daughter as an inferior. During adolescence especially, he controlled her freedom in order to shield her from sexual experiences. He threatened her with God's punishment if she tried to withdraw from his paternal authority. The woman had hoped to find in her husband a partner to counter her omnipotent father. Her husband impressed her as a tough guy. Before marriage she became pregnant. The man offered to marry her, which he regarded as an act of honor entitling him to the woman's grateful submission. From the beginning, the partner's were unable to communicate verbally. The man forbade his wife everything that was not strictly related to household activity and the bringing up of children. She was not allowed to take either language courses or driving lessons, both of which she had wanted to do. He however, took every liberty. The woman was very unhappy and threatened divorce. The man retorted that before that could happen he would shoot the whole family. Given his character, these threats could not be treated as merely idle words. In this situation, from which she saw no way of escape, the woman attempted to commit suicide, which brought her to our treatment.

Originally, she had hoped that through her husband she would gain independence from her father. She thus reverted to dependence on her husband. However, she became passively indifferent and obedient in order to withdraw from his domineering demands. She let the sexual relationship passively happen to her and slept most of the time during the sexual act.

The psychotherapy of this marriage proved difficult. We attempted to involve the husband in the treatment but he was not motivated to cooperate and merely pressed for reestablishment of the old patterns. As a result of her suicide attempt and her subsequent stay in the hospital, the woman was physically separated from her husband. In therapy, she made definite progress towards building up her autonomy and also used her freedom to have an extramarital relationship in order to counterbalance the power of her husband. She became generally more active and adventurous and gradually began to emancipate herself. This, however, increased the tension in her marriage. After returning to the old situation, she soon attempted to commit suicide again after her husband had tried every means to re-establish the master-slave pattern of relationship. This time the husband became desperate and proved more willing than before to talk with the therapist. He saw no possibility that the marriage relationship could ever essentially change, but now gave his wife the opportunity to separate completely from him. A year later they were divorced. The woman blossomed and appeared to really find her full maturity.

The active partner demands total possession of the other. The passive partner feels supported by this demand. Often they may still be very strongly attached to their parents and find it difficult to free themselves.They transfer their struggle for freedom onto the active partner, who is supposed to carry on the fight against the parents. A battle begins between the parents and the active partner for possession of the passive partner. The parents accuse him of trying to take their 'child' away. The active partner retorts that they would like to keep the 'child' as their possession. In this fight, the passive partner vacillates back and forth, trying to make peace on both sides, but also inciting one side against the other. By avoiding committing themselves to a clear position, they are able to exercise power over both the active partner and their parents.

Case 7:

The son of a Jewish businessman married an Austrian Jewish girl, who left her family and circle of friends in order to live with her husband. Her mother-in-law proved to be a possessive narcissistic character who demanded to be the focal point of the family even after all her six children had married. Each week she organized a family gathering which she expected every child to attend, along with their husbands or wives. The man was the youngest child. He was small and had a delicate build; he had never been able to defend himself directly with verbal aggression but learned sophisticated fighting techniques in childhood. His wife was physically stronger and a head taller than him. She seemed to have a straightforward and direct character, wasting no words; indeed she told everyone clearly and without hesitation what she thought of them. Secretly, the man had hoped to be able to create more distance from his mother and become more independent. He noticed, however, that he had difficulty in standing up to his wife. He could not use direct aggression against her. His strength lay in agreeing outwardly and then going his own way behind her back to reach his secret goals. Her husband's devious ways infuriated the wife. She was patronizing and easily able to crush him, controlling his every move. They built up a business of their own and were constantly together. If the man had to eat by himself, the wife would tell him what he should eat and how much it should cost. Again and again he tried to escape these orders, but this only served to reinforce the wife's control even more. She felt justified in her controlling behavior because her husband had frequented casinos before their marriage and lost money, and still remained rather careless in accounting. He was particularly glad that she took care of these annoying details for him, and yet he was angry with himself for not having the discipline and sense of responsibility to manage them. She demanded total openness from her husband, and left no room for him to fantasize on how their marriage might become more of a two-way relationship. She demanded full accountability from him and would not tolerate half-truths, and in so doing provoked him to go behind her back. The man hated direct confrontations with his wife but enjoyed his secret power over her. He understood especially well how to play off his mother against his wife by constantly vacillating back and forth and never committing himself to either one; this enabled him basically to control both women. For example, when he returned to Zurich late in the evening around 11 o'clock from a business trip, he did not dare to go into the apartment for fear his wife would make a scene. He therefore decided to wait until 2 o'clock in the morning and secretly sneak into the apartment once his wife was asleep. Of course, his wife could not sleep until he returned and then made a big scene. She demanded an exact account of his escapades and accused him of the worst things. He, however, avoided replying since it hurt his pride to have to admit that he had been sitting anxiously in his car all that time reading the newspaper. This evasive behavior was interpreted by the wife as proof of her suspicions and encouraged her to probe still deeper in her attempts to control him.

The husband's conscience was troubled and he agreed that there should be complete mutual understanding between them because his father had never done anything in his marriage without his mother. He also agreed that their relationship would fall apart if each spontaneously developed activities which excluded the other.

During therapy, the wife's recollection of freeing herself from her father was an important realization. Her father's attempts to attach himself to his only daughter by suppressing her independence had forced her to run away to Israel and sever contact with him. She realized that his control had not strengthened the relationship, but destroyed it. He had left her no choice but to withdraw completely from his sphere of influence, even though this was not her desire.

The husband had to learn to assume more responsibility for his own thoughts and actions, while the wife had to accept the risk of freedom in love.

The sado-masochistic collusion is simply an extreme form of the master-slave relationship.

As early as 1905, Freud pointed out in *"Three Contributions to the Theory of Sex"* (1938) that sadism and masochism are two sides of the same perversion, the active and passive forms of which can be found in the same individual in varying proportions.

> "A sadist is also always a masochist regardless of whether the active or passive side of the perversion has developed more strongly and represents his most usual sexual behavior."

Freud emphasizes the importance of the role of identification with the other in fantasy. When a sadistic person inflicts pain on another, he finds masochistic enjoyment through identification with the suffering object. In the fantasy, the passive ego places itself in the masochistic position, which is then forfeited to the external subject. Alternatively, masochism can be viewed as sadism directed towards oneself. Freud explained sado-masochism mostly from the perspective of the dynamics of instinctual impulses; between the libido and the aggressive impulse (death instinct).

When Freud states that the real goal of masochistic behavior is reached only when one has surrendered completely to the grace or disgrace of the other this can be seen, from the perspective of the psychology of the ego, as an extreme form of heteronomy, as a reciprocity in the subject-object dichotomy and restoration of the primal condition. Freud did not overlook the psychology of the ego:

> "One can maintain that the real stimulus for the hate reaction does not come from sexual life, but originates in the fight to maintain and assert the ego."

Sado-masochism as sexual perversion is much less common than it is as interaction of tormentor and tormented, which embraces all aspects of collusion.

Sublimated masochism can be systematically observed in sadists, as sublimated sadism can be observed in masochists. Sadists have a great fear of the unconscious, which they try to alleviate and overcome through over-compensatory acts of power. They also feel threatened by fears of abandonment and by their desire for independence. Instead of giving themselves to a partner and becoming dependent on them, they will look for a partner who is seeking exactly this relationship to them.

The extent to which sadists have to overcompensate for their lack of strength and feelings of inadequacy is illustrated in films and fairy tales in which they appear as old and sick or as deformed dwarfs who feel the touch of power in their sadistic acts against those even more defenseless than themselves. The sadist's strong belief in authority was evidenced in the personality structure of people in charge of the concentration camps in Nazi Germany. Masochists on the other hand don't simply allow themselves to be tormented. On the contrary, they are able to reverse roles so that it is the tormentor who ultimately becomes the tormented. A masochist may torment a sadist by being obedient but making no commitments. An object without a will that can be manipulated like a puppet cannot be dominated. A real experience of power is possible only where we can impose our will on someone who speaks up for himself. When an individual does not have an opinion of his own, and simply agrees to everything the other wants him to do or say, he renders his partner powerless through his obedience. Tormenting defenseless persons also produces guilt. Masochists derive pleasure from the anger they can provoke in a highly excited sadist because they feel the vulnerability behind the partner's expression of power, and also because they are never as satisfied as when they feel captured and tightly held. The excitement which they can inspire in the partner arouses them sexually. The experience of being coerced, overpowered and 'raped' is associated with pleasure.

Case 8:
        A 33-year-old woman came to us for treatment at the instigation of friends. She was humiliated and tormented by her husband in such inhuman ways that dissolution of the marriage seemed necessary and urgent.
        This woman had grown up in very unfortunate circumstances. With her red hair and large build she stood out from her brothers and sisters and was resented by her parents who had hoped for a boy. She grew up in the poorest circumstances in an industrial area. Both parents and her brothers and sisters appear to have known no restraint in sex. As a small child the patient was often spanked on her naked bottom. At the dinner table there was always a leather whip by the father's plate and the patient allegedly often had to take beatings which should have been given to her brothers and sisters. Since childhood she had experienced sexual arousal as a result of the beatings from her father, and often masturbated immediately afterwards. When she was 14 she had a serious accident, receiving numerous fractures which healed

very slowly because of her uncooperative attitude. Even at this age she enjoyed driving the doctors to distraction by making a wrong movement which complicated the healing of the broken bone. Dental treatments also aroused her sexually. In her first heterosexual relationship, she could only reach an orgasm if her boyfriend nearly strangled her at the same time.

She met her present husband when she was 27. He is almost seven foot tall and was once a successful heavyweight boxer. An accident caused one of his legs to be amputated and forced him to walk on crutches. The relationship began when the man allegedly raped the woman in the hall of the hospital during one of his visits for treatment. The woman was an employee of the hospital. Although she was different in many ways from this man, she felt compulsively attracted to him. And again, she could reach an orgasm only if he strangled or beat her at the same time. The man played the domineering role in other ways. He demanded that she wear certain clothes, and she complied despite her dislike of his choice. He never allowed her to go out alone and forbade her to read newspaper articles that he had not censored beforehand and declared unsuitable. If he found out that she had disobeyed his orders, he beat her with a stick or threatened to shoot her with a pistol. He also demanded obedience from their six-year-old son as if he was an inanimate object, and shouted him down if he wanted to answer back. The child was spiteful and like a block of wood, hardly speaking to other people.

The woman, however, delighted in secretly tricking her husband whenever she could. He still does not know that her child is not by him but an extramarital lover. She did many other things that her husband was not supposed to know about, but has recently become increasingly afraid of the probable consequences if her secrets were discovered. Protected by being in hospital, the woman immediately began to react against her husband. She changed her outward appearance on the very day that she entered the hospital. Forsaking her honest and homely look with hair tightly combed back, glasses and old-fashioned clothes, she now used cosmetics, had her hair cut short and curled, and bought herself shorts and tight pants (which her husband had forbidden). He was very upset at this change and suspected that our clinic was an officially recognized house of prostitution. For days on end he observed the movements of our patient with binoculars from a safe distance. When he came on weekend visits, the woman derived a sadistic pleasure from provoking him whenever she could. Whereas she had previously lived in constant fear of him, she now felt herself in a position of power and was surprised how much she could humiliate him. The man threatened continually to kill the doctor or the nurses who were treating her. In spite of his physical handicap his strength was tremendous and none of us would have wished to become involved in a fight with him. However, he gradually softened up more and more, becoming increasingly afraid of his wife's divorcing him, and finally threatened to commit suicide. In therapy we tried to interpret the woman's behavior. She realized that she not only feared her husband as she admitted in the beginning, but also that she derived pleasure from this fear. When she stopped behaving as she did normally and her fear-pleasure fell by the wayside, she became despondent and depressed. For a time she appeared to want a divorce because she did not experience any real attachment to him beyond the sado-masochistic sexual relationship. But, at the moment when the initial steps could have led to concrete consequences, she withdrew completely, and broke off the treatment to return to the former situation.

The Marital Power Struggle

In the majority of cases, the examples of collusion presented in this book are based on the complementary relationships between a progressive and regressive partner united by a common theme. But symmetrical collusions (see *Watzlawick, Beavin and Jackson*) also exist, where the partners compete with each other through similar types of behavior. In the marital power struggle, both partners are driven to seize power by their own suppressed desire for dependence.

Marital power struggles which lead to marriage therapy frequently prove to be very resistant to treatment. Therapy sessions become battle sessions, in which the only expectation of the therapist is that he support a divorce decree in favor of one or the other. The partners often behave like two children in a nursery school. Each accuses the other of some apparently trivial matter, and presents their point of view with hairsplitting exactness, trying to prove that they have a better case than their partner. Their arguments are carefully based on facts, but differ in emphasis and interpretation. As soon as one feels threatened by the evidence of the other, they introduce new incidents which open up the offensive. Each keeps in reserve a ready supply of events which occurred long before. They attack each other incessantly because they fear that the slightest evidence of weakness will mark them. It is difficult for an outsider to understand why these couples should constantly fight, or why they stay together at all if fighting is their only way of relating. Often the therapist will recommend a quick divorce but this misses the point entirely, because both partners want in reality to avoid separation and to continue their struggle for power.

It is, therefore, difficult in joint therapy to analyze the deeper causes on both sides of what went wrong. Each partner wants to expose the other's weaknesses and failures and yet at the same time refuses to expose himself for fear it might seem that he is confessing to weakness and injury. It is also difficult for them to express positiveness or their need for love as the partner may interpret this as a plea for dependence. And neither one can ever forgive the other or show any kind of compassion since this could be abused and interpreted as giving in. Thus even the most mundane daily problems go unsolved while the partners concern themselves with principles and implications, rather than the matter itself. If one partner suggests a film for the evening, the other will refuse to go—even though they might also have liked to see it—because they had not made the suggestion themselves. This is proof of their autonomy. The husband might be quite willing to prepare breakfast on a Sunday, but will refuse if his wife asks him to do it. The wife gets upset, saying: "If just once he would be willing to help a little and pay me some attention, but he never really does anything just for me." The husband thinks: "If I give her an inch, she'll take a mile and have me waiting on her hand and foot."

The marital power struggle is the classical example of a symmetrical relationship. In their fight both partners use similar tactics derived from a common theme. The basic mutual fantasy is: "I must dominate the other in order not to be dominated by him"; "I must make the other dependent on me so as not to become dependent on him"; "I must frustrate the other to prevent being frustrated by him"; "I must force the other to his knees to avoid being forced to my knees by him"; "As long as I have him trapped, he cannot trap me." In this struggle for power, the crucial thing is to overcome one's feeling of loss of self. Each partner tries to keep a small emergency reserve as a final guard against the danger of being dominated by the other. They want to be just one nose length ahead, and it is just this nose length that causes escalation (see *Watzlawick, Beavin and Jackson*). It is because they fear being forced onto the defensive that they both continually take the offensive. The partner's attacks will be taken seriously only if they seem to be providing ammunition for further defenses. Their interaction is typified by the common tendency of both to speak at the same time. Listening to one's partner could also be an affirmation of weakness.

Thus the fronts crystallize. In spite of much screaming, no real communication exists; there is no meaningful, relevant interchange. The struggle for power is also manifested on a sexual level as neither partner finds a way to reach the other. Each is afraid to make the first move for fear that the other will interpret a friendly advance as weakness or dependence and exploit it to make further power demands, or refuse the approach and humiliate them. This repression and fear of conceding an advantage can leave both partners unable to reach orgasm. They avoid sexual giving and ejaculation because they fear giving themselves or being manipulated. Semen is ultimately withheld as a precious possession.

Both partners will go to extremes in defending themselves against the danger of regressing to the oral stage. They are often still dependent on their parents and the struggle concerns resolving this dependency or maintaining it. Basically, they both long for intimate love and tender care, but neither is able to express their feelings and needs. As both partners have great difficulty in maintaining a level of autonomy, the struggle with the partner not only threatens them, but also strengthens them. They need one another in order to define their defensive roles. The fighting can then be seen as an attempt to gain autonomy; which is probably a more significant determinant than the sado-masochistic pleasure of the libido. Through conflict with the partner, one creates an image which becomes more distinct. The battle must never end in peace because peace implies the threat of passivity, and therefore, inferiority.

The anal power struggle is more frequently characterized by fear and pleasure (*Balint*, 1959). Continuous fighting simultaneously separates and unites, allowing both partners the joyful experience of intimate symbiosis and at the same time, the equally joyful experience of personal boundaries and individual expression. A major separation would create difficult anxiety states on both sides. The mutual provocation, involves each person so deeply in the other that distance, avoidance and separation become impossible. The marital power struggle often appears to be a substitute for a love ritual; the quarrel scenes lead directly into sexual intimacy and flare up again immediately afterwards. The danger of regressing to oral symbiosis within the relationship may be endured only if there is no potential threat of separation.

A rekindling of the anal power struggle can frequently be observed in the marriages of older people. The partners need each other absolutely and must remain close together. Loss of status, power and recognition, as well as fear of poverty, can strengthen such anal characteristics as spite, orderliness, thrift and stubbornness. The fear of being separated or dependent is increased by the threat of the partner's dying and leaving one alone, or of becoming frail and disabled and thus at their mercy. Each partner wants to prove that they have a strong and resilient ego and fights to keep up with the other. They would like to see their partner in safe, assured dependency without becoming too dependent themselves. The conflict between dependency and the attempt to assert autonomy often leads older people to grotesque forms of power struggle, squabbling and petty trickery, as in the following example.

Case 9:

A 64-year-old man had liquidated his business earlier and retired to lead a quiet life in the country. Things had gone badly in his marriage ever since. It appears that the sole purpose of his life became the annoyance of his wife. They accused each other of being mean and argued perpetually about what a wonderful life they might be having if only the other were not so selfish. Their fight for the dominant position led to a living situation in which the husband built a wall in the hall, separating the apartment in two with two rooms for each, so that they could come and go without having to see each other. In order to avoid meeting his wife, the husband had begun to sleep in the day and to live at night, while his wife continued her usual routine. The wife in turn tried to soundproof the rooms, especially those adjoining her husband's side, by hanging thick carpets on the walls. Yet, in spite of all these attempts at separation, the partners were completely dependent on each other. Shared use of the toilet, kitchen and bathroom gave them sufficient opportunity for quarrelling and communicating with each other. This was in the form of exchanged notes or insults and provocation. One of the husband's favorite tactics for provoking his wife was to defecate in the bath tub, vomit in the frying pans and urinate in the wash basin. He wrote her messages nearly every day, which usually sounded something like this: "I curse you. You are doomed. You were already cursed in the womb, you whore. I plan to poison you with something that will not kill you immediately but will make you suffer for a month before you die." He also wrote to her that he was a nuclear physicist who could produce heavy water with his ultra-violet lamps. He would sell this invention or blow up the whole city of Zurich. His wife partly believed these fabrications and was worried by his threats of setting the house on fire when she was asleep. He also assured her that he could absorb cosmic rays with a pendulum and thus determine and influence the

life and death of people. It finally became too much for the
wife and she left him.

The man then lapsed into apathy and neglect and eventually had to be hospitalized in a psychiatric ward. After he
had been hospitalized for several months, his wife spoke with
the doctors and offered to be her husband's nurse. She said
she wanted to try and take him back as he had calmed down
considerably. A year after his discharge from this hospital,
she wrote a letter to the doctor: "I am very happy to report
that my husband's condition has greatly improved since he
left the hospital. He can now take his food without first having to take medication. I walk a little with him in the open air
and try to distract him from his depression. I have the sincere
hope that although he is not really cured, he is making considerable improvement." The marital power struggle had
been this man's last attempt at exercising his own autonomy
and power. He had now given in and submitted, passively
and helplessly, to the care of his wife.

In the intensity of their power struggle, partners will often resort to
the most vicious of tactics. But when tensions have driven them to the
extreme, the threat of disintegration of the relationship will bring them
back together. And then the battle once again commences. As destructive as their efforts are, neither partner wants actually to destroy the
other or the relationship. However, it may become impossible to avoid
an escalation of the conflict and eventual divorce, despite the lack of
'willful intent' on either side (see p. 154).

Mutual spite may even cause the death of one partner. The constant
stress to which they are exposed can produce many psychosomatic symptoms. In one case, a woman had to be hospitalized for repeatedly longer
periods to receive psychiatric treatment for depression, compulsive
vomitting and recurring alcoholism, while her husband underwent medical treatment for many years for unstable blood pressure. High blood
pressure was diagnosed by the internist as psychosomatic in origin.
When he entered our psychiatric ward and was separated from his wife
for several months his blood pressure normalized. The therapy could
alter little in the marital power struggle however. The old quarrel flared
up after the husband returned home and his blood pressure shot up
again. Three years later he died as a result of hypertonia. But even his
approaching death did not diminish the fight. Shortly before he died, the
husband told his wife: "You will never find peace, because each time
you receive my pension, you will have to think: 'This is blood money

that I am receiving for killing my husband.' " This statement now weighs upon the woman like a curse.

Psychotherapy of the marital power struggle is difficult and sometimes futile. Quarrels are often so ritualized that they lose any element of realism. Therapy is a means for the partners to establish their rights and seek the support and acknowledgment of the therapist. In this situation, all analytical interpretations are rejected and are generally made irrelevant. If the power struggle has become a ritual, communication and behavioral exercises would seem to be a more appropriate therapeutic approach to the marital conflict. The ritual of communication works in opposition to the ritual of the power struggle. Clear rules of communication are established which the therapist observes and controls. In this clearly structured form of communication under the authority of the therapist, a modification of the mode of relationship often has the best chance of success. At the same time, however, methods of communication can be deceptive in the context of the marital power struggle; because the methods and rules themselves are often used as a means of disrupting communication to make the fight even more sophisticated and abstract. Wherever possible, communication exercises should serve to calm the couple down so that they may start a discussion and deal with the deeper causes of their conflict. Nevertheless, there are certain instances in which joint treatment will not be as successful as individual therapy. This occurs when a real working therapeutic bond cannot be achieved because the partners have entered therapy together only in order to control each other and uncover new material for the struggle.

The Jealousy-Infidelity Collusion

Jealousy and infidelity are complex problems which can arise in various ways. There is however, a specific, frequently recurring form that can be considered anal-sadistic collusion. In this collusion, the conflict is clearly one between the desire for autonomy and the fear of separation. An extramarital relationship is an example of the attempt to express autonomy. This forces the partner to feel solely responsible for maintaining the relationship and they therefore assume a defensive posture. Through jealousy and fear of separation, they keep close watch on the other's infidelity, controlling him and trying to force him to be faithful. But faced with this jealousy, the other partner feels all the more compelled to prove his autonomy, and goes his own way, avoiding making any commitments. And the more he goes his own way, the more the jealous partner demands possession of and control over him. In this manner the two partners reinforce each other's behavior. One says: "I am so unfaithful only because you are so jealous." The other says: "I am so jealous only because you are so unfaithful.'' The sickness of the game is reflected in the way each provokes the other's behavior. The unfaithful partner claims to be open and honest because he acts out his fantasies of infidelity. 'Openness' is a pretext for humiliating the partner and provoking them to do everything in their power to prevent the disintegration of the relationship. He presents his partner with a detailed description of his experiences—often with excessive zeal—supposedly with the intention of converting them to an open relationship, but effectively to reinforce their insecurity and fear. The faithful partner adopts the position which is also acceded to them, of being 'in the right' and represents the moral standards by which the other is declared guilty. For this they seek out the support of third parties.

In today's value system, where marital fidelity is questioned, polarization between a progressive-revolutionary partner and a conservative-protective partner is common. The attitudes of the partners are, however, interdependent. It is relatively easy and safe to be the revolutionary as long as the conservative partner tries sufficiently to maintain the relationship. While on the other hand the arch-conservative may force their partner to break the narrow bonds in an attempt to destroy the interdependence and create more freedom for choice and growth within the relationship. Each stage of development and each change in the relationship creates fear in the conservative partner, against which the progressive partner feels compelled to fight. Thus, one partner will tend towards preservation of what exists and the other will tend towards development and change. As long as this polarization does not assume exaggerated proportions, preventing a constructive understanding, the result will not necessarily be unfavorable.

Case 10:

    A trainee teacher and his wife both came from patriarchal families who were devout members of one religious sect, which is where they had met. In the beginning they had maintained a strong religious commitment in the marriage, reading daily from the Bible and praying together. They both strongly believed in keeping the vow of fidelity and trying to comply with the moral code of their sect. During the course of his studies the man came into contact with progressive student groups and came more and more into conflict with the puritanical, authoritarian world view of his wife. As the marriage progressed, increasing tensions motivated them finally to participate in group marriage therapy. The wife hoped through therapy to lead her husband back into the familial fold, while the husband sought confirmation of his ideology of liberation. In contrast to the two therapists and the group as a whole, this couple showed a noticeable faith in authority.

The polar strengthening or reinforcement of their pathological behavior became clear in therapy. The wife acted out her fears of separation in a way which increased her husband's desires for emancipation. She gave the impression of being an angry, small-minded housewife and mother who thought of little else than such domestic ideals as sitting with her husband and looking into his eyes, or reading books with him in a small universe cut off from any kind of turmoil or unrest. It appeared that she tried to do everything to prevent her husband's unhappiness. When he was late in returning home one night, she became worried and suspected a major accident. She could not go to sleep if he was not lying beside her. He, on the other hand, felt trapped by his wife's behavior, and indeed even tormented by guilt feelings because of his attempts to get free. He expressed his ideal of freedom both to her and the group in such a provocative manner that the group took the wife's side for a while, and tried to make him observe certain moral standards. He also repeatedly made blatant attempts to free himself from his wife. Threatening to spend the night with another woman, he ran away from home several times; but then had to spend the night outdoors as no such woman existed. To admit to his wife that he had only been making a scene would have been too humiliating. But he did finally start to have extramarital relationships, and initially kept them secret from his wife. At home, however, he encouraged his wife's suspicions until, as a result of her questions, he admitted what he had done. The more she persisted in questioning and trying to control him, the stronger his need became to keep secrets from her and to escape. He began another extramarital relationship during his absence from home on military service, and admitted it to the group during one session when his wife was absent. The majority advised him to keep his escapades to himself. They also made it clear to him that his need to make an immediate confession to his wife about his extramarital fantasies and experiences resulted from his symbiotic tendencies and a wish to stay together with her. He later conducted a ski camp for adolescent girls to whom he had to give classes in sex education. He insisted that his wife accompany him, even though there was really no need for it. At the camp he was surrounded by girls who adored him and with whom he flirted continuously. He thus forced his wife into the role of a chaperone seeing that things were proper. This was again an attempt to achieve emancipation by involving his wife as an approving overseer.

She, on the other hand, was able subtly and naïvely to undermine her husband's progressive ideology (see also p. 189).

During the course of treatment, her attitudes changed. She became independent and began to express her own wishes, taking an interesting and, to her, very satisfying part-time job and clearly demonstrating that she was no longer there only for her husband and the children. The collusion was thus reversed. The husband who had formerly wanted to become independent was now upset by the way in which his wife's behavior gave rise to the possibility of a separation. He tried to negate her efforts towards independence and again bind her totally to the home. Her behavior caused him so much anxiety that he was scarcely able to study, and only now did he notice how dependent he had become on this woman. She grew more confident and more free.

After a time, a new crisis arose in therapy. The man had informed his wife of a new extramarital relationship in the hope of re-establishing the former jealousy-infidelity collusion. She acted with more insight this time. She furnished a separate bedroom, refusing sexual relations with him, and gave serious consideration to a divorce. He appeared to become rather insecure about the extramarital affair and gave the impression of needing his girlfriend's support to be able to stand up to his wife.

In the jealousy-infidelity collusion, one partner acts out their wish for emancipation and represses their fear of separation, which they project onto the other. The other acts out their fear of separation through jealousy and projects their own fantasies of infidelity or desire for emancipation onto the partner.

In treatment, the jealousy-infidelity collusion is often reversed, as shown in the previous example. The partner who was initially self-assured, liberated and unfaithful suddenly becomes jealous and the previously jealous partner becomes liberated and unfaithful.

Jealousy-Infidelity Collusion

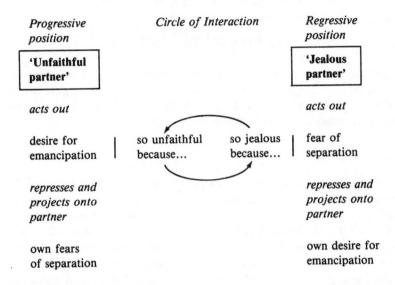

Progressive position	Circle of Interaction	Regressive position
'Unfaithful partner'		**'Jealous partner'**
acts out		*acts out*
desire for emancipation	so unfaithful because... so jealous because...	fear of separation
represses and projects onto partner		*represses and projects onto partner*
own fears of separation		own desire for emancipation

Principal Aspects of Anal-Sadistic Collusion

Both partners resist questioning of their assumption that the relationship would fall apart if they behaved freely and autonomously. The struggle for power, sado-masochism and games of jealousy and infidelity ultimately allow both partners to affirm their mutual ties and become dependent on each other. The partner in the progressive position naturally will criticize the other's dependence and helplessness, and thereby strengthen this dependency. Any move towards autonomy will immediately be punished. Should the regressive partner try openly to express an independent opinion rather than avoid an issue, the 'master' who feels threatened will quickly set them straight and push them back into line. The 'master' determines the form of freedom which the 'slave' shall be allowed.

The 'slave' on the other hand often behaves so awkwardly and irresponsibly in his apparent quest for autonomy that he provides the 'master' with justification for increasing control.

The 'master' should grow to accept the desire for dependence and the 'slave' should discover a more flexible relationship to his needs for autonomy and initiative. Both partners should learn that their relationship need not fall apart if each develops certain areas of autonomy while maintaining individual initiative.

Love as Confirmation of Masculinity in Phallic-Oedipal Collusion

The Hysterical Marriage

Social aspects of competition for the so-called masculine role. The phallic-oedipal stage of development; the phallic-oedipal parent-child collusion. The hysterical marriage. Phallic-oedipal collusion; principal aspects of phallic collusion; oedipal collusion.

Social Aspects of Competition for the So-called Masculine Role

Today phallic collusion—in particular 'penis envy,' 'passive feminine tendencies,' and castration behavior—is a very delicate subject because sociological criticism has challenged Freud's psychoanalytic beliefs. Furthermore, it is not clear whether a woman's nature differs from that of a man merely because of lack of social privilege, or because of biological differences. It would be better to speak of a collusive competition for the so-called masculine role. However, for the sake of brevity I will retain a psychoanalytic terminology. I begin with the observation derived from therapy, that competition between man and woman for the so-called masculine role occupies a central position in many marital conflicts. I believe that aspects of psychoanalytical development psychology, which will subsequently be explained, play a part in these conflicts. However, I am equally convinced that it is not biologically-based factors alone, but also socially-deviant attitudes and false expectations which play an important part (for further details, see *H.E. Richter*, 1974).

Cultural developments over the last few decades have considerably changed our notion of male and female stereotypes. Running the household and bringing up children formerly had a prestige equal to a man's work. The woman was head of the household, possibly with various domestic employees under her command. To run a household was an art demanding competence, experience, intelligence and skill. On the other hand, a man's job often offered little room for development and career, professional performance and job prestige did not have the status that they do today.

At the present time, women and men face a crisis with respect to the specific functions related to their sex. The principle of equality is difficult to maintain when a household is already efficiently run and when children are almost the only persons with whom the mother has close interaction in the isolation of the small family unit. It is also difficult for her to identify with her husband's work if she is totally excluded from it and has little opportunity to help and advise him. In addition, the feeling of self-esteem is no longer determined by the family's pedigree; it is no longer important to come from a good or aristocratic family. The woman can no longer make her identity through her husband's achievements. Only one's personal achievements count. But even raising children is hardly likely to bring the woman acknowledgment, in that it constantly exposes her to criticism and, therefore, seldom gives her the confirmation of having done a good job, but rather amplifies her failure. Many woman are understandably angry at being engaged in such an energy-consuming activity, which, on the one hand, lasts too long to be considered a temporary activity and, on the other is too short to be seen as their life's fulfillment. If the woman seeks self-confirmation and social contact through a job, she will, in the majority of cases, have to accept subordinate work whereas the man can systematically build a career for himself relatively unimpeded in the free expression of his energy. In these circumstances, therefore, a woman's behavior cannot be seen as neurotic when she reacts in a jealous, envious and destructive manner.

The woman is disadvantaged not only in relation to achievement, external prestige and career, but also because her upbringing has prepared her for a female role which is today considered inferior. Women are correct in stating that this upbringing, which results in a portrayal of weakness, passivity and need of moral support, serves to provide men with a profile of strength, courage and unshakeable domination. A woman who experiences in herself a high degree of vitality, a fighting spirit, or a need for activity and initiative has to reckon with social rejection once she develops these qualities because they are regarded as unfeminine. The feminist movement emphasizes that it is not their intention to make men out of women, but to given women equal rights and the same opportunity to develop those abilities which they feel are right for themselves. Women should not feel that they are abnormal and neurotic when they experience their so-called masculine traits and tendencies. Society should refrain from forbidding these 'masculine' qualities and forcing women to suppress them.

However, as Richter writes, it is not only the woman but also the man who suffers from out-moded role demands. The new freedom would mean that neither man nor woman feels forced to adhere to socially-prescribed norms for male and female stereotypes. This type of freedom would be a cultural innovation. Margaret Mead has written about the great differences between cultures concerning what is considered a typical masculine or feminine quality. However, no culture exists that does not define what masculine and feminine qualities are.

We know of no culture which claims that the differences between a man and a woman lie only in the way in which both sexes contribute to producing offspring, and that they are otherwise merely two human beings with different potential.

One can assume that the psychological differences between men and women are at least partly biologically based. However, it is not possible to estimate the extent to which these differences are also conditioned by upbringing. Even if it were proven that, under changed conditions of upbringing, so-called masculine and feminine qualities are no longer correlated with the actual sex, it is still possible and perhaps probable that one partner in a relationship would have more 'masculine' and the other more 'feminine' qualities, as is usually found when couples are formed. In homosexual couples where there is no biological difference, it is interesting to observe that a partner with more 'masculine' qualities will come together with another who has more 'feminine' qualities, and that a male-female division of roles emerges within the relationship.

Ethological experiments point in the same direction. *Wickler* put two male cichlidae together. After a heavy fight the defeated animal lost the magnificent color which is present only in the male. The cichlidae did not then retreat from the victor in order to escape but instead swam after it. It had adapted the typical female behavior of the cichlidae.

The problem of the division of roles between man and woman is complex and cannot be resolved at the present time. The future probably lies in the capacity of the partners to define their own roles to a large extent. The absence of specific role requirements makes it difficult to find one's identity. The more freedom an individual is given, the more intensive his education needs to be in order to acquire the skills to make necessary decisions.

When I speak of phallic collusion, I mean neurotic behavior with regard to one's sexual role. In a woman this results in pseudo-femininity and suppression of 'masculine' traits and in a man, pseudo-masculinity through suppression of 'feminine' traits. What is neurotic is the suppression of one's natural tendencies. This suppression is just as evident among today's young people as it was in previous generations. Young men still belive that they have to impress as supermen; that they have to be strong and invulnerable at all times and keyed up to meet the demands of a standard of behavior which has become out-moded. Neurotic behavior in this context is simply a set of abnormal attitudes which stem from an irresolvable conflict of incompatability between different tendencies. The cause may lie in abnormal social attitudes as well as in the individual's inappropriate upbringing. Parents frequently raise their children inappropriately by complying with abnormal social attitudes. The family is the smallest social unit and a place where abnormal social attitudes are most readily put into practice. The boy is brought up to value toughness, success and achievement, and the girl to value flirtation and attractiveness over professional training and pursuit of a career. The parents are concerned that the boy may grow up lacking masculinity and the girl lacking femininity, and this is often conveyed neurotically to the child.

In the following discussion, I shall employ psychoanalytical terminology since it is in general use but I would like briefly to point out how it should be understood. When I speak of the woman's 'penis envy' I do not mean this literally, but rather as an expression for the envy of male privileges. The castrating attitude does not refer to more or less conscious intentions solely to render the man sexually impotent, but also to wound him totally in his manhood and overturn his privileged position. Similarly, the man's castration anxiety is his fear that all his male functions will be harmed and that he will fail in them. Sex can be seen symbolically. It presents the problem of male role fulfillment in a highly concise manner.

In the examples of narcissistic, oral and anal-sadistic patterns of collusion, the division of roles did not correlate directly with sex, although in anal-sadistic collusion the active role is more often ascribed to the man and the passive-masochistic role to the woman. Freud described 'activity' and 'passivity' as precursors of 'male' and 'female.'

The Phallic-Oedipal Stage of Development   (Girls can be Have Phallic Pos.)

Freud's presentation of this stage of development, particularly for girls, is regarded critically even by psychoanalysts. He paid too little attention to the effects of socio-cultural prejudices and compulsions in upbringing and family atmosphere.

According to psychoanalytical development psychology, the phallic-oedipal phase comprises roughly the fourth to seventh years. Whereas previously sexual differences had barely been evident, in this phase an increased awareness of the difference between male and female acquires great importance.

We should, therefore, now differentiate between the development of the boy and that of the girl.

The boy

In the phallic stage, the physiological activities of the penis affect the relationship with the mother. The boy wants to show off his member, have it admired by his mother and to try to have his mother share in his pleasure. He begins to feel like a little man and sees his father as a rival. He wants to possess his mother and push his father away. Here he comes up against the limits that both parents set for him. The mother will gradually reject the boy's demands. The boy feels inferior to his father's great strength and has to cope with castration anxiety, that is to say, he fears his manhood to be far inferior to that of his father and that his genitals could be harmed by him. He frees himself from this conflict by identifying with the authority and power of his awe-inspiring father. The boy can give up the fantasy of his mother as sexual object with the idea: "When I grow up I will be like daddy and marry a mummy."

According to Freud, the Oedipus complex is repressed and is followed by a latency period. By repressing the Oedipus complex, the boy escapes the conflict between narcissistic interest in his penis and libidinal possession of the parental object (mother). The authority of the father introjected in the ego forms the seed for the superego, which takes severity from the father, perpetuates his prohibition of incest and thus protects the ego against the return of libidinal object possessiveness.

The need to be loved and cared for is stronger than the phallic urge, and so the latter can be given up. The Oedipus complex contributes considerably to the development of the child's sexual identity. The boy learns that he has to give up his mother as a sexual object, that his mother belongs to his father and that he has to find his own loved one.

In every crisis and conflict, the Oedipus complex provides an opportunity for an important step in development, as well as the risk of traumatization. In favorable circumstances, the boy will be able to accept the reality of the situation. The fantasized love relationship with his mother should be given up in such a way that he can transfer these love feelings without difficulty to another woman.

The girl

The oedipal stage begins with the discovery of sexual differences. In particular, the girl discovers that she does not have a penis. This may give her the feeling that her brother is more adored by her father and more loved by her mother. She may also feel herself to be organically worse off. The so-called penis-envy develops. Gradually, however, she learns that through her more receptive tendencies she becomes a woman for her father. The mother now becomes a rival for his affection and like the boy who identified with his rival, the girl acquires in a similar way a new source for her growth as a woman.

As with the boy, the girl's ability to overcome the Oedipus complex can be hampered by unfavorable external circumstances. On the one hand, the father may behave seductively towards her and at the same time frustrate her, and on the other, the mother may be a totally inadequate figure to identify with, either because she does not sufficiently identify as a woman herself, or because she permits the father to humiliate her in this role.

In puberty, there is a reawakening of the Oedipus complex, but with the crucial difference that the conflict now assumes a more real character; a real danger of incest exists. This Oedipus complex is particularly pathogenic because it can develop into a family conflict and have adverse and lasting effects on the child's behavior in his own marriage.

If the child's oedipal demands are rejected and frustrated, or if he is tempted into relationship traps, the phallic-oedipal developmental patterns can be lost. The child may regress to the pregenital stage. That is, he may form a relationship in which he is more accepted and responded to by the parents, for example through expressing his needs for affection, security and dependency. Here the child finds a level on which he can communicate with his parents relatively free from conflicts.

If the parents understand the child's difficult oedipal conflict, they will show him the boundaries that he must keep and avoid inconsistent temptations and rejections. The child will then overcome the oedipal stage without continually feeling his self-esteem threatened. In this respect, the Oedipus complex can be a training for heterosexuality. During successful resolution of the Oedipus complex, the child has experienced in play and fantasy the learning situation of 'husband', 'wife', 'mother' and 'father'. Gradually the child has learned the responsibility, limitations and, to a certain degree, the acceptability of these roles. He thus experiences a kind of trial marriage. This trial marriage forms the basis for couple relationships, both leading to and shaping the behavior patterns of later marriages. The cases presented have clearly shown to what extent marriage can be influenced by earlier object relations, even when both partners consciously attempt to be quite different from their own parents. It is therefore important to examine more closely to what degree marital behavior is influenced by previous object relations. Freud emphasizes that the core of all neuroses is the unresolved Oedipus complex. I would add that it is also the core of all neurotically-disturbed marriages.

The Phallic-Oedipal Parent-child Collusion

Resolution of the phallic-oedipal conflict is closely connected to the behavior of the parents. The child in the developmental stage and later more realistically the adolescent, makes the oedipal demand of pushing aside the parent of the same sex in order to have a relationship with the parent of the opposite sex. This demand can create a conflict in the parents themselves, which makes resolution of the Oedipus complex considerably more difficult. Thus the mother may feel aroused by the sexual demands of the boy and support him in his advances in order to derive pleasure from the relationship. This tendency may be especially encouraged by the mother if she feels sexual dissatisfaction with her husband. With her unconsciously seductive behavior she can meet the boy's expectations, only to harshly and immediately reject and disappoint him. Such inconsistent and changeable behavior makes it particularly difficult for the boy to give up his mother as a sexual object without injuring his self-esteem.

Frequently the father's relationship with his son is ambivalent. It is pathogenic for the boy if he dominates his father or is strongly dominated by him. In the former case, the boy may be able to outwit the father which leads to guilt feelings; and in the latter the father may be so superior that the boy has difficulty identifying with him and may tend to submit to him on a homosexual level. However, it is not only the son who competes with the father, but also the father who competes with the son. The father can actually feel threatened and completely rejected by his son. If the father is a manual worker and his son a student he will often be proud of him, but at the same time jealous. His jealousy is often aroused by the mother who idolizes her son. The mother will experience a similar conflict if her growing daughter is more attractive than she is and if the father is madly in love with her. On the other hand, the daughter will feel guilty if she succeeds in usurping her mother's place in her father's affections.

The Oedipus complex can, therefore, result in real partnership conflict between parent and child; a neurotic interplay in the sense of a collusion. Often the child has not overcome the conflict by the time he reaches adulthood. The daughter remains tied to her father and the son is unable to free himself from his mother. The son will not be able to resolve where his boundaries with his mother lie and will include her in his marriage. The fear of incest is at least as strong in the parents as it is in the children. The father is frequently jealous of his daughter's lover or feels deposed by his successful son. The mother is often jealous of the daughter-in-law and tries to dethrone her and ruin the marriage of her son. These intense relationships between two generations, motivated by unresolved oedipal parent-child collusion, exist outside the family situation as well; at work for example.

The Hysterical Marriage

Phallic collusion is best represented in the hysterical marriage syndrome, which is the subject of previous works (*Willi*: 1970, 1972). Although I shall be describing in detail this form of collusion, it should be noted that certain hysterical marriages result from oral-narcissistic disturbance.

The Hysterical Woman

The hysterical marriage syndrome occurs frequently. The hysterical female character will be described with particular reference to her way of relating to her partner.

Women with hysterical character structure are often accused of being whimsical and superficial in their emotional life. However, people fail to see that these women suffer from their own inner emptiness. Their emotional expressions are adopted and dramatized in order to give themselves a greater feeling of identity. They often find it difficult to be alone and have no inner strength on which to depend. They thus tend to push aside any conflicts and project themselves externally, living outside themselves. In order to escape from their personal conflicts, they try to transfer them on to others. This they find very satisfying and effective because they usually have a natural beauty and much feminine charm. An important method for manipulating others is to demonstrate weakness by being ill, crying helplessly or attempting suicide. It can be said that their strength lies in their weakness. They entrust people in relationships with the solutions to their conflicts, and feel an especially enhanced sense of self-worth when they are 'forced' to witness the bloody feuds between two of their rivals. In this way they become the onlookers to a drama which they have initiated.

The hysterical woman avoids intimate, personal contact for fear of being at the mercy of her partner and being overpowered and used by him. In her strong impulse to externalize all conflicts, she needs her partner as an ego support; someone who takes the helm, a protector who guides, directs and controls her. For a marriage partner she needs someone who is absolutely stable and dependable, and who will guide and hold her, keeping her safe from all danger. Men often see the hysterical woman as the embodiment of the seductress. Most of these women have led intense sexual lives before marriage and many, particularly the phallic-exhibitionists, have a tendency to flaunt sexuality in their relationships—by making obscene jokes for example. This strong demonstration of sexual drive is, however, frequently a defensive maneuver directed against the partner. Her offensive directness is an effort to intimidate the man and escape him. But this strategy occasionally fails and she is seduced ostensibly against her will.

Other hysterical women may shy away from the intimacies of a personal encounter and flee into sexual relationships which lack any emotional content. They believe they can bind the man to them by yielding to him sexually, without giving anything of themselves. Other more orally-fixated hysterical women create situations in which they will be cared for by producing symptoms of illness which men find particularly seductive. In such instances they appear child-like, innocent and shy and

are apparently quite surprised to find that the man becomes sexually excited by this naïve helplessness and can even think of 'such a thing.'

The background to this sexual behavior is usually an unresolved
Oedipus complex. These women have an ambivalent relationship with
their fathers. Usually they were the father's favorite. He is often described as fascinating and contradictory: on the one hand, instinctive and
impulsive and on the other, childishly naïve, soft and pitiable. The
seductive behavior makes it difficult to overcome the Oedipus complex
and above all hinders later marital relationships in the course of which
the oedipal situation is reactivated. The mother was usually a difficult
figure with whom to identify, either because she herself identified insufficiently with her own womanhood or because she was unable to set an
example due to her own feelings of inferiority.

Thus in most cases we find definite problems in early childhood
making it more difficult for these women to overcome their oedipal conflicts. In contrast to the so-called masculine woman, who behaves and
dresses like a man, and who treats men as rivals, the hysterical woman
works out her conflict in another way. She consciously represses her
needs for developing 'masculine activities' and contents herself with
forced 'feminine passivity.' Her attitude is: "All right, then I'll just be
an inferior woman. But then no-one can make any demands of me."
The man should prove at all times to the weak woman that he is a man:
"Let's see if he really is so strong!" She stubbornly rejects any other
form of behavior and challenges the man to recognize her female weakness while secretly fantasizing, often unconsciously, that she is thus
revenging herself on him. Although she pretends to be a sexy woman for
men who have a strong sex drive, she achieves satisfaction by first ex-
citing him, and then brusquely refusing him at the moment he thinks he
is nearing his goal. However, in considering a stable relationship she can
only imagine choosing a man who stimulates neither her unresolved
'penis envy' nor her Oedipus complex, but instead alleviates these
conflicts.

The regression to passive needs is further encouraged by pregenital
fixation. As Freud has already pointed out, the strong bond with the
father is overlaid by an even stronger bond with the mother. Because of
her oral fixation she longs for a man who will mother her and strengthen
her infantile, passive attitude.

The Hysterophilic Man

The husband of the hysterical woman appears to be a pleasant, rather
shy man; a little lame, but a harmless, lovable and kind person. Most of
these men grew up as spoiled mother's boys. Some live with their
mothers as adults and leave only when they marry, which is usually late.

Their mothers are generally described as extremely possessive, active, phallic personalities in contrast to whom the inconspicuous and pallid father is notably withdrawn. To enter into open rivalry with such men would create feelings of guilt. Their mothers, too, prevent sadistic-aggressive or phallic-exhibitionist tendencies from developing, demanding instead from their men a devoted attention. It is only their passive needs—for warmth, caresses and protection—which are acknowledged. Regression to this early infantile position makes avoidance of the oedipal conflict possible.

These men find it difficult to free themselves from an attitude of mother-dependence. In order to defend themselves against bondage to the mother, they may engage in overcompensatory activities which prove their manhood, such as enthusiasm for sports like mountain-climbing, parachuting or flying. These kinds of athletic endeavour can be understood as attempts to overcome and seek relief from an unresolved mother-earth bond. In compensation for the loss of the mother they identify with her, yearning for a woman whom they may care for as they wish their mother might have cared for them. Being protector and helper for the partner provides a defense against their own need for care and mothering. They try to sacrifice themselves in order to gain their family's respect. They consider themselves indispensable to, and take sole responsibility for, the success of the marriage. Their low self-esteem makes them seek the position of center and focus of the family. Satisfaction of their passive needs is rejected, and the needs themselves are denied, as they are seen as signs of weakness and dependence. Thus the overcompensatory defensive posture is directed against their own passive-feminine tendencies, which could in turn be a defense against unresolved oedipal and castration problems.

In contrast to the hysterical woman, an hysterophilic man completely inhibits his behavior. He is quiet and withdrawn and seems not to want to create a fuss. However one may observe his need for exhibitionism in his altruistic behavior towards the woman. He has an absolute compulsion to dramatize his wife's position. He wants to see her as a completely unique being, someone who cannot be reached in any ordinary way. He arouses and intensifies the dramas which his wife creates, providing himself with the opportunity to function as a helper or rescuer. He can therefore be described in his alignment to the hysterical woman, as hysterophilic.

The Development of an Hysterical Marriage

At the time of the first meeting the woman is frequently in an unhappy situation, from which she needs urgently to be rescued by the man.

Often it is an unhappy love affair or an unresolved parental bond. Commonly, her feeling of being in love with the man ceases when the word 'marriage' is mentioned. Under pressure from others and in an attempt to no longer repeat her misgivings, which she herself cannot understand, she forces herself to end all her avoidances and 'be sensible.' Although she does not feel in love, she decides to get married expecting that love will come of its own accord.

The hysterophilic man considers himself especially capable of rescuing this woman from her worries and entanglements, as everything in him urges him on to prove himself in a difficult task. He is relieved to be told by his wife that sex is of no great importance in her relationship to him, that she really chose him because he emanates security and confidence and is disgusted by carnal men who, like animals, seek only sexual satisfaction from women. The hysterophilic man feels relieved because he is not required to be sexually potent, but rather can prove himself on social and psychological levels by performing this difficult task. He senses a future with this woman because it appears that she will have a life-long need for support and protection. Her grateful reliance on him represents a great narcissistic achievement and guarantees the security of continual female dependence. In return he offers his boundless love, which allows her to manipulate him without his awareness of it.

Thus the relationship is idealized from the outset, on both sides. The woman denies both her own 'masculine needs' and the weakness of her chosen husband. In wanting to see the man as strong, she manipulates him through her expectations. Objectively, she is better off because of it. Any existing conversion symptoms disappear, her phobic symptoms recede and she becomes much more contented, emotionally balanced and happy.

The man is identified with the image his wife projects onto him. The need for him to be a motherly helper and chivalrous knight gives him great strength. The relationship which the hysterical woman projects, compliments the hysterophilic man's need to direct the confirmation of others onto himself. The hysterical woman inflates him with her projections. She keeps a hold of the valve, however, in case she needs to control his size and possibly deflate him again. The inflated man, as the carrier of her projections, feels elated with his volume.

Usually, however, this happy state ends in disappointment. The husband's growing feeling of self-worth becomes overwhelming. His self-doubt reappears, and the former need for passive childlike security from a protective mother becomes imperative. But he cannot express his regressive demands as they are firmly rejected by his wife. She cannot and does not assume any motherly functions towards him, having already committed herself to being childlike and needy. When the man collapses under his aspiration of knightly glory, he lays himself open to her ridicule and angry contempt. She is disappointed and pours criticism on him. Rather than defend himself, the man supports and reinforces her rebukes. He is ashamed of his weakness and feels that his wife's contempt is appropriate punishment for his failure. The conflict between his need to be the inexhaustible, undemanding mother figure and his need for passive mothering, often results in ridiculous behavior. Although he remains willing to assume the role of the considerate helper, he does it in such a way that his wife is forced to watch over him as if he were a child. Her rebukes correspond to his need to be punished. He finds the parasitic life style of his wife increasingly exhausting, becoming paralyzed with lethargy and passivity. Everything is directed towards avoiding arguments and diminishing conflicts.

However, this type of behavior from the man is also the worst thing that could happen to the woman. She depends on constant disputes with others for her self-awareness. She finds it easier to tolerate passionate hatred and rejection than indifference and lack of response. In order to elicit some sort of reaction from her husband, she may insult him and embarrass him in public or try to arouse his jealousy.

Although the husband does become jealous, he does not become more active in any way. Ever on the defensive, he claims to be in the right and tries to explain this to his partner in a long-winded manner. Her relationship with her lover only convinces him all the more that without him she would be morally degenerate. This 'saint-like' behavior often enrages the woman. The husband tantalizes her with his endless patience, evoking feelings of guilt and also leaving her face to face with her own conflict and feeling of helplessness. His position is reflected in the statement: "Look what I can put up with." Friends and observers, and many doctors, side with the husband, sympathizing with him for having to suffer the cruel fate brought upon him by his wife. The woman's claims that her husband is a mean, hypocritical sadist are not taken seriously. However, a closer look into the circumstances confirms a pronounced masochism and disguised sadism in the 'passive-feminine' man.

The sexual life of these couples parallels that of brother and sister. The woman shows disgust at the awkward and clumsy advances of her husband. Usually she shudders at the mere touch of him. When she does consent to sexual relations she feels like a prostitute, because she cannot feel any love for this man. She also complains about his lack of sexual aggression, although in reality the belief that she could freely manipulate the man's sexual activity played an important part in her choice of partner. The hysterophilic man often bears total frustration without complaint, and frequently suffers from impotency. His basically frigid wife ridicules and mocks him until his sexual confidence is completely shaken. The woman now behaves more and more as the 'revengeful type' (*Abraham*, 1921); someone who uses all her feminine attributes and qualities to render the man powerless and revenge herself.

To the hysterophilic man, immediate sexual satisfaction is of secondary importance in the relationship with his wife. An intimate union will succeed on condition that she be willing to accept and support him. His potency is completely at her mercy; he even wants to put his potency at her disposal. Aggressive-phallic behavior is far from his mind and he thus contents himself with impotence as an expression of refined and sublimated manhood, in contrast to the aggressive and selfish brutality of other men.

The overly-considerate behavior of the man and his need for a sign from her to initiate sexual intimacy proves especially difficult for the hysterical woman as she is highly ambivalent about sexual relations. She would only be able to give herself without guilt if she were raped. On the other hand, such coercion would be difficult to accept because of her castration complex. This conflict remains active in her; she is both demanding and frustating in any sexual approach, always rejecting her partner's attempts to please her. She wants sexual intimacy when he is not interested and refuses him when he shows signs of wanting her. If he makes direct advances she wants him to be patient, delicate and considerate. If, however, he takes his time and acts with delicacy and sensitivity, he can no longer project the masculine power of the rapist.

The marital disturbance increasingly becomes a fixation on rigid character behavior. The wife complains about her husband's lack of drive, interest or masculinity, while the husband attempts to hide more and more behind the righteousness of a saint and martyr. This form of relationship is in the long run adequate for the passive woman. She needs to feel the effect of external forces in order to avoid disintegrating and falling prey to inner chaos. She therefore begins to search for other ties for support and respect outside her marriage. One means is the development of conversion symptoms and other illnesses or symptoms of addiction which will elicit the attention of doctors, hospital staff and social workers. Extramarital relationships are another means. Some men feel called upon to save these women who yearn for love and are so unhappily married. In her relationship with her lover, the hysterical woman once again projects the fulfillment of all her fantasies. In contrast to her feeble husband, her lover is manly, supportive and not afraid of restraining and subduing a woman. She feels protected and supported by him. Enraptured, she feels that it is only through her relationship with her lover that she has come to realize the meaning of life and love. But closer acquaintance with her lover reveals that he is a caricature of her husband. The woman chooses on a conscious level, a lover who will lead her, although it is she who determines how this will be done. To all appearances she is repeating the game she played with her husband. But now she flaunts her capacity for orgasm in front of her husband and renders him completely impotent. He completely denies his sexual needs and allows the lover to take his place without protest. Despite the adversity of his situation, he never complains and may even say that he would marry the same woman again even if he knew that things would end in the same way. He is proud of his undying love for his wife. He may become chronically depressed, feeling exhausted. He may also have difficulties at work and complain of neurasthenic pains. However, in principle, he has resigned himself to his fate.

The situation becomes especially unhealthy when the children are involved. They are often initiated by the hysterical woman into all the intimacies of the conflict. The helpless father may turn to his children for support and understanding, evoking strong sympathy from a daughter. This behavior places a heavy burden on the children. More importantly, they grow to realize that personal relationships can be used to one's own advantage if one is able to play two persons off against each other. They learn that partner relationships can be manipulated and begin to doubt that they can ever be genuine, stable and strong. Daughters in particular become precocious and affected. The unhealthy and contradictory intimacy between their parents frequently becomes the cornerstone of their own hysterical marital relationships.

The Phallic-Oedipal Collusion

In both partners we find a prior conflict in their relation to masculine roles. They both usually have an unresolved relationship with the parent of the opposite sex and lack a model to identify with in the parent of the same sex.

At first the woman tries to sublimate her feelings of inferiority by identifying with her husband. A special thrill for her is to feel that she has complete control over his sexual power. In a wider sense as well, her husband is a man only to the extent that she makes a man out of him. In the long run, however, she is unable to identify with him. Supposed problems, especially her fantasies of revenge and castration re-emerge. This creates a painful dilemma in that she wants a potent man but cannot sustain a partnership with him. If he is potent, her envy is reactivated. If he is impotent, she loses sexual satisfaction and the fantasy of having found a masculine substitute in the man. However unsatisfactory the relationship with an hysterophilic man may be, it is often the only relationship possible for her.

For the man, aggressive-phallic sexuality is ruled out because of his own Oedipus complex and unresolved role conflicts. He can only conceive of a delicate and chivalrous relationship with the woman. Sex is permitted only in as far as it is desired by the woman. He wants to give his potency to her. He feels greatly appreciated if the woman makes a man out of him sexually, helping him to overcome his fears about his potency. However, since he relies on her initiation for his potency, he fails as soon as he is no longer sure of his wife's support. It is very difficult for the woman to give him this support because of her own problems. During courtship, the man's message to the woman is: "I will be potent because you give me confidence," to which the woman replies: "I can give you confidence because through me you become potent." During the partnership conflict, however, the man's message is: "I'm impotent because you castrate me," to which the woman replies: "I castrate and despise you because you are such an impotent wet blanket."

Phallic Collusion

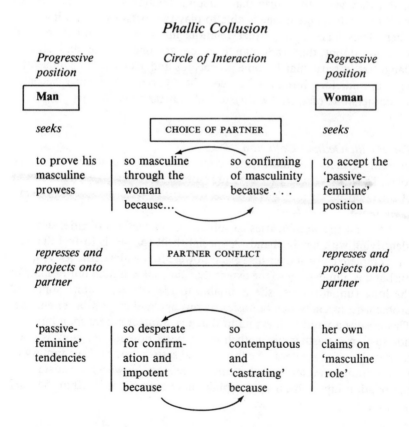

In the hysterical marriage the joint oedipal and castration complex of the couple is by no means acted out on a purely phallic-genital level. On the contrary, the added effect of an oral fixation causes both partners to regress to the oral collusion level of caring and being cared for. This gives the man greater freedom because he has learned through his mother that considerateness and courtesy are acceptable forms of manhood. He therefore wants to feel 'manly' in carrying out these caring functions. This oral caring role also serves the purpose of helping him to overcome both his oral dependence on his mother and his tendency to passive femininity.

The woman also regresses, to the demanding oral position, and expects a high degree of tenderness, devotion and care from the man. For her too, these needs have their origin in her oral need for her mother. But she conveys her oral needs to the man in a way which has a castrating effect on him. In a specific and general sense, her demanding behavior renders him impotent. The phallic collusion can therefore be seen to be acted out on an oral level as well.

Digressing from the hysterical marriage described here, there is another form of accentuated phallic collusion in which the man seeks to impress in a phallic-exhibitionist way. He flaunts his masculinity through success at work, or conquests over women and continually seeks confirmation of his potency. This enables him to circumvent his castration anxiety and 'feminine tendencies.' Through their phallic behavior these men are dependent on the admiration of women. If the admiration is withdrawn, their manliness immediately crumbles. Here the woman is in a different position. She knows that her husband required constant phallic confirmation. She feels the presure to convey this to him although deep down she considers him a weakling. She knows, however, that if she denies him confirmation, he will seek it from another woman.

Principal Aspects of Phallic Collusion

Neither partner would question the belief that the man should always be strong and superior and that the woman should be weak and in need of leadership. Both expect to help the man become more masculine so that the woman will finally be able to acknowledge his superiority. But by their unconscious collusion the couple sabotages this fantasy and it is never actualized. The therapeutic solution would consist in the man's overcoming the need to present an appearance of pseudo-masculinity, and the woman's overcoming her need to present an appearance of pseudo-femininity. The man would learn to be open about his weaknesses, passivity, softness and helplessness and the woman would learn not to suppress her initiative, the immediate experience of her vitality, activity and strength. The solution frequently proves very difficult for the partners. The woman's contempt and envy of the man's 'masculinity' will continually humiliate him, preventing him from admitting his weakness without feeling deeply wounded. Filled with guilt, the man will either give in to her demands to be more masculine or will become phallic-active elsewhere. He can hardly demand that his wife take over the male role which she values so highly. In the final analysis, 'masculine privileges' and the responsibility and expectations involved therein should be shared more equally between the partners rather than becoming the focus of a battle for prestige.

Oedipal Collusion

Oedipal collusion is basic to the marital relationship, because in the couple one again experiences the relationship to one's parent of the opposite sex through identification or contra-identification with the parent of the same sex. The love and hate one has for the parent of the same sex must play a part in every heterosexual relationship. In the partner, one experiences the oedipal lover.

The Oedipus complex shapes a marriage positively as a repetition of the parental marriage and negatively as an attempt to reverse the parental marriage. In joint therapy, attention should always be given to the degree to which memories and experiences from the oedipal stage influence the marriage.

An unresolved Oedipus complex often prevents a marriage from taking place. The old love for the parent need not be given up, for instance, if the girl looks after her father when her mother has died. Some have an irrational need to offer themselves as lovers to partners who are already married, and take a particular pleasure in breaking up marriages. Others in their flight from incest cannot enter into deeper relationships and may be able to have sexual relationships only with partners who have nothing in common with the parent of the opposite sex; for example someone with a different skin color or someone young enough to be their own child. Some fail sexually only after they have actually become married.

In other types of marriage, the oedipal component manifests itself in the choice of partner who does resemble the parent of the opposite sex. Frequently a partner is chosen who is old enough to be the individual's father or mother. If the husband is more than ten years older than the wife or the wife more than five years older than the husband, oedipal components are often involved. What interest in this relationship does the partner have who has been chosen as father or mother? Frequently, it can be shown that he or she also has an unresolved Oedipus complex which they are attempting to overcome by playing the role of the admired-despised parent. They try to carry out the parent's function through identification with them. Often the older partner is found to have paternal or maternal feelings towards the younger partner. For instance, as father he may have the idea of initiating the young girl into married life, or moulding her according to his preconceptions and, given his superiority, making her completely dependent on him. These paternalistic men usually spoil their 'children'; worry about them, give them a lot of attention and go to much trouble to be helpful. However, they do not allow their wives to grow up, and make no expectations of them such as asking for assistance or an opinion. A collusion of the oral-symbiotic or anal-sadistic type is frequently formed. As much as these women initially enjoy leaning on a man of experience, they eventually need to do something in accordance with the principle of equality in order to compensate for their own inexperience. The considerably younger woman is, therefore, often superior in terms of her youthful charm, vitality, enthusiasm for dancing, sport, movement etc. She experiences the paternal guidance—justly or unjustly—as patronizing and oppressive. Spoiling and overindulgence lead to hysterical behavior, domestic dramas, intrigues and manipulation. The question of jealousy frequently arises because the fatherly husband lives in constant fear that his wife might be more sexually attracted to a younger man. This is compounded by the fact that the problem of incest in these marriages often creates sexual failure.

If the woman is considerably older than the man and acts as a mother, a similar problem exists. Young men are often soft, childlike and lacking in independence. The rationale for the choice of a considerably older woman is their lack of skill in dealing with a younger less mature woman. They also have difficulty in maintaining a balance of influence in their marriage and resort to various defenses against the threat of inferiority. Some begin to drink at home or in bars and, under the influence of alcohol, boast about their strength or even try to display it. On the one hand, they are drinking to escape the patronage of their wives, and on the other, they are giving them greater authority and a stronger position.

Case 11:

    The owner of a riding school, a woman who was fifty-two, had been married for three years to a twenty-one-year-old photographer. It was her third marriage. She had previously been friendly with a man thirteen years her junior, but in retaliation against his unfaithfulness she had married her present husband. The man's age put him between her older and younger daughters. For two years the marriage went well. Then he started having extramarital relationships with younger women and, like a boy, confided his experiences to her each time. During this time he had become a man, although he made himself out to be much more of a man than he really was. He had tried to dominate the woman and even beaten her up, but she had resisted him. More than anything else she found it difficult to forgive his adulteries. Initially their sexual relationship had been good but during the sexual act she now suffered from cramps and persistent pain. He had also infected her with venereal disease a few months earlier. The woman presented an image of liberated masculinity. Her eyes sparkled as she talked about what a splendid man her father was. She herself would have preferred to be a man. All her friends had been weak and helpless men who had wanted to be protected and led by her. In reality, she had no need of a man. Her present husband too was soft-hearted and childlike. When she informed him of her intention to divorce him he lay in bed sulking and went on a hunger strike.

A few days after the conversation with his wife, the man made his first parachute jump which was apparent proof to him of his manhood. He promptly broke his ankle and had to be hospitalized. In his conversation with me he was obviously at great pains to make a more adult impression. According to what he said, he was devoted to his wife because younger women were too inexperienced and it was only older women who could understand him. He threatened to commit suicide if his wife left him. However, he agreed to the divorce after several individual and joint therapeutic sessions.

Oedipal aspects probably play a part in every marriage. A partner is chosen because they resemble the parent of the opposite sex (what *Abraham* calls incestuous dependence) or because they are quite unlike them (escape from incest, exogamy). Since the bond to the parent of the opposite sex is ambivalent, it remains so with the partner. It is especially true of neurotic exogamy that the partner is consciously chosen in opposition to identification with the parent to ensure that there can be no repetition of the parent-child dependence or the parental marriage. *This intention time and time again turns out to be an illusion*, as was shown in the introductory example in Chapter 4. If dependence on the parent of the opposite sex remains strong, the partner will constantly be compared to him. The partner is either loved or hated because she resembles the mother, or loved or hated just because she does not resemble the mother. If there is in reality no resemblance between the chosen partner and the parent who is the object of ambivalence, the choice of partner can be seen as an avoidance. However, in such cases, the partner loses their fascination after a certain time. No resonance is created through living together. A woman who hates her tyrannical father while being fascinated by him at the same time will quickly tire of her dutiful but dull husband. Henry *Dicks* has written a particularly lucid study of this unresolved ambivalent dependence on the parents and the resulting love-hate relationship.

Collusion Patterns Are Not Marriage Categories

In the preceeding chapters, we have described four patterns of collusion which are intended to show how the interaction of two partners escalates into a conflict with typical structural characteristics. This results from disturbing or unconscious fantasies which they both share. There is a danger of seeing these four patterns of conflict as types of marriage or marriage categories in terms of which all married couples could be classified. Such a conclusion, however, would be one-sided and could have disastrous consequences.

The four patterns of collusion are four dynamic principles which as such do not form a whole illness. Rather one must realize that every married couple is affected by all four of the previously mentioned basic themes, namely *'love as oneness,' 'love as caring and nourishing,' 'love as security through belonging,' and 'love as confirmation of masculinity.'* Although all four basic themes touch every married couple, the emphasis will usually fall on only one of these collusion patterns. In treatment I usually focus on this specific collusion pattern although the other basic themes play a part. However, the couple may undergo a change during treatment; they may regress to an oral collusion or progress to a phallic rivalry or power struggle. Alternatively, it becomes obvious that sado-masochistic excitation serves to fill a narcissistic hole and contributes to greater self-awareness and confidence in one's own boundaries.

The description of the hysterical marriage gave an opportunity to show how the phallic-oedipal problem occupies a central position in this marital syndrome as well as showing how other collusion patterns play an important role. Thus narcissistic collusion often plays an important part in the hysterical marriage in that both partners have poor feelings of self-esteem and weak ego-boundaries. In the woman, narcissistic difficulties appear in her exaggerated relationship to others, her merging and identification tendencies and her 'being outside herself.' In the man, narcissistic difficulties are manifested in his tendency to live only for the woman, offering himself as an extension of herself, or as an actual substitute for herself. Oral collusion is particularly evident in the hysterical marriage when the woman approaches the man with her insatiable demands for care, affection and attention, while the man tries to sublimate his oral fixation through overcompensatory mothering and caring. Neither the woman's hunger for titillation and almost addictive need to be fed continuously with new dramatic effects, nor the corresponding needs of the man, can disrupt this. To participate in it involves narcissistic as well as oral aspects. Anal collusion is demonstrated by a woman's talent for intrigue through which the woman seeks to dominate the man, and by the man's masochistic martyrdom and saintliness through which he can torment and dominate the woman.

As already shown, the phallic problem can also be acted out sexually. The hysterical woman can give her husband a sense of failure in his attempts at being caring (she castrates him in this respect). Conversely, a symptom such as sexual disturbance may have its origins elsewhere and need not necessarily be only a phallic-oedipal problem. Thus it is not uncommon to find sexual hyperactivity in men who are jealous of their children and who are afraid that their wives may not be sufficiently devoted to them. Sexual overactivity may also prove to the man that he completely possesses and dominates the woman. Or sexual refusal and failure may be justified in a narcissistic sense since orgasm is feared as loss of self. Sexual denial can also be orally justified because caring for the partner has been so exhausting that there is nothing left to give, or anally justified because one partner torments the other by retaining semen.

The above treatment of the concept of collusion is intended to show the different ways in which marital conflicts can be viewed without placing them in rigid categories or systems of classification. Collusion patterns should be taken as guide-lines rather than be treated say, as plant taxonomy in a botany book or cooking recipes. They should aid in introducing both thematic and dynamic accents to couple therapy.

6

COLLUSION: THE UNCONSCIOUS
INTERPLAY OF PARTNERS

Intraindividual Balance

Interindividual Balance

Conjunction of Intraindividual and Interindividual Balances

Partners' Common Unconscious

From Partner Choice to Marital Conflict

Collusive Stalemate

Divorce and Resolution of Collusion

In the preceding chapters, I have attempted to describe the behavior of marriage partners by means of a standard collusion model. In this chapter, I shall describe dual psychodynamic principles which may govern these patterns of collusion.

Intraindividual Balance

Each of the collusion themes, such as *love as ego-confirmation, love as caring and nourishing, love as security through dependency* and *love as confirmation of masculinity*, contains both a regressive and a progressive element. Thus, sacrificing oneself completely to a partner in order to gain from him a better self would represent the regressive extreme of the *narcissistic collusion*, whereas the notion of the partner giving himself completely to oneself and thus attaining growth and inner transformation would be the progressive extreme of the same pattern.

A partner who allows himself to be mothered, protected and looked after without reservation, represents the regressive extreme of *love as caring and nourishing* in the pattern of oral collusion. The progressive extreme of the same pattern would be the image of a partner as self-sacrificing mother or knightly protector.

The regressive extreme of *love as security through dependency* in anal-sadistic collusion would be the passive, completely dependent partner, whereas having a partner completely under one's control and leadership would be the progressive extreme of the same collusion.

The theme of *love as confirmation of masculinity* in phallic collusion includes the progressive fantasy of the man who is a hero in every situation while the woman worships him, regressively, for his achievements.

Every individual, in the course of sharing life with another, becomes involved in these patterns both in their regressive and progressive aspects.

Free interplay of regressive and progressive fantasies and conflicts is essential to the health of every human being. Every individual needs to be cared for by someone sometimes—to allow himself a moment of carefree abandon and dependence, and to assert his identification with the partner—although the image of passive, regressive satisfaction is associated in everyone's mind with the fear of vulnerability and frustration. On the other hand, it is natural to hope to receive recognition or confirmation of one's autonomy, self-sufficiency and identity from one's partner, just as it is natural to fear going too far in satisfying these needs. Because of unresolved conflicts in his earlier development, a person may be particularly predisposed towards one aspect of a given pattern with the result that, when confronting a real partner relationship, he fixates on the type of behavior intrinsic to that aspect while rejecting or avoiding the opposite. For example, a man who felt continually repressed by his mother during his childhood may only be able to conceive of a relationship in which he does not need to adapt to his partner, but either shapes the partner to his will or surrenders to her.

An orphan may have been so strongly frustrated by his unsatisfied needs in early childhood that it is difficult for him to enter a relationship unless he receives extra care and attention and does not have to given anything in return. A man who was ridiculed as a mama's boy may tend to behave in every relationship like a knightly protector or a nurse, in an attempt to counter any idea of his maternal dependence. A girl whose father used to drink may do her best to reform her husband of his liking for alcohol simply because she missed the opportunity of reforming her father, and thus appears motivated towards an oral mother role.

The repression or unfulfillment of behavioral potential is accompanied by fear, and a sense of guilt or shame arising from thematically-related experiences and emotionally-charged memories of childhood, as was shown in greater detail in the discussion of collusion patterns.

I think that an essential pre-condition of a healthy relationship is the flexibility which enables an individual to assume either a progressive or regressive role depending on the specific relationship. Or expressed negatively, an essential cause of the disturbed relationship lies in clinging rigidly and one-sidedly to either the progressive or regressive extreme. The aim of psychotherapy is to bring out those fearful, repressed fantasies through which an individual entrenches himself in a single extreme position.

Any notion partners may have about their marital relationship can therefore be traced back to an extreme position which is either sought after or rejected in order to compensate for chronic fear, shame or a sense of guilt.

Therefore, for those who seek the *regressive role* in their relationship, marriage means:

—*narcissistic tendency*: I want to surrender to you because I am so worthless that I am in no position to make any demands or judgments on my own. You are my world. You are the master of my fate.

—*oral tendency*: I want to be cared for and protected. I was so frustrated (or spoiled) when I was a child that I am incapable of assuming a maternal function and I am also afraid of failing as a mother.

—*anal tendency*: I will remain passive with you and let myself be guided by you in all circumstances, in the same way that I did in my family. I will refrain from making any demands for independence and leadership, fearing to be rejected or abandoned by you.

—*phallic tendency*: I wish to confirm you in your male role while confining myself to the passive and feminine role, as a true wife should.

For those who see themselves as playing the *active and progressive role*, marriage means:

—*narcissistic tendency*: I want, given your approval, to dissolve myself and become the embodiment of your ideal.

—*oral tendency*: I wish to offer myself to you as an ideal mother and no longer to be treated like a helpless child.

—*anal tendency*: Since someone has to lead in marriage, I shall assume this function to which I shall adapt and resign myself.

—*phallic tendency*: I want our relationship to confirm my masculinity and no longer be criticized by my mother as a failure.

Characteristic of an early disturbance in a relationship is the conjoining of essentially dualistic progressive and regressive images into a single extreme excluding the other. Such self-imposed repression serves as a defense mechanism against behavioral potentials rejected in the relationship.

According to the psychoanalytic theory of defenses, the more strongly an image is repressed, the more insidiously it forces its way in through the back door, as it were. Every basic drive which remains an unfulfilled potential plays a specific emotionally-charged role in the choice of partner and in the conflict between the couple.

A strong drive for an independent power position is accompanied, for instance, by an equally persistent but repressed need for passive dependence. Likewise, it would seem that an increasingly strong need for passive dependence creates an even stronger distortion of the power position.

On an interpersonal level, a balance occurs between the desired behavior pattern and unconscious experience. The more extreme marital behavior is, the more persistent will be a parallel unconscious fantasy, and the more strongly this fantasy is repressed, the more extreme the parallel compensatory drive in marital behavior will become.

Interindividual Balance

In addition to the above-mentioned *intra*individual balance in which marital behavior is determined by the individual's inner dynamics, there is also the *inter*individual balance in which the marital relationship is determined by the interaction between the partners.

On an interindividual level, the role which the dynamics of the couple plays in determining the behavior of each partner is greater:

1. the more the couple constitutes a closed system; and
2. the more the couple becomes exposed to internal or external

stress while trying to remain self-sufficient at the same time as being socially active.

For the sake of the present discussion on couple dynamics I shall assume that the above conditions do exist. To what extent the dynamics are modified when these conditions are not fulfilled will be demonstrated in Chapters 8 and 9.

An individual's behavioral pattern is affected by another's not only in marriage but also in any group. This is particularly true of institutions where serious expectations about the role to be played determine to a large extent the behavior of those who carry out a given function. Every group is a unit in which the nature of its behavior is determined by and dependent upon the relationship between its members.

Considered as a closed system, a couple enables each partner to behave in a specific pattern only insofar as this is allowed by the other partner. *A* can give intradyadically ('conjointly') as much as *B* can take, and *B* can take no more than *A* gives him. The sum total of what has been given equals the sum total of what has been received. Or *A* can lead in the dyad as long as *B* follows him. *B* can let himself be led as long as *A* is willing to lead. The sum total of leadership behavior equals the sum total of subservient behavior. Alternatively, *A* can perform a mother function in the dyad insofar as *B* allows himself to be taken care of. *B* can receive no more care than *A* is able to offer.

The principle of interaction operates as follows: the more active the one is, the more passive the other; the more selfish the one is, the more altruistic the other; the weaker and more careless the one is, the more controlled the other; the more despondent the one is, the more determined the other, etc. A couple constitutes a structured unit that needs to be functional. One partner can modify the complementary behavior of the other by making him responsible for the social well-being of the couple. Through excessive passivity or agitation, carelessness or extravagance, a partner can bring the dyad into a state of imbalance. Living as a couple also becomes difficult when both partners try to compete with each other in terms of efficiency, control and leadership behavior. *A* can hardly play a mother role when *B* tries to be solicitous at the same time. *A* is best at caring when *B* consents to being taken care of. *A* cannot lead when *B* wants to lead as well. *A* is best at leading when *B* allows himself to be led.

A homeostatic coping mechanism operates within the couple by means of which the partners bring their behavior patterns into a state of harmony that balances all extreme deviations. The inactivity of one partner results in a parallel increase of activity in the other, whereas the hyperactivity of one brings about a corresponding decrease in the other's activity.

Conjunction of Intraindividual
and Interindividual Balances

When one partner tries to protect himself through a defensive role because of personal problems, it will be conducive to the stability of the relationship if the other initiates compensatory counter-behavior. Thus the partner he tends to choose is one who will make him feel accepted or even needed because of extreme behavior, such as progressive hyperactivity. His prospective partner would make it easier for him by freely adopting regressive behavior themselves. The *inter*individual balance between the partners would reinforce the *intra*individual balances since the partner would embody the regressive passivity which one is trying to suppress in one's own personality.

It is difficult to form such a relationship, however, unless the prospective partner is self-motivated to behave in this way. And, similarly, the partner too will seek a relationship in which their intended regressive defense behavior will be recognized by another willing to assume the progressive role.

Each individual externalizes through his behavior a repressed behavioral potential of another.

Behavioral potentials that an individual represses in his unconscious correspond to the social behavior of the other. There is a conjunction between the intraindividual balance of each partner and the interindividual balance of the dyad. Each person feels not only that his behavior is needed by the partner but also that there is no pressure on him to assume the opposite role which he dreads, since the partner is already motivated to assume this role.

This process is usually described in terms of projection. Since the beginnings of psychoanalytical study, it has been known that the unconscious fantasies of one are projected onto the other. However, the concept of projection should be used carefully in the psychology of marriage. In marriage, the image one has of the other is not so much a type of fantasy or imagined ideal as a specific perception. The attributes of particular significance to a partner are those which correspond to the cut-off or repressed aspects of himself which he tends to project onto the other for the sake of an even better defense. *Laing* (1972) writes that "the person does not use the other merely as a hook to hang his projections on. He strives to find in the other, or to induce the other to become, the very embodiment of projection."

What effect do these projections have upon the respondent? In what way will his behavior and his unconscious be influenced by them?

The person receiving projections is not without his own motives, in that he tries to attract the partner's projections towards himself and adapt them to his own life-style. Projections are by no means empty fantasies. Indeed, they are of real consequence in a relationship in that they affect the social behavior of the respondent.

Partners' Common Unconscious

Partners are bound to each other by a mutual agreement, a largely unconscious acceptance of each other. Sharing the same images and unconscious fantasies creates as much an emotional basis for mutual attraction and passionate attachment as it does for conflict within the couple. Thus the mutual unconscious agreement lying at the core of the couple's relationship may become an infrastructure for mutual resistance.

In the narcissistic couple conflict, behind all the bitter fighting, there is a common yearning for an absolute ideal of peaceful symbiosis whose unreality demands continual accentuation by the addition of frustrations.

Despite all the arguments in the oral marital conflict, partners agree that love should function as a mother-child care-oriented relationship.

In the anal-sadistic conflict, the partners draw up an unspoken agreement knowing that their relationship would disintegrate were it not safeguarded by bondage, control and authority.

In the phallic conflict, both parties assume that the husband should always be superior to the wife.

These common unconscious biases are easily discernible through all the quarrels and arguments. The latent conjunction or agreement between partners often becomes obvious only after a long therapeutic process.

Common unconscious biases involve specific dynamics which often correspond to the pattern of collusive complements, as described above.

The entanglement of the partners' social behavior with their unconscious experience is of great significance for marriage and family therapies. When carrying out the joint Rorschach test our research team developed an investigative procedure which might be instrumental for the study of this question. The partners, taking the Rorschach test together, are requested to reach an agreement about one meaning for each card. While they are making their decisions, it is possible not only to determine their different modes of social behavior but also to evaluate, on the basis of their discussions about the imagined meaning of the ink-blots, the unconscious dynamics, fantasies, fears and defense mechanisms working within the dyad. The divergence between social behavior and unconscious dynamics can be seen in the following example of an alcoholic couple. At the joint Rorschach, the wife suppressed any sign of initiative, active behavior or cooperation from her husband through her authoritarian attitude, although the same 'authoritarian' wife revealed passive needs and strong dependence fantasies in her response to the test. Another example is provided by an hysterical couple where the husband left the leadership position to his seemingly passive wife although his phallic needs and castration complex became obvious when interpreting his wife's responses.

From Partner Choice to Marital Conflict

When falling in love, the partners develop a mutual self. It is formed as each attempts to modify his individual self to unite with the self of the partner and thus create an harmonious whole. During the course of their relationship, the parties differentiate themselves from each other through their roles, as was shown in the discussion of collusion patterns. Consequently, the connection that remains between them during this process becomes very restricting. The larger the territory one partner maps out for his behavioral use while the other shares it in fantasy only, the greater is the threat to the relationship both on an intraindividual and interindividual level.

On an intraindividual level, each partner finds in the other a substitute for their repressed personal potential. As long as both partners feel committed to each other as a unit, they find it interesting to act as extensions of each other. Yet in the routine of everyday life each retreats back into the individual self while the closed system of mutual self loses its value. Certain layers of individual personality that were previously repressed in the unconscious re-emerge and undermine the stability which the partners have created through collusion.

On an interindividual level over longer periods, the progressive partner may not allow the other that regressive satisfaction which he denies himself. Thus he frustrates his partner by forcing him into a regressive role, but at the same time frustrates himself because he must assume progressive ego-functions within the dyad without the reward of full recognition. He criticizes his partner's regressive behavior, but cannot accept their desire for true self-awareness and independence.

A person playing a regressive role despises his progressive partner because being dependent makes him feel weak. He delegates ego-functions such as control, leadership, decision-making and initiative because he is not willing to take responsibility. Indeed, rather than perform these progressive functions himself, he undermines all his partner's progressive efforts. However, he despises himself for it, because he knows that he is continually dependent on the partner.

The husband who gets drunk every night expects his wife to look after him and keep on nagging him about it, as she cannot just sit back and watch him go from bad to worse. But his need of a nurse damages his self-esteem and so he becomes stubborn and drinks even more. The problem can only be solved when the husband decides to assume responsibility for himself.

In another example, a man might run a business with his wife and live beyond his means leaving the accounts in disorder. He forces his wife to control him and keep a check on him all the time. He thus threatens her with becoming even more careless. In reality he hates himself for his lack of will power. The conflict will be resolved only when he is willing to manage his finances himself.

At best the individual will realize that he may use his partner as a vehicle for those levels of his own personality which he should integrate within himself rather than those which he has suppressed, despite the fear of what this process might cost him.

Many fail, however, to reintegrate these delegated elements of their psyche, finding the idea unacceptable. They react with anger to any suggestion that they destroy the vicarious transference which once made marriage appear so attractive.

A regressive partner should come to terms with projected progressive potential; that is, with his own desire for autonomous development and active responsibility. When all goes well, he will take this step towards maturity by himself, even though he has always viewed himself as a mediocre, dependent parasite living in fear of rejection and abandonment.

Similarly, a progressive partner should confront the reality of his regressive personality to see the falseness of his strength, enterprise and 'maturity' and recognize his own passive tendencies such as a need for dependence and an instinctual desire for pleasure.

Ideally, the partners are fully capable of cooperating with each other in taking these steps towards maturity and thus helping each other on the path to realization. Usually however, one or both partners will try to recapture the original sense of their relationship.

The characteristics of an unsuccessful relationship can now easily be recognized. One, or both, of the partners not only holds on tightly to the mutual self at any price, but also struggles to reinforce their original behavior and keep the partner bound to a set of complementary reactions (interindividual balance). At the same time, the extreme emphasis on their own behavior serves as a defense against the return of repressed levels of their own personality (intraindividual balance).

Ultimately, this reinforcement works against their own intentions. The *progressive narcissist* originally demanded self-sacrifice from the partner because it strengthened and supported him, but now he realizes that the partner's adoration is immobilizing and imprisoning him. His anger is aroused and he tries to break free of the partner or destroy them. Yet the more he humiliates the partner, the less capable he becomes of discovering his real self, and thus of freeing himself from the moral obligation of carrying them along with him.

The *regressive narcissist* will be enraged by his partner's failure to embody the ideals he projects onto them and therefore tries to force them into the ideal. However, his total commitment to the partner will no longer be expressed in self-sacrifice but rather in feeling responsible for and essential to the partner's development. He will see himself as indispensable, having no doubt that without him, his partner would be doomed to destruction.

Thus the extreme 'egoism' of the progressive narcissist leads finally to dependence on external forces, while the extreme 'altruism' of the regressive narcissist results in his being manipulated from without. Clashes will continue as long as the progressive narcissist is unwilling to support or acknowledge the partner's individuality, or as long as the regressive narcissist refuses to be responsible for his own development.

The *oral mother*, who expects his partner to behave like a helpless child, seeks to deprive himself of all direct satisfaction from the partner. As the nurturer in the relationship he can have no needs of his own, yet he drains himself to exhaustion. And exhausted, it is he who becomes the deprived child.

The *oral child* will continue to make demands, fearing that the partner might become unable to continue mothering him. He regards himself as incapable of assuming a maternal role and feels unwanted and rejected by the partner in this role. Because he persists in forcing the partner *ad absurdum* into the role of mother, by increasing his demands and regressive behavior, he will gradually destroy the oral collusion altogether. He therefore does eventually succeed in obtaining what he wants: a mother substitute.

The conflict may continue until either the progressive 'mother' allows the partner to look after himself or satisfy his oral needs or the regressive 'child' realizes that he cannot make child-like demands and must give as well.

The *passive regressive anal* who avoids any form of autonomous development and overt, aggressive self-assertion will try to use his passivity in order to dominate and control his seemingly authoritarian partner. This is not all that difficult as he has a precise understanding of his partner's weak points and their dependence on followers. His nearly slavish obedience and superficial deference become passive resistance, opposition and eventually an autonomous bid for power.

The *active leader* will doubt whether his partner really is close to him: "Won't she see my leadership as tyranny or manage to take control of my thoughts by insisting on complete openness?" Because he punishes the partner for every original thought, he gives encouragement to lies, exaggerations and evasions.

The conflict will seem irresolvable unless the passive-regressive partner starts to make an open and honest demand for autonomy, seeking the partner's recognition of himself as a separate being without the fear of divorce; and also unless the active-progressive partner allows him autonomous territory and initiative without feeling threatened, unwanted and abandoned.

A husband with the responsibility of playing the *masculine role* treats every situation he encounters as a proof of a test of his masculinity. Failure means to him the collapse of his carefully-constructed male identity. The wife, confirming his inflated masculinity, will strengthen it through her false display of female weakness until she rejects him as a failure.

An endless battle will ensue as long as the husband represses any trace of weakness or passivity in himself and as long as the wife continues to identify with an extreme image of herself as a husband-worshipper.

The fundamental cause of conflict, therefore, lies in both partners' resistance to confronting repressed layers of the personality, whether their own or the partner's. Moreover, refusal to confront the unconscious creates a sense of guilt which, projected upon the other, makes them appear responsible for one's own failure. "I am how I am only because you are like you are. If you were different, I would be different too." The other's poor performance serves as an alibi for the self's poor performance. The partners lock each other into a collusive circle of interaction.

Characteristic of the collusive relationship is an implicit agreement between the partners concerning their mutual disinterest in the unconscious. Accusations from both sides appear merely to be rituals performed in order to dissolve the collusion. Any real attempt to alter the partner's collusive role and involve him in his own repressed share of the conflict is immediately undermined. The 'oral mother' might complain of being too exhausted by the burden of his caring duties to allow himself to be looked after and spoiled by his partner, but in reality he can tolerate very little care and attention, and this is what he has in common with his partner who is certainly not willing to look after him.

Although the *anal leader* criticizes his wife for her dependence and passivity he thwarts every move on her part towards independence and ultimately reinforces her passive behavior. The *phallic* wife mocks her impotent husband, leaving him no room for satisfaction of his passive and feminine attributes, as this would presuppose integration of her own masculine desires. Although they both suffer and provoke each other in their marriage, ultimately they agree that they do not wish to change their relationship in any way. Often a long therapeutic process is required before a couple can realize how they reject an idea of change.

Collusive Stalemate

In the course of life together, the collusion appears to be a trap which binds the couple to their original fears with little chance of escape. Far from discovering in marriage the means to overcome a sense of inferiority, rejection and weakness, the partner's fears are accentuated by endless accusations, humiliation and guilt. Someone who once considered marriage as a paradise in which to find fulfillment of his infantile needs, finds that he is more frustrated by the behavior of his partner than that of anyone else. Collusion has become a destructive arrangement, breeding rage, hatred, feelings of revenge, despair and bitter disillusionment.

An outside observer would find it difficult to understand how two rational human beings could hurt and victimize each other so incessantly, apparently oblivious to the futility of their attacks. If these arguments are about trivia long-past, why are the partners so stubborn and hard on each other? If the things this woman would like to have seem to cost so little, why on earth can't her husband give in and become a little generous and a little more considerate? Why doesn't he buy her flowers, accompany her to his parents-in-law, serve her breakfast in bed on Sundays, put the newspapers away, compliment her on her cooking, etc.? It wouldn't cost much, would it? Why can't the wife be a little more tolerant, flexible, allow her husband to go out by himself once in a while without interrogating him afterwards, let him read his newspapers, cuddle him a little on Sundays, support him in his troubles at work or offer a word of praise or appreciation for his being a good provider all year long? For heaven's sake, is this too much to ask?

Nowadays there are many best-sellers on marriage counselling and confrontation techniques, handbooks and instruction manuals offering a wealth of information and advice on behavior. By fixing specific times for talking over decisions, through clearly formulating what a mate expects from his partner, by drawing up a priority list of demands or by devising an exchange of roles, constructive information is offered to help people resolve their differences in a fairer fashion. The point I would make against behavioral counseling is that the soundest and fairest confrontation techniques become distorted and misused when the background from which these trivia tend to inflate into serious matters remains unclarified and unchanged. For how can a person express clearly what he feels or what he wants from his partner when he is unaware of his repressed feelings and expectations? If the subject of argument alone was at stake then it would be impossible to explain why two persons, otherwise performing rationally in social relations, carry on year-long battles over so little. Moreover, if these problems could be settled rationally, people would find the solutions themselves without having to seek advice elsewhere.

The trivia that are fought over usually reveal one dominant characteristic. A husband who refuses to bring his wife flowers realizes that if he did so and failed to come up with caramels the next day, his wife might say "You don't love me anymore." Possibly the deeper motive results from an oral collusion originating in unresolved childhood experiences. Alternatively, the wife might suspect him of a secret affair with a woman to whom he offers a diamond ring while buying her only flowers (anal collusion). A wife might refuse to acknowledge her husband's professional achievements because of her own deep frustration as a housewife and mother (phallic collusion). Indeed, it is difficult to praise what you consider to be the cause of your inferiority. The wife has no interest in being nice to her husband on Sundays if it is only to help him be able to work during the week.

Thus the cause does not actually lie in trivia. Stubbornness and rigidity come about as a result of the countless frustrations experienced in the past which make all changes in behavior appear meaningless. This is as true of disillusionment about one's own childhood.

The inability to be flexible in trivial conflicts is a clear indication of how inhibited the partners are in their interaction. Thus the unconscious dynamics of the dyad most often determine the behavior of the partners.

Divorce and Resolution of Collusion

Collusion is a dynamic group process in which the behavior of one person exercises an overwhelming influence upon the behavior of another who in turn conditions the behavior of the first through their own behavior. This process is reinforced by mutual unconscious patterns which, although repressed by both parties, merge together when a polarization of roles comes about. In what way does this escalating vicious circle lead to separation and divorce?

In a situation of serious crisis and strong emotional pressure the couple's relationship tends to lapse into two negative patterns:

1. the reinforcement of collusion—renewed commitment or even stronger attachment to each other, and

2. a degeneration of the relationship—the estrangement of the pair because of their refusal to unite in the dynamics of the dyad (or more simply 'each goes their own way').

The mutual self has collapsed. The structural principles, which delineated clearly regressive and progressive roles and maintained the self-esteem of both partners in a state of balance, are no longer observed. The partners' behavior has ceased to be interdependent.

It can repeatedly be seen how people involved in a marital crisis find no option other than either to continue their neurotic collusive attachment or to withdraw from the game altogether. At the onset of a marital crisis collusion usually intensifies. At this point one or both partners may try to break loose of the vicious circle. This is possible if the dyadic system, which has until now been closed, is opened and other persons are brought into the conflict. However, if a partner is intent on confirmation of his self-worth or satisfaction of the other's primal needs, he will not be willing to allow them to escape from the collusive arrangement. The progressive partner then tries his best to draw the regressive mate back into their role, by arousing fear of the future or by undermining the partner's autonomy and assertiveness: 'Go on, see what it's like being on your own and see where it gets you. Just don't expect anything from me when you come back begging on your knees.' The regressive partner will try to hold the other in collusion by sowing the seeds of guilt: 'I trusted you so much, gave up everything for you, but now I realize that I overestimated you.' If, in spite of all the games of fear, guilt and shame, the partner refuses to be drawn back into collusion, the crisis begins moving towards divorce. For continued co-existence, the game of collusion may still be played, or one partner may try to realize his unfulfilled potential outside the marriage. However, unless other factors intervene, the relationship will sooner or later dissolve. Only in retrospect can one see how real and healthy that step towards overcoming collusion had actually been, and there is no better time than when entering a new relationship.

However, initiating a divorce does not necessarily imply a healthy resolution of a neurotic arrangement. A collusive partner may seek a divorce because of the other's refusal to continue playing the role he would like. He would, therefore, start looking for a partner who might be more favorably disposed. Occasionally people divorce contrary to their own intentions. The threat of divorce often becomes the only weapon left in anal collusion. Always inclined to escalate their counterattacks when provoked, the partners may trigger off a process with its own momentum, leading them to divorce when neither one really wants to give up. Drawn-out divorce proceedings result when separation is very painful. These partners can turn their lives into a living hell, seeking to annihilate each other in deadly hatred. And even when the divorce is complete, they may continue their harassment of each other.

7

COLLUSION AND PARTNER CHOICE

A Key-in-Lock Operation
or a Process of Mutual Adjustment?

Is Every Marital Conflict Collusive?

Bibliographical References to Collusion
and Collusive Group Processes

The problem of collusion warrants further discussion and will, therefore, be dealt with in this chapter in a theoretical manner with professional references. A closer look needs to be taken at partner choice
because partners often initiate a neurotic game from the time that they
start dating each other. Here the question arises: 'Do the defense mechanisms of the partners work like a key-in-lock operation or does collusion come about during a process of mutual adjustment?'

The concept of collusion will become clearer once we have examined non-collusive marital conflicts and disturbances caused by a neurotic
relationship for which only one of the partners can be held responsible.
In addition, I would like to refer to sources in which assumptions similar
to those I suggest have been made, but which for the sake of clarity I
have thus far refrained from mentioning.

Finally, I would like to demonstrate that the concept of collusion
need not be limited to marital conflicts but can be expanded to include a
wide range of group processes.

A Key-in-Lock Operation
or a Process of Mutual Adjustment?

To begin with, let us consider whether similar or opposite personality structures are the decisive factor in partner selection. Two apparently obvious rules have frequently been quoted: 'Like attracts like (homogamy)' and 'Opposites attract (heterogamy).' Literature in which partner choice is discussed in these terms is abundant. The complexity of the problem gives rise to diverse opinions. Results of statistical studies concerning class, race, religion, world-view, value systems, attitudes, habits and interests denote a closer link between similar individuals, but indicate that the probability of meeting a certain type of partner in a given social or professional context is greater than in another. In relation to personality traits, however, partner choice is an essentially difficult process to determine. It is around this question that the conclusions of a number of investigations appear controversial. On a methodological basis, emotional factors such as fear, instinctive behavior, needs, defense mechanisms, etc. are difficult to evaluate. Winch assumes that the complementariness of needs is decisive. Others emphasize the similarity of partners' personality traits as crucial. More often than seems credible, *Kreitman* with co-workers *Penrose* and *Nielsen* has reported homogenous mental disorders between similar marital partners, the so-called homogenous psychiatric diagnosis. The fact that studies in homogamy and heterogamy have yielded such differing results is, in my opinion, due to a lack of clarity and, to a certain extent, distortion of concepts:

1. an assumption underlying similarity or divergence of personalities in a couple is that two individuals commit themselves fully in a marriage relationship and therefore every mental process is examined from the point of view of this similarity or divergence. However, it would seem that as far as partner selection and couple conflict are concerned, only specific aspects of personality traits become involved and therefore the question need only refer to those qualities, wishes or fears which are relevant to that specific relationship;

2. the similarity theory does not necessarily exclude the divergence theory since polar opposites may constitute two extremes of the same entity. The two sayings can then be combined together: 'Like opposites attract.'

The collusive bias is apparent in both the progressive and regressive characters of each partner although partner-oriented behavior commonly reveals that one partner adopts the progressive, and the other the regressive aspect of the same theme. Eagerness to help may stem from a need to give help, from a commitment to a mysterious grand endeavour or from an attempt to compensate for an overdeveloped maternal tendency. Depending on the method of investigation, partners may appear as opposed to or similar to each other.

Is the partners' collusive complementarity attributable to their personality structures or to the process of their mutual adaptation? For many years the spokesmen for the similarity hypothesis have discussed whether partners are psychologically similar prior to coming together (assortative mating theory by *Slater & Woodside*) or whether they become similar during the course of their marriage (interaction theory of *Kreitman* and co-workers). *Kreitman* has demonstrated a high convergence of mental pathology and marriages of long duration. His studies offer statistically valid confirmation of how strong assimilation can become between mentally disturbed marriage partners. I have encountered the same problem when carrying out joint Rorschach tests. Although these have not been rigorously systematic, they do demonstrate that, in the majority of cases, the interpretation of the blots differs considerably from the previous individual tests. The joint test thus provides a different image of the personality. In the case of families of schizophrenics, for example, I have often found that clinically-healthy relatives scored results characteristic of schizophrenics in joint tests, but that these were quite absent from their performances in individual tests. Following these results, I began to speak about interaction-personality, that is, the 'personality' in interdependence with a specific partner which is often substantially different from the personality which appeared in individual Rorschach tests.

In terms of everyday life experience, every individual exists and behaves as a different personality, depending on the partner with whom he interacts. Thus with partner *A* he may feel superior and high-ranking, with partner *B* inferior and mediocre, with partner *C* shy and inhibited; partner *D* may make him feel like a conversation leader and story-teller, partner *E* may evoke in him a need to help and give warmth; he may feel secure with partner *F*, take initiative with partner *G*, educate partner *H*, feel neurotic with partner *I* and healthy with partner *K*.

These different personalities correspond to the process of mutual adjustment between the partners.

The interaction-personality is not necessarily the 'false self' (*Laing*) nor the persona (*Jung*), but a manifestation of previously-latent qualities which emerge under the influence of a specific partner or situation while qualities which were previously manifest, recede into the background.

In a social and psychological study quoted by *Argyle* (1967), it was shown that behavior varies considerably depending on who it is one is relating to. Every person has several modes of behavior or subpersonalities. Two people can relate to each other in more than one way. Owing to the available subpersonalities, the problem of finding compatible and well-adjusted interaction patterns has several possible solutions. Similarly, there are several different states of balance for each dyad, depending on the situation. Dyads can be more compatible in some situations than in others. In their studies, *Heider* and *Newcomb* (cf. *Wienold* 1972) have shown that two people tend to exchange those patterns of behavior, attitude and approach which will assure them of a positive, friendly response. Deviation from a known attitude or way of perception may put a dyad under stress. According to *Wienold*, the more an individual is appreciated and confirmed by his partner, the closer he feels to them.

Let us consider what happens when we lay the groundwork for a new relationship. This obviously involves an intensive adaptation process during which we try to determine how much the new setting confirms or restricts certain aspects of ourselves, while the others in this setting are also observing which concept of themselves we will form. As *Laing* (1972) said, "Every relationship means defining oneself through another, and defining the other through oneself." Let us take the example of a family in which the wife keeps her husband under her thumb, permitting in him only a child-like dependence. Even if this is not his normal behavior, the husband will want to be cuddled and cared for sometimes. Yet, if he wishes to resist this type of relationship, he will not allow himself to indulge in this role for any length of time, and even then in only a limited manner. A situation in which someone feels most comfortable is one in which they feel recognized and accepted in the same way as they perceive themselves or would like to perceive themselves.

A similar testing of reciprocity occurs in partner choice. When two people meet for the first time, they start an intensive process of reciprocal evaluation. It is usually known right from the first encounter whether closer contact will follow. *Watzlawick, Beavin* and *Jackson* describe this process as an exchange of I-thou definitions.

Reciprocal testing through light conversation can be extremely intense, even though the topics may include trivia such as the weather, holiday travels etc. Conversation may offer the opportunity for exchanging a whole range of quasi-verbal and non-verbal I-thou definitions, as the following example of party conversation shows:

A: "The weather's marvelous!"

B : "Yes. It must be great to be in the mountains."

A : "The mountains! What a fantastic idea! Are you any good at climbing?"

B : "I climb a lot."

A : "You do? Wow, that would terrify me. Don't you get dizzy?"

B : "That's easy to get over. It only happens to beginners."

A : "What a fascinating sport! Actually, I've been dreaming of mountain-climbing for years, but you need to find a guide if you want to do it, someone you can trust completely. Do you really think that women can overcome their fear of great heights?"

In this short interchange, the polarization between a 'manly leader' and a 'feminine follower' seeking protection is clearly apparent.

The following example reflects different attitudes:

A : "The weather's marvelous!"

B : "Marvelous! It looks like a great time for the mountains."

A : "Do you climb a lot? I prefer riding. Nothing feels better to me than gliding through the air alone on a horse. . . ."

Here we have a woman with no faith in masculine leadership. In contrast to the former dialogue, where mountain climbing conceals deep personal needs, the latter does not serve to bridge the gap.

Collusive partner choice does not appear to be a key-in-lock process where both personalities fit tightly together. Instead the couple emerges as a result of mutual adjustment, a blending of the latent and manifest personality traits of both partners. Of particular importance in this matching process is the degree to which a person feels that a description of himself which closely approximates to his ideal is both accepted and supported, and similarly that the partner feels confirmation of that self-image which makes them feel understood or appreciated. A neurotic pattern of collusion can be dangerous because any neurotic disturbance creates suffering; despite the belief that one will be fully accepted by another human being and released ultimately from the fear associated with former relationships. These expectations provide the strongest motivation for entering and forming a couple relationship.

Partner choice, therefore, appears to be a dyadic adaptation process in which certain needs, fears and ideals assume unusual predominance while other aspects of the individual psyche are not affected. Mutual fascination and adaptation can only take place within a framework of unrealized personal potential. Some degree of interpersonal potential does not enter the actual marital relation, but remains repressed in fantasies or is directed toward external individuals such as professional groups, a circle of friends, immediate family, club etc. The preponderance of socially desirable traits, as shown in statistical analysis of couples, may have a stabilizing influence on the couple relationship, but it does not make the partners' hearts beat more strongly nor will it provide incentive for a 'marriage of love.' Collusion concerns that aspect of partner choice which is capable of generating the strongest emotional attraction between partners and which plays a crucial role in falling in love.

Is Every Marital Conflict Collusive?

Collusion means to me that a couple engages in neurotic warfare. By 'neurotic' I mean that the partners are unable to objectively evaluate and resolve their differences because of unconscious fixations on conflicts experienced in childhood. Marital conflicts, consequently, need not be collusive in the sense used here.

A couple is planning their next holiday trip. She would like to laze about at the seaside while he would rather go to the mountains. For him, the seaside is boring and hot; she feels that the mountains would be too strenuous and dismal for her. These differences of opinion may lead to heavy clashes. Each may stick to his or her point of view with good reason. So far, it looks like quite a normal argument. The battle becomes neurotic when each begins to impose his or her will on the other rigidly, based on deeply hidden motives. A power struggle results that has nothing to do with the holidays but instead with self-confirmation caused by an irrational fear of giving in and losing face. This fear reaches exaggerated proportions because of childhood experiences during which the partners learned that differences of opinion could be settled only on a master-slave basis.

The wife may think: "He doesn't want to go to the seaside simply because he doesn't have time for me anymore. Off he goes climbing and leaves me all by myself. Really and truly, he doesn't want me at all!" The discussion about holidays becomes a test to determine whether one partner loves the other, indulges the other or wants to leave their narrow relationship altogether. For the husband, however, climbing may be an attempt to overcome his maternal-dependence—in psychoanalytic terms, 'inology'. He may loathe the seaside holiday because he fears a regression to infantile passivity. This conflict over holiday plans may activate a strong underlying desire for argument and control which has no rational link with the subject under discussion.

Although the majority of marital conflicts originate in intimate problems between the partners, these problems are not necessarily neurotic. Among those problems that are not neurotic are the conflicts specific to a particular stage in the relationship (see Chapter 3). As their freedom increases, it becomes difficult for the couple to make adequate decisions about the pressing problems of everyday living. Greater freedom presupposes greater competence and autonomy and places heavy demands on the maturity of the couple. Freedom brings uncertainty, differences of opinion and the tiring though invaluable search for solutions. Clashes are imminent in discussions about how to live together: in marriage or legalized union; with children or without; in a community or privately; in a permanent or a looser relationship; in a symmetrical or complementary division of labor and roles; allowing extramarital liaisons or in absolute fidelity; etc. Practical crises or aging may put additional pressure on the couple. There are no simple solutions other than cooperating in a process of maturation and enduring the long search for a way out of the crises.

Traumatic experiences which were not resolved in childhood are carried into later life. In parallel interpersonal conflicts, stress situations and crises of maturing, these early experiences are reactivated and determine the 'solution' found. Non-neurotic couple conflicts cannot be clearly distinguished from neurotic collusions. However, when resolution of a marital crisis proves to be particularly difficult because of irrational fears and defense mechanisms, we have a case of neurotic collusion.

The neurotic game of collusion can be assumed to take over when both partners become caught up in a formalized fighting ritual which drains them of mental energy for long periods and thus prevents them either from reaching a solution or from escaping the trap. The battle itself may become the very substance of living for scores of years, as if the partners came to daggers and effectively tore their lives to shreds. Psychosomatic illnesses can develop under these conditions of continual stress and may prove fatal. It is difficult for an observer to understand how two people could become enraged over such childish trifles. They do not seem to draw the obvious conclusion about the split between them and the torture they cause each other, which is to go their separate ways. The partners often behave as if they were not quite sane, they cannot tolerate rational discussion and lack the ability to see the relationship objectively. They maintain their narrow attitudes towards each other and reiterate their stereotyped accusations and demands, always failing to grasp the basic cause of the conflict. In all matters external to their relationship, however, they appear to be open, approachable, understanding and in harmony with others. They frequently threaten to divorce during therapy, but decide to discontinue therapy just when it might have had a real impact on their relationship.

Essential to collusion, therefore, is an extreme commitment between the partners made irrational by deep personal difficulties. It is sometimes difficult to recognize this irrational attachment as an inadequate form of behavior as it may be socially approved or even encouraged, despite its abnormality. Thus we often see individuals, seeming as saints or martyrs to their partners, who quietly put up with the grossest humiliation and altruistically drain themselves of their energy, all the while presenting an image of complete disinterest and humanity. These extreme modes of behavior can usually be explained in terms of one partner's relation to the other. Thus, for example, if one partner plays a complementary role, he may behave like a devil incarnate, a lecher, a deviant or egoist. There is reason to believe that the polar role of one, a collusive symptom, causes the other member of the dyad to be willing to be helpful, to tolerate and to suffer; it is through these qualities that this partner becomes fixated on their polar opposite. 'Where there is light, there is shadow,' appears to be true both at an interindividual and intra-individual level.

The partners may structure their joint defense mechanisms in such a way that they diminish their mutual receptivity and responsiveness, and it is in this state that they are trying to cope with the inadequacies of the behavior confronting them. A couple who quietly accepted years of total sexual abstinence may suddenly experience during therapy an unreal sense of improvement, an impulsive urge for reconciliation or a rapid change of behavior, all of which are maneuvers to withdraw from the pressure of treatment as quickly as possible.

Couples frequently believe that they lived a happy life together 'until that time when' a specific external event occurred. This might have been when a child was born, a job was changed, one partner showed signs of professional strain, a new worker was hired, the couple moved to a new house, a child moved out, one of their parents died, etc. Any such event appears to trigger off a pattern around which a latent conflict has long been smouldering; this pattern manifests itself as 'love as self-confirmation,' 'love as mutual caring,' 'love as completely belonging to each other,' and 'love as confirmation of masculinity.' Any such event may undermine the compensatory defense mechanism of the couple and force them into an escalation of collusion. In therapeutic treatment, we have to trace back through these petty issues to find the deeper, personal motives, and at the same time make a connection between the deeper disturbances in the relationship and the actual situation in which they have become manifest.

Although not every marital conflict is collusive every marital conflict can degenerate into a destructive and irrational search for solutions. This is what I describe as collusion.

Therefore, by the term 'collusion' I mean a neurotic game, rather than just any game between two partners. The division of roles within the dyad, complementary behavior and the integration of behavioral patterns into an overall system are all normal processes of group dynamics that enrich the lives of the partners, and give fulfillment. *What makes the game neurotic is its defensive quality. The assuming or rejecting of roles is determined by irrational motives originating in unresolved traumatic childhood experiences and conflicts, and does not lead to a free interplay between the partners.*

In the therapy of collusion, I begin with the working hypothesis that the neurotic element and therefore the cause of the marital dispute involves both partners equally. *Are there marital conflicts whose cause can be assigned to a relationship disturbance in one partner only?* When one partner tries to draw his partner into a neurotic game or provoke complementary neurotic reactions in them, this partner does have a choice of whether or not to become caught up in the collusion.

A man who had been married for ten years reported the following sadistic fantasies about his wife. His fantasies became particularly vivid during intercourse and were crucial to his sexual arousal. He fantasized that he ripped his wife's belly open and cut off her skin and genitals. These fantasies disturbed him deeply, especially because of his fear that one day he might try to act them out. With great trepidation and after a long internal struggle, he revealed his fantasies to his wife, who was unaware of them. He was astonished and disappointed to discover that she listened to his confession without any display of emotion or agitation, nor indeed did the knowledge of his fantasies affect her sexual behavior in any way. No collusion came into being. The husband's sadistic fantasies, unshared by his wife, remained entirely his problem. The wife refused to construct a collusive bridge for her husband and thus denied him his collusion.

Thus, in principle, a partner may or may not become involved in a proposed collusion. As *Laing* (1972) writes, "If one refuses collusion, one feels guilt for not being or becoming the embodiment of the complement demanded by the other for his identity. However, if one does succumb, if one is seduced, one becomes estranged from one's self and is guilty thereby of self-betrayal." *Laing* also emphasizes that aspect of the self which allows the other to impose, or project a false self upon it. My own view is somewhat different. I think that one does not necessarily enter a collusive relationship simply to avoid a sense of guilt, but that one is predisposed towards that self which the partner posits as an ideal. Collusion appears on the first level as the mutual neurotic-reactive predisposition of the two individuals involved. If this mutual predisposition is lacking, a partner may suffer because of the neurotic disturbance of the other but he will not, however, impose his own conflicts, personal traumas, irrational fears and rigid defense mechanisms upon him. While one partner may try to avoid becoming involved in the other's relationship disturbance, he will not build a wall against him. In therapy, collusion is assumed to be a neurotic game when one partner reports that the marital disturbance is entirely his fault. When one partner is brought to therapy on the initiative of the other, some evidence is already provided that the case is not collusive. Since collusion arises in the course of a mutual process of adjustment, *it is not a predetermined phenomenon. An individual with a neurotic relationship disturbance is not necessarily compelled to seek a partner with whom to develop a corresponding collusive connection.* I would also qualify another assumption often made by therapists, that a neurotic in his second or third marriage will act out the same neurotic drama he did in the first. This may be the case, of course, but it is equally true that the second marriage often differs distinctly from the first. An individual can become involved in a neurotic relationship with one partner, yet create a healthy relationship with another. *Collusion occurs when similar neurotic relationship potential begins to resonate between the partners.* Everyone has a number of weak points which predispose him towards a neurotic pattern. Yet, as psychotherapists know because of their counter-transference involvements, it is possible to recognize and modify abnormal tendencies.

Bibliographical References to Collusion and Collusive Group Processes

In the literature concerning partner relationships, the concept of collusion appears to have a variety of meanings. *Laing* writes in *The Self and Others* (1972) that the notion of collusion means "secret accord." 'Lusion' comes from the Latin 'ludere' which can mean not only to play but also to deceive. "Collusion is a game played by two or more people whereby they deceive each other during the entire course of the game." Collusion, according to *Laing*, reaches its full stage of development when one person finds another who will confirm the false self which he is trying to realize and vice versa. Each finds another who, by confirming his false image of himself, gives this appearance a semblance of reality.

The incentive to develop my concept of collusion came from *Henry Dicks* (1967) who has worked out a dynamic concept of collusion along the lines of *Fairbairn* and *Melanie Klein*. His book, *Marital Tensions*, contains the best of what has been said from an analytical point of view on the psychodynamics of marital crises. Dicks holds that the essential motive for partner choice lies in the search for rediscovery of the repressed or missing elements of self in the partner, under the drive of the libido. The essential cause of marital conflict would then appear to be the projective pursuit of blocked and repressed elements of self in the partner, under the pressure of the antilibido. The paradox that the very motive which fostered a relationship becomes in the course of time the cause of marital crisis is thus clarified. A sense of belonging would, therefore, arise from viewing the other as part of one's self. A couple would thus constitute a kind of ego territory in which each partner gains the opportunity, through projective identification and in co-existence with the other, to rediscover the missing, cut-off or sublimated elements of his primary object relationship. In their conflicts, each partner reacts as if the other were an object from their past. 'Cat and dog' marriages are the essence of collusion, the partners tossing some 'bad object' from one to the other, trying in effect to put the other 'totally in the wrong.'

Dicks's observations clarify the way in which repressed levels of the ego—which are associated with the 'bad object'—continue to be associated with corresponding levels in the partner. A question which has received little attention, from Dicks or other marriage analysts, is: What makes the partner decide whether to identify with the positive or negative aspect of the repressed object material? What personal factors are at work when the partner enters the collusion offered to him, and how does his behavior provoke the other's collusion?

The observations from marriage therapy which led me to develop a concept of collusion appear to correspond to a number of points made in recent literature on analytical group therapy. It is therefore all the more surprising to find in therapeutical groups that the partners are guided by a therapist in selecting each other, rather than being left to make their own choice. In an analytical group, once a common unconscious is established, collusion cannot be adequately interpreted in terms of pre-existing personality structures. Indeed, because collusion presupposes a dynamic group process, the dominance of specific personality traits of a participant is a function of their resonance within the group. Many of the individual's personality processes may not stimulate any response, or the group may outlaw some of them, excluding them from making a contribution to collective activities. *Bion* (1961) found that individuals in a group are subject to a process of homogenization by which their unconscious experience is equated with the common unconscious fantasy of the group. In the course of being with each other, an unconscious group process unfolds and a group structure becomes prominent, which results from the integration of several personality structures of individual members. A shared unconscious fantasy begins to govern the members' dialogues as well as their behavioral patterns. The group itself begins to speak, using the members as a medium. The feelings and reactions of the group become mirrored separately in individuals who reinforce similar feelings of their own in this manner. Every individual initiative fulfils a role within the group. Each member of the group tries to influence the others through the role which corresponds to his own prevailing unconscious fantasy. A partner will accept a role thus designated for him when he finds that it is in agreement with his own prevailing unconscious fantasy. In this way, roles within a group are assigned a kind of common denominator and a shared group culture comes into being.

Similar observations, though expressed somewhat differently have been made by *Bion* (1961), *Ezriel* (1950, 1960/61), *Stock-Whitaker* and *Lieberman* (1965), *Argelander* (1972), *Heigl-Evers* (1972), *Grinberg, Langer, Rodrique et al* (1957). The effects of shared common feelings and fantasies in marital conflicts have been dealt with by *Henry Dicks, K. Bannister and L. Pincus* (1971) and *June Mainprice* (1974).

As was mentioned in the preceding chapters, joint regression is characteristic of the mutual disturbance of partners in marital conflict. This process may activate fixations on conflicts which have been unresolved since childhood. *Dicks* views marriage as an arena in which unresolved object relations emerge with specific clarity. Regression into earlier childhood conflicts during marital crisis results from a number of parallels between marriage and parent-child relationships. A similar regression may occur in all the participants in group therapy. *Bion* points out that every therapeutic group has two aspects:

1. a work-group aspect, which means reality-oriented, goal-directed cooperation between group members whose various ways of functioning correspond to different levels of maturity

2. a basic-assumption aspect, which presupposes the expression of stronger emotional drives originating in a common basic premise and resulting in strong group cohesion. These emotional drives reveal decidedly underdeveloped traits. In a therapeutic group, regression into the basic assumption aspect is desirable on therapeutic grounds.

Bion describes several types of basic assumptions which *Heigl-Evers* modified.

Bion's remarks are applicable to marital conflicts. The work-group aspect, therefore, appears to be lacking in collusive conflicts. Regression into a common basic assumption is marked by an increase in emotional drives and creates strong, though immature, cohesion between the partners. It is always surprising to observe how an individual whose ability to cope maturely with conflicts in his professional life is ever increasing, can regress into antagonistic behavior as soon as he finds himself in marriage territory.

Collusion as the regression of partners into a common unconscious basic theme is a phenomenon in the sphere of group dynamics and one of wide application, although this book confines itself to dyadic relationships. Collusion can play an important role in all types of group conflict, including politics. Wherever radical groups become polarized, one may observe how one group pursues its own repressed elements in its opponents. Thus, having brought about a total victory for one party, a revolution often establishes a system of power which in some dread fashion resembles the one it originally sought to overthrow.

8

TRIANGULATION OF COUPLE CONFLICT

Alliance Against a Threatening Third Person

The Third Person as a Buffer and Mediator

The Third Person as a Partner in a Unilateral Alliance

Distribution of Roles in the Marital Triangle

The Role of Children in Marital Conflict

So far I have confined myself essentially to the psychodynamics of the couple—to the interaction of marital partners in collusion—as if this interaction was acted out in a closed system, although no dyad is completely closed. Nevertheless, being a semi-closed system, the dyad does have its own internal dynamics. When it comes under stress in a collusive conflict, the arrival of a third person becomes one of the most important additional coping mechanisms. *Murray Bowen* describes the triangle—a three-person system—as the molecule of any emotional system; whether this applies to all relationships remains to be seen. It is certain that under stress the dyadic system becomes a triangular set. Creating a connection with a third person may strengthen one's own viewpoint in opposition to one's opponent or, alternatively, bind the couple more tightly together.

It will be remembered that the closing-off of the couple from within is symptomatic of their pathological state. The freedom to become involved in creating connections with a third party is necessary for the healthy behavior and continuing development of the partners. This chapter confines itself to one specific form of triad, however, the involvement of a third person in marital conflict. The third person of the triangle has in this case a specific role to perform: he or she helps the couple to avoid bringing an open marital conflict to its conclusion, or provides them with a better argument for becoming involved in their conflict. The relationship with a third person will therefore be treated in this chapter from the point of view of its function as a coping mechanism.

We shall look at four different forms of the triangle used in collusive conflict:

—two reunited against the threat of a third person;
—a third person as a buffer and mediator;
—a third person as a partner in a unilateral alliance;
—distribution of roles in the marital triangle.

Alliance Against a Threatening Third Person

Focusing outside marital territory may help to neutralize intradyadic tension. Partners *A* and *B* approach a third person *C* in order to experience in him a common challenge or threat and thus become reunited, pushing their intradyadic tensions into the background.

$$A \dashv \vdash B \longrightarrow \quad \underline{A \mid B} \atop C$$

So *A* and *B* become close to each other when they oppose *C*. It is a well-tested political maneuver to neutralize insoluble internal frictions by amplifying the dangers from without. At a social gathering, the best way to liven up a conversation stifled by inner tensions is to encourage those present to talk about an absentee, who is in some way related to them. In reference to a marital context, a couple in rift can find a new togetherness when their child faces difficulties at school requiring the cooperation of both parents. Alternatively, a couple may feel threatened by their own parents who try their best to sabotage the relationship. A couple may have to come together because of the aggressive behavior of neighbors, relatives, a housekeeper, an employer etc.

Case 12:
    A nineteen-year-old girl came for extended treatment with a diagnosis of acute *Anorexia Nervosa* (self-emaciation

in adolescence). She was a year older than her sister. The sister was a charming girl, popular with boys and apparently free from problems while the patient had a long history of being oversensitive, withdrawn, overly religious and peculiar. From her parents' point of view, particularly the mother's, her behavior was considered extremely egocentric, complicated and a burden to those around her. In the many parties at their home, people were to look cheerful and carefree, nobody dared to sit around and mope, and conflicts were to be avoided. The elderly couple was beset with increasing tensions, hidden power struggles and competitive behavior, however. Since the tension between the parents had no means of expression, they could only unite against their disturbed child, our patient. They saw their daughter's illness as nothing other than proof of how wrong it was to become involved with personal problems, which trapped one in unhealthy fantasies, and how important it was to avoid conflicts, protecting oneself by enjoying an active social life, sports and other conventional pleasures. Their daughter's illness gave the married couple, helped by the younger submissive daughter, a tool with which they could bind themselves together against the anorexic patient.

Case 13:

The son of a rich Jewish manufacturer fell in love with a Catholic German girl. For his parents, his choice was the worst thing that could have happened to them on religious and especially racial grounds. From the son's point of view, he was asserting his independence through his choice. A turbulent emotional battle broke out as a result.

The parents combined their threats with attempts to destroy their son's relationship. When the young couple hastily and secretly married, the parents fired their son from the family company and cut off all relations with him. Being an only son, the young man had expected to take over the business one day. Exclusion from his family led him to a hard trial of self-assertion. Determined to prove how happy they were in their marriage, the young couple lived for many years in idealization, habitually repressing all aggressive impulses. The parents gradually found their son's marriage easier to accept and began to show signs of reconciliation. Soon afterwards, the young man had a nervous breakdown with panic and anxiety states. In the psychotherapy that followed, he admitted, not without strong resistance, that he had felt increasing doubts about whether his wife was really the right match for him. The threat from his parents, which left no space for disturbance of their love-harmony idealization, had prevented any honest critical debate between the young man and his spouse for a long time.

If the complementary relationship within the couple has proved unsuccessful for both, each finds in the third party a chance to rally together. Both partners can externalize a regressive need such as asking for help by locating a helpful third party in an old friend, therapist or priest. Alternatively, in oral collusion, both marriage partners may assume a maternal role towards a helpless child. Should the role of the third person actually be played by a child, there is a risk that the child will be kept in a state of dependence and submission and not develop his own autonomy, since his parents need him in order to avoid reverting back to their dyadic collusion.

The Third Person as a Buffer and Mediator

Using a third person as a buffer and mediator is a common method of preventing or counteracting marital tensions. Many couples protect themselves against excessive intimacy by avoiding every opportunity of attaining a strictly one-to-one relationship. They must have their children nearby all the time, or bring their parents home, or roam restlessly from one party to the next, solely to avoid being alone with their partner. Such relationships can be particularly detrimental to the children in the family, who often find it hard to reject the role of being the link between their parents.

Case 14:

A nurse of twenty-one was directed to us for inpatient psychotherapy after attempted suicide. For several years her family situation had been the following. She lived in the same house with her maternal grandparents, a mongoloid aunt, an unmarried uncle and her younger sister and brother. The grandparents were tense most of the time. The grandmother was a tyrant, telling everyone what to do; the grandfather was a drunkard who spent most of his time in the pub and was on the brink of collapse. The patient's mother believed very strongly that her parents could not live together without her as mediator. After she married, she felt obliged to remain with the elderly couple in order to keep them together. Thus she stayed on with her husband in her parents' home, although this meant being subject to her mother's authority and having her interfere in all their affairs. The husband was a lively vital man of bearlike strength, in contrast to his spouse who was fragile, socially timid and introverted. Marital tensions were never allowed to be expressed openly. They thus began to use their youngest child (a son) as mediator. He had to be with them constantly and slept in their room. His father spent every free moment with him. The son developed acute asthmatic bronchitis and was confined to bed until the age of twelve (both illnesses indicate regressive parental dependence). Of the three children, only the son agreed to follow the parents in their sectarian beliefs and read the Bible with them every day. Soon however, the family underwent certain inevitable changes. The mongoloid aunt died and the uncle married and moved out of the home. The grandmother passed away, giving the mother an opportunity to become independent and to be with her husband more often. Soon afterwards, the son died as a result of an electric shock. This came as a heavy blow to the parents, particularly the father who explained with forceful grandiloquence how a piece of himself had been torn from his breast. For the first time the parents were alone; their two daughters worked away from home and visited only at weekends. This situation aroused the father's fear of relating to his wife. He sought to find an outlet first by exaggerating his religious fanaticism and then by making overt erotic approaches to his daughter, demanding that she never leave him.

$$
\begin{array}{l}
\text{GM} \\
\ \mid \\
\text{M} \ \text{—} \ \text{S} \ \text{—} \ \text{F} \ \longrightarrow \ \text{M} \ \text{—} \ \text{D}_1 \ \text{—} \ \text{F} \\
\ \mid \\
\text{GF} \quad \text{D}_1 \\
\quad\quad \text{D}_2 \quad\quad\quad\quad\quad\quad \text{D}_2
\end{array}
$$

GM = *Grandmother*, GF = *Grandfather*, M = *Mother*, F = *Father*, S = *Son*, D_1 = *elder Daughter*, D_2 = *younger Daughter*

Up until this time, both daughters had been relatively free of pathological impingements by their family, but their brother's death created a difficult situation. On the one hand they were just reaching maturity and had to face all the problems of growing up, and on the other they felt obliged out of loyalty (*Boszormenyi-Nagy & Spark*, 1973) to take the place of their dead brother and offer their lives to their parents. This affected the elder daughter more strongly. Under the stress of this untenable conflict, she made an unsuccessful attempt to end her life. The parents were shocked by this continuing threat, which nevertheless made it obvious to them that they would lose this child as well, either through her death or her future autonomy. By generating in her a sense of guilt and fear the parents attempted to keep their daughter as mediator.

The Third Person as a Partner in a Unilateral Alliance

Partner *A* brings Partner *C* into the conflict as his ally, receiving support from him in his battle against Partner *B*.

$$A \dashv \vdash B \quad \longrightarrow \quad \genfrac{}{}{0pt}{}{A}{C}\Big\} B$$

B feels betrayed and tries to find an ally for herself, thus expanding even further the circle of conflict. Many people feel a need to offer themselves as unilateral well-wishers, be they relatives, friends, children or therapists. This unilateral ally usually adds to the dyadic friction, aiding one parent at the expense of the other. Escalation may easily come about when the husband takes the third as his mistress. His wife may then attempt to commit suicide, and she will be hospitalized. The doctors appear to be full of understanding for her. The husband meanwhile, feeling concerned, stirs up the children against their mother. Her parents and relatives visit her in hospital and become involved in the battle. Her mother begins to take an active role in family life, looking after the children and managing the finances; at the same time, she tries to enlist the children's support against their father. The husband, on his side, attempts to oust his mother-in-law from her new role and replace her with his mistress. The wife then seeks psychotherapy.

Unilateral turning towards a third person in a situation of marital conflict is one of the most common and perhaps most dangerous coping maneuvers both on psychological and social grounds. Moreover, it runs counter to two principles which I think are important for a healthy marriage. The demarcation principle is undermined by the initiation of an exclusive relationship aimed against the marital partner. Similarly, the balance of equal-worth is upset by one of the partners arbitrarily elevating their position through involving a third person; this is surely what makes the other feel defeated and betrayed. They then feel forced to take counter-measures in order to restore the balance. Women of hysterical disposition will do their best not to become directly involved in a fight with their partner since they lack confidence in their own strength. They look for another person who will be willing to fight their partner not only with them but also instead of them. Third persons may already be brought in, of course, when the other partner has violated the rule of battle with equal weapons. For example: the husband uses his physical strength against his wife, whereupon she brings in the neighbors and her father for help.

In discussing the demarcation principle, I mentioned how important it is that boundaries be neither too rigid nor too diffuse. The freedom with which modern couples are ready to approach their conflicts, and their willingness to talk about them with friends is to be welcomed. For these discussions to be constructive, there are certain guidelines that need to be considered, in accordance with the demarcation principle. It is dangerous to have an intimate conversation about one's marital conflicts alone with a member of the opposite sex, since it is probable that in this situation they would offer themselves as a unilateral ally. However, there may be a real need to clarify one's relationship through a third person. Such a conversation requires of both people a high level of objectivity, fairness and critical control over one's relationships.

Distribution of Roles in the Marital Triangle

Another way out of unbearable dyadic tension is a triadic distribution of roles. With the voluntary or unconscious consent of both partners, the third person assumes those aspects of the relationship which the partners cannot share in marriage. For example, a husband with homosexual tendencies may persuade his wife to take a lover. A wife may keep her husband's extramarital affairs alive, fighting against them 'officially' but in reality becoming their spectator. A husband may be quite agreeable to his wife's discussing her mental problems with a psychotherapist, when this will relieve him of his endless caring for her. Occasionally, the couple may realize the value of the third person only once he or she has left them.

Case 15:

A couple requested marriage counseling because of the excessive and apparently ungrounded jealousy of the husband. As an only child, the wife had been deeply attached to her father. At the age of twenty she married a man who was also very young. The husband had spent most of his childhood in orphanages and foster homes and rejoiced in finding compensation for deprival of his parental home. After ten years of happy marriage, the wife's father died and a crisis erupted within the couple. They had previously both maintained a parallel, child-like attachment to the father. Both had remained rather dependent on him during their marriage, finding in him protection and reliable guidance. After his death, they felt abandoned and obliged to assume adult functions unaided. The wife demanded that her husband replace her father in the protective role, which was very difficult for him to do. He developed an irrational jealousy of a man he thought his wife was attracted to who might replace her father better than he could.

To a limited extent, a triadic role distribution is necessary and valid, yet insisting on reciprocal freedom to satisfy needs can place undue pressure on the marriage. A triadic role distribution should not be a defense tactic but should allow for the fact that the partners cannot be everything for each other. Similarly relationships to parents, relatives, friends and children can become triadic processes which enable specific, otherwise problematic, relationship modalities to be realized. As to the performance of the dyad, it will be essential to see whether both the demarcation principle and the balance of equal-worth are observed and to what degree the third member is necessary for the existence of the dyad.

Marital triangles

Extramarital affairs are one of the most common reasons causing couples to seek professional help, either from a marriage counselor or therapist. In such cases, the psychotherapist will try to avoid making value judgments and instead make the couple decide whether they are willing to tolerate an external relationship, dissolve the marriage or terminate the external relationship completely. However, when going through psychotherapeutic literature, what one finds most striking is the change that has occurred in the therapist's notion of value judgments. Not many years ago, a person breaking away into an extraneous relation and incapable of leading a permanent, stable-couple existence would be suspected of neurotic social inadequacy, fear of intimate relations, desire for phallic self-assertion, etc. Those facts in the client's life-history would be emphasized which appeared to hinder the exclusivity of his marital relationship. Today, an opposite paradigm seems to hold sway in that the demand for fidelity may well be viewed as symptomatic of neurosis. Jealousy is now associated with urges to infantile dependence, fears of being alone, possessiveness, etc., giving cause for psychotherapeutic treatment. Although I think that it is necessary in principle for a therapist to have a position that is as unbiased as possible, it is equally important not to conceal one's own therapeutic point of view, which one should clearly reflect. It would be naïve to expect a therapeutic approach to be free of any evaluative projection. In the case of an extramarital relationship, for example, evaluations may vary considerably depending upon whether the therapist admits a married couple for joint treatment, and, if necessary, places the lover with another therapist, or admits all three for joint treatment. Through the type of framework the therapist chooses for handling a couple's therapy, he already provides appreciable demonstration of the bias which is bound to influence the outcome of the therapeutic process. Joint treatment of both partners will in itself increase the probability of bringing the partners closer together than would be possible in a triadic setting. Since I have not yet found adequate evidence to believe that a triangular relationship can evolve smoothly for all three members, I am inclined to support the demarcation principle. At the beginning of therapy I arrange the therapeutic setting and at this point I have already made a conscious value judgment. This is a point on which many therapists tend to disagree, finding it unethical to exclude the lover and not treat them as an equal partner.

Case 16:

A German woman lived with her Swiss husband, his former wife, and the eight-year-old son from his former marriage. She registered herself for treatment of hysteria, suffering from depression caused by these living conditions. She had met her husband three years earlier on a business trip and began an extramarital relationship with him, initially without the knowledge of his wife. They loved each other passionately and the man promised to divorce his wife and marry her. The patient consequently moved to Zurich a year later. However, the man did not keep his promise of divorce and at this stage had not mentioned a word about his affair to his wife. Only under pressure from the patient did he finally tell his wife everything, following which she agreed to a

divorce. Yet just before the divorce the man's wife fell into a
state of depressive despair with hysteria and self-destructive
attacks in which she beat herself with crockery, threatened
suicide and cried continually. The divorce took place but the
patient and her husband now began to keep the former wife
in their apartment, offering her help and consolation. However, the former wife, a social worker by profession, had
enough knowledge of group dynamics to realize that she
might bring the newly-wed couple even close together by as-
signing them the common task of caring for and comforting
her as 'patient' (extradyadic polarization). She therefore
decided to move out with her eight-year-old son and live in
another town. After six months, she appeared to have pulled
herself together. She realized that she was submissive to and
dependent on her ex-husband. Because he was very attached
to the child, she offered to come back and start living in the
same house with his wife and other friends. In contrast to the
character she had previously portrayed, she now behaved as a
fully autonomous, self-confident person, which had a
specific effect on her former husband who began to be with
her more and more frequently. A new intimate relationship,
both mentally and physically, began between them. The two
women were overtly friendly towards each other. The first
wife advised the other concerning her attitude towards her
difficult and obviously neurotic husband. She appeared very
sympathetic to the fact that in his second marriage, her ex-
husband seemed to be encountering difficulties. There was
never an open clash between the two women but the second
wife, who had no other social connections in Zurich, secretly
suffered from the presence of her husband's former wife. She
lacked the courage to insist that her husband break with his
former wife once and for all, as he was showing phobic
symptoms and might not have been able to stand any
pressures placed on him. When the patient decided to come
for treatment, I initially considered involving all three but the
husband failed to attend an appointment because he did not
feel ready to carry on an open conversation about the triadic
conflict. Instead, I talked to the two women; one, an attractive young German with an air of helplessness and anguish
about her, the other, the divorced first wife with a radiant expression, spirited and seemingly blissful. Although the latter
made it clear that she had no intention of remarriage, she did
not want to stop sharing the same community either, for she

had no doubt that it was a case of a neurotic marriage. It was not because of her that the marriage was not working out, but rather because both partners had not resolved infantile neurotic relationship disturbances. With subtle skill, she knew how to wound the other deeply under the guise of generous therapeutic advice. I took the other wife into our psychotherapeutic ward so that the husband and the first wife could remain in the communal home. After a short time the man took a job in Germany and broke off with both women. This was not quite to the first wife's liking. She decided to move out and live in another community.

Situations like the one described are not uncommon particularly among young people of today. In their strivings to realize a communal philosophy they often take the ideals of freedom, solidarity, openness and collectivity to extremes, becoming joyless, oppressed beings in the process. In these cases I try to apply the demarcation principle so as to create a framework conducive to peace and a reduction in tension.

Extramarital relationships are no longer unusual. It is indeed a virtue to be open and straightforward, and, because this is so, many partners will color their attitudes of self-disclosure with indirect motives. Some will confess their secrets to a partner only to reinforce his fear of the possible peril of an extramarital relationship. Willingness to confess may also spring from a need to cling and a fear of separation, states which were mentioned when discussing the jealousy-infidelity collusion. Some may directly propose to the partner an 'open' extramarital relation and, through their tolerance, safeguard control of the partner's prospective actions outside marriage. Being willing to confess one's secrets may serve as a weapon in marital power struggles, a means of humiliation or intimidation to put the partner at a disadvantage. Others may prefer to resign themselves for a long period to an idealized relationship with a lover, rather than bring the marital conflict out into the open. This would preserve the trump cards they hold in readiness should they need to blame their partner for the stalemate in the marriage. Alternatively, they may exploit the situation to elevate themselves in their own eyes, or their partners' eyes as indispensable and reliable persons. An external relationship may represent an attempt at playing with fire to keep the marriage in a state of tension, or a status symbol designed to prove that a partnership is particularly progressive. Escalation often occurs on both sides and the partners vie with each other in detailed reports of their sexual exploits or the stimulating conversation they have had with others. The partner may listen, trying his best to show no trace of jealousy or tension. In the course of therapy, the two often realize, much to their surprise, that although an external relationship brings them much suffering, neither of them has had enough courage to admit this to the other. They may then see that neither was really interested in maintaining the outside liaison but only in demonstrating that he could perform no worse than the other, as well as be independent. There are also those who embark on an extramarital path simply to avoid excessive mutual demands and expectations.

When living within the confines of marriage appears too demanding, when partners feel they have ceased to be everything to each other, when sexual relations with another clearly become more gratifying, or when a third person understands and advises them better, partners still try to maintain certain aspects of their relationship. They want to ensure that sex within their marriage remains a common need, that problems between each other are shared and that contacts with friends and time together remain mutual priorities, even though these are no longer their only needs. Absolute openness about extramarital relationships seems to have an adverse effect on the majority of couples. Those who have these relationships should bear the responsibility themselves. After all, it usually proves to be beyond an individual's ability to maintain a long-lasting relationship with more than one person at the same time.

In my own experience, having an external relation for a long period of time with the partner's knowledge is not conducive to happy married life. However, brief extramarital experiences may bring an essential enrichment at the individual and intermarital levels alike, despite the stress this places upon one or both of the partners. How serious this stress will be is a function of the individual idiosyncrasies of the partners. A high degree of flexibility is required in defining and applying structural principles in these cases.

However, some couples do manage to perpetuate long-lasting triangular relationships with the complete knowledge of all parties concerned. They are those who, after many years of conflict, reach the conclusion that they cannot fulfil specific expectations in marriage. This is particularly true if one of the partners rejects sexual relations. Their sexual activity will then have to find an outlet elsewhere in terms that are acceptable to both. From this perspective, triangular relationships can be considered as the best if not the ideal solution to a marital conflict. However, in most cases the external partner is given a function to perform which, to his dismay, may not be equivalent in status to that of a marriage partner.

Examples of several types of domestic triangle follow.

Case 17: *A third party as safety valve in phallic and oedipal collusion.*
A successful businessman, aged 45, had been married
for twelve years. The reason for marriage therapy is his rela-

tionship of two years' standing with a 17-year-old girl who urges him to marry her. The couple expect to ease the difficulties involved in divorce through marriage therapy.

The spouse is the only daughter of a well-to-do businessman who was authoritarian at home but surrounded the patient with affection tinged with incest. During puberty, he guarded her jealously from all possibles dates; when dancing with her he would embrace her, holding his body firmly to her, and kiss her more ardently than would be expected from a father. She entered marriage with strong sexual inhibitions accompanied by highly-colorful sexual fantasies. Primarily, she detested the idea of making love to her husband. Her first complete sexual experience occurred a few years before her husband's affair, when she had an intimate relationship with a working student. With him she achieved orgasm for the first time and discovered sex to be a fascinating experience. She tried to arouse jealousy in her husband who reacted, however, by finding himself a girlfriend. As soon as he became involved in his extramarital relation, he became impotent with his wife. She broke off with her lover to attack her husband for his infidelity while fantasizing vividly about his love-making. In this manner, she began to use marriage as a means of reliving the oedipal configuration of her childhood. In very much the same way as she had done with her father's mistresses, she experienced sex in a projective fashion, imagining her husband having those sexual experiences which she had to deny herself. And in replacing her husband by her father, she took revenge on him, persecuting and punishing him for his infidelity.

The husband also used marriage to re-enact the oedipal configuration of his youth. His mother had been an energetic, self-centered and castrating woman with a volatile spirit, who repeatedly made him feel insecure by first encouraging him to be emotionally open and then rejecting him for it. Her incessant criticism and belittlement destroyed his self-confidence.

When it came to dissolving his marriage, the most important issue for the man was confirmation of his masculinity. It was his wife's sensitivity, lack of aggression and the support she gave him in his power struggle against his parents which had attached him to her. Through her, he had become confident in his profession. He had been delighted to find in his spouse someone who would accept and appreciate him. During the course of his marriage, however, patterns from his childhood began to re-emerge more forcefully. His wife adopted the same grumbling attitude that he had had to put up with from his mother. He interpreted everything she said as criticism of himself; he feigned illness, became uncompromising and sexualiy inhibited. Entering into a relationship with another woman was revenge for his wife's humiliations, using his sexual prowess as a trump.

Essentially, the marital crisis developed into an oedipal collusion. The wife's drive to set up a triangular relationship came from her fear of incest and her need to take revenge on an unfaithful father. The husband's drive came from his resistance to a castrating mother. Marriage activated childhood fears of incest. Satisfactory sexual relations were only possible for each partner outside their marriage. Defense against incest manifested in their married life in that the man played the role of the unfaithful one while his wife took the role of the jealous bully. Both roles were interdependent or complementary. By putting her husband down, blaming him for misdeeds—particularly his promiscuity—the wife reinforced his reactive behavior to his mother and encouraged him to seek self-confirmation through another woman. On the other hand, the longer her husband's relationship with his girlfriend lingered on, the more the wife saw herself in the role of the frustrated third person. She felt the need to punish her husband as a substitute for her father on whom she wanted to take revenge. Each partner's behavior thus provided an alibi for the other's neurotic behavior. The husband could say: "I want to fulfil myself by having a girlfriend because you keep putting me down." The wife could say: "Of course I put you down when you try to find fulfillment by having a girlfriend." As a result, their neurotic behavior becomes a closed loop.

During therapy, the man discovered the true function his girlfriend performed for him. The worst thing that can happen in a neurotic configuration between two partners is that one of them abruptly discontinues his abnormal behavior. At a certain stage of his therapy when the husband thought of breaking up with his girlfriend, his spouse, who had urged him all the while to make this move, panicked at the thought of having to have sex with him. Her reaction was extreme, including incessant vomitting and severe migraines to an extent previously unknown to her. They were unable to sustain sexual relations and the husband was able to abandon the idea of dissolving his extramarital relationship.

At a later stage of therapy, the wife overcame her humiliating and nagging attitude and timidly admitted that she loved her husband in spite of his faults; indeed she felt she actually needed to be dependent on him and controlled by him. Much to his surprise, now that his wife showed him the affection he had missed for so long, he became fearful that she might suggest a sexual relationship with him in which he would prove incapable of performing well. His resulting clumsiness caused his wife soon to revert to her bad temper. Because of the existence of a lover, the couple did not have to cope directly with the fear of incest; they could cope with a third person much more easily. Rather than overcome her aversion to marital intercourse, the wife could then channel it towards her husband's girlfriend. Rather than come to grips with his fear of sexual impotence, the husband could boast about his extramarital potency and use his girlfriend as a shield against his wife. Thus the existence of another woman enabled the couple to avoid a confrontation with their real marital conflict and freed both partners from recognizing the reality of their responsibility for the conflict.

Case 18: *A third party as prestige symbol*

The marriage of an office employee was unhappy. His wife, a beautiful dark-haired woman, had married him allegedly for the sole reason that she could not find a better husband because of traumatic childhood experiences and her consequent lack of self-confidence. She felt that the marriage did not fulfil her ambitions, especially when she compared herself to her former friends. They had made their careers in the meanwhile and were well-off, whereas she had to drive a cheap car and could afford only one dress a year. She would provoke her husband with frequent outbursts, belittling him in the hope that this might stimulate an advancement in his career, but in vain. Her husband's only reaction was to develop impotency. To earn more money they took in a tenant, a German doctor who soon began a sexual relationship with the woman, with the husband's knowledge. It was obvious that the relationship strengthened her self-esteem since she could now engage in stimulating discussions with her lover and felt fully satisfied in the sexual relationship with him. The husband was glad to see that his wife looked satisfied and now left him in peace. They rejected the idea of divorce; besides, the doctor did seem to be a little immature. The husband derived consolation, however, from the thought that in contrast to the robust gusto of the Berliner, he, the little Swiss, was definitely inferior. He constantly emphasized the distance between himself and his beloved by picturing her as beyond comparison.

Case 19: *A third party as dividing line in narcissistic collusion*

In a narcissistic marriage, the wife plagued her husband continually with her suspicions of his infidelity. Her father had married three times and had never been faithful to his wives. His daughter was deeply mistrustful of marital relationships. However, she was adamant in insisting that her husband was the only man in whom she had ever had complete confidence. She claimed it would be horrible for her were this trust to be jeopardized. By worshipping and idolizing her husband she bound him in ever tighter fetters, while he began to feel increasingly eager to break away from the responsibilities she imposed upon him in order to be able to remain himself. And so an extramarital love-affair really happened, whereupon the wife, finding her mistrust confirmed, showered the man with invectives. Although his conscience was not clean, it was impossible for the husband to split with his lover as it would have seemed like breaking with his real self. The relationship with his lover served as a dividing line between himself and his wife; the third party both divided him from, and led to a confrontation with, his spouse. During therapy it became clear that the wife, while appearing to fight with all her strength against her husband's liaison, behaved in this way to guarantee its continuation. Eventually, confronted with the man's serious attempt to split with her, the lover threatened to commit suicide. The wife then insisted that he give her special care and not "take her for a ride." Consequently, at the wife's instigation, the husband's liaison continued. The wife's refusal to understand the real meaning of her relationship to her husband demonstrated that she could not bear the undisturbed intimacy of married life and had to manipulate circumstances so as to be in a position to accuse her husband of all the trouble she felt he had caused her.

Case 20: *A third party as nourishing mother-substitute*

Caught up in oral collusion, a love-hungry husband feeling unsatisfied in his relationship with his wife, tried to find consolation with a much older woman, whom he occasionally stayed with for the night. Though a little jealous initially, the spouse was in reality quite happy that her husband freed her in this way from having to satisfy his excessive demands for attention, tenderness and care.

In hysterical marriages, the husband frequently does not object in the least to his wife's having an extramarital affair. He considers this insufficient ground to threaten divorce and refrains from attacking his wife's liaison. On the contrary, he can maintain a distance from his wife because she has a lover and thus, firmly entrenched in his role as martyr, can free himself from sexual obligations. This husband will not consider an external relation as a serious threat to his marriage for he feels that his love is indispensable to his wife. He does not feel that she will desert him since he is so willing to sacrifice himself.

The Role of Children in Marital Conflict

Through involvement of the children, a marriage conflict may expand into a family conflict. To avoid confrontation, the tension in the dyad can be extended to create a larger system and will then elicit reactions from the whole family. Under the stress of the conflict, one of the children may fall ill, probably the one who allowed himself to become most strongly involved. The family then begins to focus upon the sick child, and members begin to feel responsible for the child's illness. Thus the parents may avoid confronting each other with their marital conflict, although within the family there is a tacit understanding that the conflict proper concerns only the parents. But there is also a tacit agreement that it is not through the parents that the conflict will ever be resolved. Under these circumstances, the sick child offers himself as a substitute in order to neutralize the conflict. This means a partially narcissistic victory for the child since he now feels indispensable and has cause to believe in his parents' inability to carry on without him.

The way in which marital conflict escalates into family conflict will not be discussed in great detail since it falls beyond the scope of this book. As this subject has been treated extensively in literature on family therapy (e.g. *Stierlin, Minuchin, Boszormenyi-Nagy & Spark*), I will confine myself to marriage dynamics. An American family therapist once told me that child therapy could just as well be replaced by marriage therapy, for the origin of family conflicts usually lies in marital conflicts. If this principle has not yet been realized, it is due to the unwillingness of most parents to undertake marriage therapy. Moreover, it occurs to me that most therapists would prefer to treat children rather than married couples.

Thus the child can serve as a medium for acting out collusion themes. Instead of being presented with marital conflicts, a therapist will be introduced to his client's views on education. Each parent presents his attitude to bringing up children as nothing but a reaction to balance the bad approach of the other. When one says: "I am hard on the kids because you are too soft," the other will say, "It's only because you're so authoritarian that I'm not." When one says: "I want the children to obey me because you lack discipline," the other will say, "I am undisciplined because you always expect obedience." When one says: "I nag the kids simply because you idealize them," the other will say, "I idealize them only because you are always putting them down."

Excessive harshness from one partner leads to a gentler approach from the other, just as excessive leniency from one partner leaves the other with no alternative but to adopt greater severity. Thus the child's lot will closely depend on a specific pattern of reciprocity: when a parent takes one extreme, his partner reacts with the opposite extreme. However, success in educating children depends upon developing attitudes of harmony with social models rather than disharmony. The operating principle in the family disturbance is again the circle of mutual reinforcement, which makes it impossible to say who is responsible for the events which take place.

It is unfortunate that many parents unintentionally create behavioral disturbances and symptoms of disease in their children. But this exploitation, resulting from their collusive tensions, is a means of 'getting at' the partner. "Look at what you have done with your behavior." In an atmosphere where accusations are tossed from one side to the other, the child often has to be sent to a child therapist. When the father complains, "My wife spoils the children outrageously," one must question how much this man feels wronged and consequently is hard on the children out of repressed jealousy.

Similarly, when a woman reports her husband's harsh treatment of their children, or his neglect of them, one may ask how much she herself suffers from his coldness and bullying and how much she feels he takes too little notice of her in the first place. When a person does not dare to make his own demands directly, he uses a common psychological defense mechanism which is to find another person with whose satisfaction he can identify. "Aren't you cold?" one asks when one would like to turn on the heater. "Would you like something to drink?" one asks when one is ready to have a drink.

Case 21:

A couple called on a child psychiatrist because of their alleged differences of opinion about bringing up their children. Their seven-year-old son was reported to show symptoms of brain damage with corresponding behavioral problems which the couple described in vivid detail. The child was said to be prone to outbursts of screaming and rage during which he lost all self-control. He appeared to be unable to discipline himself and would not accept authority. The husband and wife blamed each other for making mistakes and came to a marriage therapist, although they were unaware of any marital conflict between them.

A marital problem which was indicated in the first interview was an anally-oriented collusion. The husband played the guardian of law and order, an authority-figure seeking absolute obedience from a slightly-infantile wife who apparently bowed down to him, but angered him with her sloppiness, passivity and laziness. Rather than come to terms with the problem in their partnership, they projected it into the sphere of their child's upbringing. The husband who had grown up during the war tended to apply a harsh military approach to the child's education whereas the wife kept undermining his authority, secretly allowing the child every liberty.

The emergence of symptoms gave the husband justification for keeping a tight rein on the child (and therefore the wife also) and strengthening discipline at home. The wife, for her part, took advantage of the child's behavioral disturbances since the husband was now placed in a position where he had to take care of the child, and thus proved his inability to do so properly. In reality, she brought out her husband's authoritarianism *ad absurdum* by demonstrating, through their child's state that, both with her and the child, he behaved like a narrow-minded fool. She secretly cherished the child's reactions and identified with them.

It can thus be seen how behavioral anomalies of the child enable the partners to bypass the subject of tension between themselves.

Case 22:

Another example of anal collusion, mentioned on page 116 concerns a student teacher who was a keen radical. In theory, he supported the emancipation of women. At home, however, he demanded respect for patriarchal authority. He spent most of his time away from home with his books, but on those rare occasions when he studied at home his wife would allow the children to run quite freely, even encouraging them to be as noisy as little monsters, until they managed to make the student jump up from his chair in his study,

screaming at them to "shut up." He would then retreat
repentantly into his study to reflect upon the theory and practice of anti-authoritarian education while his wife laughed up
her sleeve.

Here again, the wife used the children to jeopardize her
husband's authority, without attempting to confront him
directly.

Frequently, one partner may manipulate the other into the role of
the 'evil bully' so as to secure the children's love for themselves. Or they
may try to make the other feel jealous by ignoring them and devoting excessive attention to the children. A child may be encouraged to develop
those qualities which make the other partner feel disappointed and
angry. A boy may be praised for being strong, tough, chivalrous and
gentle while the daughter may be dressed up prettily to give her an air of
being a sexy female with a touch of motherly warmth and devotion.

What is unfortunate about these parental efforts is that qualities
which can hinder the child's development are not moderated or brought
into the right proportions; on the contrary, they are inflated and used as
weapons. *Richter* (1967) shows how parents seek a narcissistic extension
of themselves in their children, regarding the child as a substitute for
various aspects of themselves. In my experience, a narcissistic collusion
can also arise between parents and child in which the child no less than
the parents is conditioned to treat his parents as a substitute. Frequently
I have observed how adolescents often fail to become self-sufficient and
mature adults simply because they have an image of themselves as being
indispensable and of primary importance to their parents. This image
may contribute to the child's heightened awareness of himself and ab-
solve him from pursuing his own development. Cutting oneself off from
one's parents may then not only generate guilt feelings and fears but also
a loss of self-identity in as much as one identifies with the roles one plays
for one's parents.

Involving the child in a unilateral alliance within the relationship is
also discussed in detail by *Richter*. This form of relationship often has a
devastating effect on the child. One or both parents may try to win the
child to their side to set him against the other parents. The child thus
becomes an arbitrator in parental disputes. Each parent expects him to
act as a shield, as champion of their cause, or as a spy, liar and trouble-
maker, etc. As though the parents themselves have become children,
they seek consolation, protection and help from their children, thus
placing often unbearable loads on their offspring. These games of intrigue are particularly harmful in that they make it almost impossible for
the child to overcome the Oedipus complex. When a mother clings to her

son telling him terrible stories about his father and encourages him to rebel against the father, or when a father confides in his daughter about his sexual frustrations and complains about her mother, occasionally trying to approach the daughter herself, these children will suffer traumas which may often handicap their intimate relationships for their entire lives.

Since family therapists in the U.S.A. have dealt with the role of the child as substitute carrier of conflicts and substitute for negative identity in greater detail, as *Richter* has done with the role of child as scapegoat, the subject is mentioned here for the sake of completeness only. The type of relationship involved corresponds to a collusion with extradyadic polarization in which the married couple, or possibly the whole family, unites against the child. The child then becomes the crystallization point of family conflicts, a vehicle of projection of all that the family lacks the courage to face. He is a disgrace, a black sheep, a traitor whom everyone rejects. During this time the family remains fixated upon the vehicle of its projection and is passionately involved in all the scandals the child creates. It does not suffice to consider the child in juxtaposition to the marital dyad alone, although this is an important aspect. Rather this type of conflict should be viewed as an overall *family collusion* in which every member, as in a drama, plays a specific role. However, family collusions fall beyond our present subject.

In addition to children; mother-in-laws, friends and other relatives and even ideologies may be used as vehicles of collusion in the form of allies or scapegoats in the relationship. However, it is the child who in the modern nuclear family most frequently becomes 'the third party' constantly exposed to pathological influences.

9

PSYCHOSOMATIC ILLNESS
OF THE COUPLE

Psychosomatic Symptoms as Neutralizers

Psychosomatic Illness as a Joint Defense Syndrome

Psychosomatic Communication

Dialectics of Debit and Credit

Help-Rejection as a Symptom of Illness

Forms of Psychosomatic Illness of the Couple

Psychosomatic Collusion in the
Doctor-Patient Relationship

Psychosomatic Symptoms as Neutralizers

The preceding chapter showed how a couple under stress will tend to open their boundaries to include a third party. Relating to a third person may neutralize intradyadic tension as both partners must close ranks to oppose him. Alternatively, a third person may be used as a unilateral ally by the partner who does not feel prepared to continue the struggle on his own. In dyadic dynamics any psychosomatic symptom can play a similar role to this third person. If, as a result of dyadic tension, the balance of equal worth is threatened and shifts to the disadvantage of one of the partners, there are several means at that partner's disposal for restoring the type of balance acceptable to him. The partner can be disarmed by tears, fits of fury, fist attacks, or avoidance mechanisms, all of which exert the necessary pressure. When these tactics are no longer successful and the situation becomes so difficult that the weakened partner can no longer rely on conventional methods, an extraordinary step must be taken in order to restore balance in the relationship. In this situation psychosomatic illness commonly develops.

'Psychosomatic illness' means any organic illness or symptom which has psychological causes. In a more specific sense, the term denotes illnesses involving organs, particularly certain types of gastrointestinal ailments such as duodenal ulcers or ulcerative colitis, but also bronchial asthma, eczema, dermatitis, primary chronic polyarthritis, essential hypertension, etc. In a more general sense, the term encompasses more common vegetative and regulatory dysfunctions such as migraines, palpitations, constipation, insomnia, menstrual disturbances, sexual problems, obesity, anorexia nervosa (emaciation in puberty), nervous breakdowns, etc.

The illness causes a change in the nature of the dynamics of interaction of the couple as a whole, rather than affecting one partner alone. Indeed, the dyadic relationship enters a different phase, receiving a new "gauge," as it were (*Watzlawick, Beavin & Jackson*). On one level the illness brings the partners closer together, but on another level it emphasizes more strongly the division between them. A sense of inner distance arises in them and many issues which used to cause controversy are no longer mentioned for fear of exposing one or both partners to excessive stress. All that is not directly related to the illness appears to be irrelevant. In this way the couple distance themselves from their collusive conflict. Further external separation can occur due to hospitalization, a stay in a convalescent home, long-term confinement to bed or other physical restrictions.

Symptoms may develop once a third person is drawn into the dyad's field of stress. Often totally involved in their collusion, the couple may have had limited contact with the outside world. Illness now breaks the isolation; intense contact with the outside becomes a reality caused by the illness. Depending on the interest the doctor shows, the conflict will be made known to him first in a veiled manner and later quite openly. Thus illness becomes the couple's plea to society to help free them from their collusive entanglement.

Case 23:

A housewife aged thirty-nine, the mother of an eight-year-old son, requested treatment for acute palpitations (cardiac neurosis) from which she had suffered for six months. Her husband was an office employee, a kind of pedantic, correct and conscientious bureaucrat. The client had married this man after being mistreated by her first husband, a man with criminal tendencies. In her second marriage she chose to forego adventure or experiment and lead the stable, secure life of an upright citizen at the side of her reliable, if narrow-minded, consort. As she was a charming woman, sensitive to all the pleasures in life, she found it difficult to keep her sexual fantasies under control. At a school reunion she met an old boyfriend, a real sportsman with a fast car, who had always fascinated her. During that brief encounter she underwent her first neurotic crisis, experiencing an accelerated pulse, a fear of suffocation (dyspnea) and heart attack, and a piercing pain in her chest accompanied by agoraphobia. As a result, the client was unable to leave her house without the help of her husband. He even had to do most of the shopping for her. He took up the challenge without a murmur of complaint, urging her to pull herself together and not worry too much.

The client was admitted to in-patient psychotherapy. Eventually, during analytically-oriented individual therapy, she became overwhelmed by growing fears and felt threatened by her forbidden sexual fantasies. Following the therapist's advice, she took a part-time job, which was not very well-received by her husband who had long been very possessive about her. He would have preferred keeping the client entirely to himself and in fact seemed to look upon her as a mother figure. He also had a deep feeling of being eclipsed by her eight-year-old son. After three months of therapy, the client's neurotic anxiety symptoms subsided. She could walk out of her house by herself and though her fears returned on occasion, she was able to carry on without undue distress. After her return home, considerable stress developed in what had initially appeared to be a problem-free marriage, as the client refused to give up her newly-won self-confidence.

Her husband was notably jealous and insecure. One day he came to see me with his wife, producing a copy of the

Swiss civil legislation code-book which proved in black and
white that by virtue of the law (article 160) he was the head of
the family by whose side the spouse was bound to stand in
word and deed, supporting him in his efforts towards the
welfare of the state in accordance with her ability. In this for-
malistic manner he attempted to defend his threatened patri-
archy. One Sunday afternoon he suddenly appeared at my
door, desperately seeking my advice because his wife had remained stubbornly sitting on a bench in the forest and refused to accompany him home. It came out that earlier, while
tidying up the house, he had thrown out some of her personal
effects. He now expected me to hospitalize the woman saying: "She is obviously a lunatic."

Yet in spite of the increase in arguments at home, the
client's condition showed steady improvement and she was
consequently released from out-patient treatment. Since then
she has written short letters to me at the end of each year
which are interesting to reproduce here as they show clearly
how the client initially used her mother as an ally in the relationship and how the marital stress appears to have become
unbearable. In the second letter, the situation appears externalized as the man develops a psychosomatic illness. The
relationship then became concerned with the sphere of illness
alone.

In her initial letter, when life with her husband was most
turbulent, the client wrote: "He (her husband) kept on sending
me typed letters through my son Dieter. He wanted me to
visit you again next Friday, or else he would punish me
severely. So the biggest storm was yet to come. He was still
nervous and stubborn and yet feeling down, so you see, having no alternative I telephoned my mother, something he
never expected. She asked him to come to the telephone and
gave him a good talking to. It worked. He always thought he
could treat me as he liked. It will soon be a year since we have
been here, a hard year and the fight goes on. I can see that.
Today my husband had the courage to tell me that I could
have a room for myself, that he would grant me a residence
permit or something. After all, my part in building the house
is not less than his, if not greater. To make matters worse, he
likes to drink, which doesn't do him any good. That's why he
has got so irritable, disrespectful, aggressive and authoritarian. I am no longer going to be so humble, saying
Yes to everything. I am determined to stand up for myself

and call upon my family for help. He hurt me several times by saying that I had not been at a mental institution for nothing and when you think about it, it's obvious that my case is really serious. . . ."

A year later, I received a second, much shorter letter: "So we have made it through another year and the new year is beginning. At the end of November my husband had an operation after gall-stone colic. He has always had to be careful about his diet. He finds it easier now. He is still weak when he walks but we all hope he will improve. Dieter had bad 'flu and was coughing a lot. He had an infection in his little finger that the doctor had to stitch. So I cannot complain of being bored and having nothing to do."

Thus, thanks to her husband's illness, the client's situation seems to have been alleviated.

The motives underlying the specific symptoms which the client develops often become most evident after the disappearance of these symptoms during therapy. In many cases previously inhibited sexual fantasies, which used to give rise to fear, come to the surface. When this type of client finds himself unable to control urges which he once freely enjoyed, he feels helplessly victimized by his sex drive and begins to associate it with danger to his marriage and with self-denial. Although therapists do not recommend it, the client may often enter an extra-marital liaison in order to provoke the partner and thus relieve himself of guilt. This transfers control over the newly confessed fantasies to the partner. He feels that the partner should become responsible for his moderation in sexual matters and enforce the limits he has assigned to him. The partner is usually jealous and insists that he exercise moral restraint. But because he feels capable of greater personal autonomy as a result of therapy, he begins to defend himself against the partner. If the marriage has been monotonous, free of tension and focused only on the development of symptoms up until now, conflict will tend to arise as the symptoms subside. Thus we clearly see how the illness of one partner has helped the couple keep their marriage within narrow bounds and free of stress. When the partner who has borne the symptoms abandons his illness, the other may feel particularly restless. They will be anxious at the possible alteration of their role and loss of influence. When they reaffirm their role with coercion and threat the client becomes even more ill than before therapy, and may even need to be hospitalized in a mental institution or require special custody. A stage of derogation follows in which the client is told, "I preferred you when you were sick." The partner fears that now that the client is all right, he will want a separation. It is not uncommon for the partner to begin showing symptoms of illness at this point. I found this to be particularly true of cardiac patients admitted to our in-patient psychotherapy, where I took great pains to bring partners together for joint therapy. Generally, as the client acknowledges his repressed fantasies and becomes more autonomous, his symptoms may disappear but the marriage will be subject to increasing tension.

Case 24:

A woman, aged 31, and mother of two children was sent to our psychotherapy clinic as an in-patient. She suffered acute phobia with symptoms of cardiac phobia and agoraphobia. She had shown symptoms of cardiac neurosis for eight years and had received treatment from a number of internists as well as psychiatrists. She had been hospitalized twice in psychiatric clinics, without any substantial change in her symptoms. In-patient treatment was recommended because the client was unable to leave her home by herself.

Her illness first appeared when the client was being examined by her doctor for a throat infection. The doctor, a handsome man, had supposedly made some ambiguous remark to her. When the doctor was later visiting her neighbor's home, the client was seized with the first onset of fear. In a state of panic, she ran to see the very same doctor. The client had been married for ten years to a baker, with whom she ran the business. She was forced to stop work, however, because of her illness. Since then the man had been active as an agent. He seemed to live as a playboy away from home, in contrast to the client who gave the appearance of being a humble, if not dull, housewife. She was jealous of her husband, who had several affairs with other women.

During in-patient treatment, the client was beset with fantasies of extramarital affairs. She also had a sexual experience with another patient, an event which her husband greeted with cynicism but later turned into a joke. However, the client's condition showed steady improvement. She became independent and began to exert her autonomy. However, she did not do this in a very constructive manner, provoking her husband at every opportunity and arousing his jealousy. A marital crisis consequently erupted, to which marriage therapy was applied without much success. The husband entrenched himself in his imaginary role of carefree cynic and tried as best he could to treat his wife as a silly, irresponsible crank. A power struggle arose between the two. In terms of her individual symptoms, the wife was in better health after being discharged from the clinic than at any time since the onset of her illness. She was again able to move around without problem and took a part-time job. But the stress in their marriage reached intolerable proportions for both partners. Each lived in fear of being dominated by the other and constantly sought out new weapons with which to attack them. The husband's health started to decline, he looked pale and exhausted and lost 20 lbs. He was temporarily unable to work, was fired from his job and had to take a lower position. In a rare moment of calm he said to his wife: "Now that you are well you don't need me anymore, do you?" He began to squander the money his wife earned, which would have ensured her independence from him. He appeared in my office quite unexpectedly one day to say that his wife was "freaking out" and should be hospitalized. He became possessive of her, jealously controlling and guarding her all the time. By taking a job and learning to be self-assertive, the wife lost all previous apprehensions about divorce. Her continued involvement in other relationships led the husband finally to request a divorce. The divorce proceedings were tedious, as the couple toyed with the idea of temporarily separating and coming together again. Finally, the client decided on her own to carry out the divorce in an organized manner,clarifying all aspects of the divorce suit. She overcame her provocative manner towards her husband and was able to treat him amicably once the divorce case was completed.

For the purpose of therapy it is desirable that the couple express their conflict directly, rather than resort to the indirect method of illness. As the symptoms of illness subside, the stress within the marriage generally escalates, so that most couples yearn for earlier days when the sickness of one partner rendered the relationship calmer and more stable. Role-reversal is not uncommon; after the one playing the role of invalid has been treated, the other falls ill.

Psychosomatic Illness as a Joint Defense Syndrome

In simplified terms, psychoanalysis relates the development of psychosomatic symptoms to the following process.

When libidinal or aggressive impulses towards the partner are not allowed free expression, they become repressed. The individual consequently stops relating these emotions directly to his mate in order to obtain satisfaction. The first stage of defense then begins, in which the individual tries to switch to substitute fantasies through which to re-evaluate his relationship and achieve some level of security. However, when the measures taken towards overcoming emotional stress prove a failure, the process of displacement continues into a second stage involving the dynamics of organic defense. It is in this second stage that psychosomatic symptoms begin to develop. The individual ceases making overt demands of the partner and appears to be fully reconciled with them and 'back to normal.' The emotionally-charged tension will now manifest itself in physical symptoms. In this way the partner frees himself from the existing conflict, though at the price of taking on the load of physical illness as a sort of *mnemic* symbol (*Freud*). A considerable amount of his psychic energy must now be devoted to the development of symptoms, and this leads to a narrowing of his sphere of interest.

According to *Mitscherlich* (1967), an emotion—to the extent to which it is allowed access to consciousness—releases the tension contained within it by relating to an object, that is someone with whom the subject has a relationship. The object and I experience each other meaningfully in our interaction. Now repression does not consist only in preventing an emotion and corresponding fantasies from entering the sphere of the conscious. In a psychosocial sense, repression means inhibiting the emotion's direct relation to the object and preventing it from becoming identified with the object. When repressed, emotion clings tenaciously to its own state of inhibition and becomes equally incapable of expressing itself in its prior affective gestalt or of relating itself to the partner. The emotion begins to operate 'autoplastically' inside the organism, directing itself towards the subject's body in a libidinal, aggressive or self-destructive manner. The helpless individual stops directing his emotions hopelessly towards external objects, trying to change them or derive pleasure from them. He directs them instead towards his own body which becomes the object of his narcissistic regression.

Mitscherlich speaks of two stages of defense. In the *first stage* emotions are banned neurotically, by fantasizing about imaginary fulfillment of one's desires and daydreaming about one's omnipotence. Object relations come to be characterized by neurotic demands and defensive attitudes. Ultimately, psychoneurotic symptoms become manifest. Psychoneuroses are forms of illness which, by confining themselves to feelings and desires, maintain a secondary process called *desomatization*

(*Schur*, 1945). However, when neurotic repression mechanisms cannot handle the personal crisis, a second stage follows in which the crisis is displaced into the dynamics of organic defense processes.

In the second stage therefore, psychosomatic symptoms develop and social defense behavior disappears. Acute neurotic impulses diminish in the subject's consciousness and behavior. His reactions begin to show a certain standardization, while his character acquires a definitely monotonous quality. One part of the neurosis changes and becomes repressed. The subject is no longer able to meet the challenges of adjustment because of the psychoneurotic distortion of his behavior. His actions cease to relate to external objects in any direct way.

Resomatization (*Schur*, 1945) which follows, entails diminution of the conflict-governing emotion, which finds its substitute in a psychosomatic symptom. Now, as a result of resomatization, repression becomes reinforced and so prevents the subject from being confronted with his forbidden emotion.

Development of symptoms can thus be considered as the assertion of the ego through its regressive-oriented defense in order to derive the primary gain from illness. To quote Freud:

> "By this means the ego succeeds in freeing itself from the contradiction (with which it is confronted); but instead, it had burdened itself with a mnemic symbol which finds a lodgement in consciousness, like a sort of parasite, either in the form of an unresolvable motor innervation or as a constantly recurring hallucinatory sensation, and which persists until a conversion in the opposite direction takes place."
>
> (*Standard Edition, 3, 49*)

The energy which the ego expends on the development of symptoms is draining for the subject. As a result, the ego's field of interest diminishes. As compensation for the weakening of ego-functions, the psychosomatically-ill person may become very demanding of care, sympathy and support. This can be described as the secondary gain from illness (*Meerwein*, 1969).

This two-stage process of defense, as outlined by Mitscherlich, can easily be applied to the psychodynamics of couple conflict.

When partners are unable to overcome their conflict, by using either familiar psychological means or models which they have developed in the course of living together, and do not find it possible to maintain a distance from each other or involve themselves in substitute fantasies, their conflict is likely to shift into the somatic sphere.

In the desperate situation where tension cannot be resolved on a verbal level, the couple revert to 'organic language' and somatize their conflict. In other words following psychoanalytic literature, the stages that an individual goes through in the development of symptoms are equally true at a dyadic level. Although dyadic behavior and models of interaction may have been dominated by neurotic tendencies, the dyad reaches a state of peace and 'normalization' once the couple retreat into the realm of illness.

A similar observation was made by *Richter* (1973) following his study of phobic families, and another study he conducted with Beckmann on heart phobia. The symptom creates both intimacy and distance at the same time. The partners have no choice other than to relate to each other more intensely than ever and to become involved in each other to the exclusion of everything else. At the same time, they can make no demands of each other and must avoid all conflict which might be incompatible with the nursing and care due to the invalid. *One is simultaneously imprisoned and protected by one's symptoms. Although the conflict does not vanish completely, it will be played out on a different level where it is usually easier for the partners to be flexible and approach each other with a certain degree of tolerance, without fear of humiliation.*

Psychosomatic Communication

In the terms of communications therapy, a symptom constitutes an adequate behavioral reaction to an untenable marital or family situation *(Watzlawick, Beavin & Jackson)*. A symptom enables one partner to communicate to the other something which escapes his verbal grasp for which he cannot be held responsible. The pathology of the system is dependent upon the partners' allowing each other exclusive access to these irresponsible, non-verbal forms of communication.

Let us examine how the couple modify their collusive conflict by means of the development of psychosomatic symptoms.

In *oral collusion*, the partner playing the role of the adopted child can now expect more care and concern since his demand is legitimized by his illness, while the partner playing the mother figure can give help more freely. Alternatively, if the sick partner is the one playing the role of the overtired mother, he will now be relieved of his maternal obligations and can himself regress orally. He is now in a position to make demands of those around him without undermining in the least his self-image as a person free from personal needs and inwardly secure.

Case 25:

A 32-year-old woman has been virtually bed-ridden for twelve years with hysterical abasia. Her husband, an electrical engineer, is the same age. They married six years ago and have had no children. After being treated in numerous clinics and institutions, the wife was sent to our psychotherapy clinic as an in-patient. She has the looks of an artistic young woman with long flowing hair, radiant features and a sophisticated, dramatic bearing. She approaches everything in a lofty and sweet manner which conceals her preoccupation with her physical ailment. Her husband is a technician, short and inconspicuous with hidden ambitions and high ideals. He had no pre-marital relationships and was formerly head of a religious youth movement. He began an evening course but dropped it in order to devote himself entirely to his sick wife.

The couple became acquainted at catechism classes when they were sixteen years old. At about this time the girl decided, not without parental pressure, to discontinue her love affair with an artist and become acquainted with her future husband. As a result of her mobility problem, which appeared to be directly related to their first walk together, she has been bed-ridden for the past twelve years. For her this was a means of rejecting her future husband and putting him to the test; she was convinced that no man could ever really get close to her. But since the man urged that the union be continued—solemnly declaring that he was unable to live without her—she decided that this was a man she could marry, and someone on whom she could surely depend. After five years of friendship they were married in a house-wedding ceremony, as the client had to remain in bed. There she has rested, until now, in the care of her husband and parents, who live nearby. She cannot be left alone at any time since this would cause her suffering. Her husband treats her with great self-sacrifice and tries to occupy her with music and reading. The man sees his wife's illness as beneficial to the marriage. "We have come closer to the objective of marriage than others. Because we spend a lot of time together, we are very close." He spends every free moment he has at his wife's bedside. He is a keen cook and willingly looks after the household. The picture his wife paints of their marital bliss is less pleasant, but when the couple introduce themselves to a doctor they give out a loving chirp and a feeble whisper. The husband accepts, with great understanding, that sexual abstinence is a requirement dictated by her illness. Thus oral collusion, caring and being cared for, can be maintained through the development of symptoms without introducing conflict.

The question of the 'master' and the 'slave' in *anal collusion* is rendered meaningless or becomes veiled as a result of illness. The ill person can use his illness to tyrannize the healthy partner; or, in the converse situation, the healthy partner can now feel stronger and place the weakened, ill partner in a position of even greater dependence. It is not obvious who is dominating whom in an extraordinary or emergency situation. In the fight for rights of ownership, a compromise acceptable to both partners can also be reached, as shown in the following example.

Case 26:
    This couple married late in life and were childless. Both partners sought to take everything from the other, without giving anything in return. Their conflict centered around money matters. The husband believed that their money should be held in common while the wife wanted to keep the money she earned herself. After years of struggle over the question of possession, the wife developed neuralgia. Her illness helped to solve the conflict since a great amount of money had to be spent first on obtaining diagnosis and then on treatment. A compromise became possible because, as the husband wished, all the money now had to be handled jointly while at the same time, suiting the wife, almost all the money had to be spent on her alone. After she had been treated by a number of doctors she was finally operated on and her suffering ceased. Subsequently, she returned to hospital for treatment of depression. The doctor handling her case recommended marriage therapy. The conflict then focused on another problem: her husband's lack of interest in their sexual life. She insisted that the cause lay in an illness of his and produced his yellow-stained underpants as evidence. The fight now developed into the question of possession of sperm; the wife wanted it all for herself, while the man tried to keep it all for himself. She tried to prove that he was ill and he fought back in protest. Her motive for obtaining a diagnosis of his physical illness was to help neutralize the conflict.

In *phallic collusion*, with the onset of one partner's illness, the rivalry subsides as illness excludes the possibility of sex and also hinders the masculine drive for prestige and status as well as the capacity for initiative and success, etc. In the following example there was strong competition over sporting achievements in climbing and skiing.

Case 27:

An experienced German mountain-climber was humiliated to find that when he tried to hasten his pace his Swiss wife still drew further and further ahead of him as they approached a peak. A further blow to his pride was the fact that she was carrying a pack all the while. In a slightly condescending tone, his wife made it clear that she found it boring to go climbing with him and would prefer in future to go alone, accompanied by a guide. On all subsequent holidays her husband would already have sprained his ankle at the end of the first day, and his doctor would then recommend that he discontinue his tourist programme. The man's holiday-time marital competition thus came to an end.

Dialectics of Debit and Credit

I. Boszormenyi-Nagy and *G. Spark* (1973) proposed a system in which each family's performance is assessed in a kind of accountancy ledger recording the debits and credits of each member. Each family member's behavior combines, dialectically, debit and credit alike. In fact, every family unconsciously tends to abide by a law of fair exchange, which balances all its assets and liabilities.

Analysis of the couple's behavior from the point of view of asset and liability appears to be the most successful approach to their psychosomatic illnesses, particularly because literature on the subject abounds with arbitrary assessments and hasty conclusions. To some authors the psychosomatically ill partner is the one who uses his symptoms to gain definite benefits from others, the so-called 'secondary gain from illness.' Others consider him to be a victim, a scapegoat through whom relatives resolve their own neurotic conflicts. He may be seen as a bearer of symptoms tyrannizing those around him or, conversely, as the one who falls ill first because he is the weakest member of the family. Some say he develops his symptoms in order to escape family problems while others suggest that he is the most loyal member of the family, the only one who engages seriously in family conflicts and is therefore subject to decompensation. He may be accused of concealing the real conflict behind psychosomatic defenses or he may be praised for introducing the whole family to treatment through the offering of his illness.

In my opinion, the question of who is debtor and who is creditor in family and marriage illness is best answered from a dialectical standpoint. The symptom-carrier and his partner—let us call the latter 'the host'—relate to each other through the illness in terms of their mutual debit and credit accounts. The accounts of each partner usually balance each other.

For the *symptom-carrier*, illness has roughly the following meaning. He feels relieved of family and professional obligations, and the sphere of his external activity shrinks dramatically as he concentrates instead on the changing course of his illness. He decides that he can detach himself from other conflicts and feels released from engaging in all types of quests and dangerous situations. He sees himself as the center of attention and allows himself to be passively dependent on those around him. While surrounded by sympathy and care he can regress into fantasies and free himself of all responsibilities. By means of his symptoms he can assert himself, have his own way and even excuse himself from participating in his collusion: "I don't take part in arguments now that I'm ill." The host may be infuriated by the presence of these symptoms, and feel betrayed and abandoned. But the host generally acquiesces to the symptoms because of his guilt feelings and reconciles himself to the fact that the collusion now has a different basis. The symptom-carrier has to accept that his limitations and loss of prestige all result from his status as patient. He may adopt a more flexible attitude towards the partner, however: "Now that I'm ill, I can't . . . I have to save myself from getting angry and so I have to give in to my partner a lot. . . ."

The *host* not only sustains his ill partner but also their symptoms, as he too enjoys a certain amount of protection and benefit from the illness. He can give in to the symptom-carrier more frequently because the partner is no longer considered fully responsible and much of what they say can be dismissed as being conditioned by illness. Because the host is healthy he can feel superior to his ill partner, but he must also deny himself many things and take on new responsibilities. Yet he gains greater flexibility in their conflict and can now say: "I must always spare my wife too much strain on her nerves. . . .I wouldn't take it too seriously as her condition makes her very irritable. . . .So I wouldn't take what she says at face value. . . .She is simply ill and receiving treatment. . . ." The host also finds that his sphere of activity is reduced by his partner's illness. The previous tension in the relationship becomes completely meaningless, for the host must now look after his partner, refraining from making any demands; but in so doing he can also excuse himself from any attempt to solve the dyadic conflict. He can or must deputize in the task of taking over all family duties and responsibilities and this makes him feel indispensable, reliable and powerful. He gains a sense of superiority over the ill partner which feeds his narcissistic pride.

I have not attempted to draw a clear distinction between psychosomatic and psychoneurotic symptoms (i.e. hysterical, compulsive, phobic, depressive, schizophrenic, etc.) since both seem to affect a relationship in a similar way. Admittedly, the dividing line between a difficult personality and symptoms of mental illness cannot be accurately defined. People usually have a greater understanding of the pathological behavior of the mentally ill than of the obscure personality of someone with psychosomatic symptoms. In fact, compulsive symptoms cause people to react with compulsive rituals, the meaning of which escapes them. In psychosis, the individual retreats from people into a remote and ominous realm. Symptoms of mental illness provoke defensive reactions of shame, guilt and fear in others, whereas organic symptoms are calmly accepted as ordained by "the will of God."

Help-rejection as a Symptom of Illness

This could well be interpreted as the reinforcement of psychosomatic defense. The client deliberately refuses to accept all the secondary gains from illness, which he could easily enjoy. He disguises and belittles his illness, which is often organic though psychosomatic in origin; such as chronic primary polyarthritis. However, the same reaction may occur—and this is not a well-known fact—in connection with *conversion* symptoms. In both cases the client refrains from discussing his symptoms with anybody; yet they nevertheless appear. He makes no demands and is calm, resigned and reasonable. He insists that he is doing quite well—"not too bad, really"—and seems to be both healthy and happy. Judging by his symptoms, however, the client is in quite a miserable state and certainly qualifies for careful medical attention, and perhaps intensive care and treatment. In fact he may even be in critical condition. But the client tirelessly emphasizes his independence, constantly apologizes for any possible inconvenience he might be causing, refuses any assistance offered him and asserts in no uncertain terms that he is scarcely worth attention and should not cause any trouble for anyone else.

Such patients tend to attach themselves to the kinds of people who show precisely those characteristics which they describe in themselves. As partners, they do not wish to be troubled by the partnership; they seem to have decided that the relationship must not create any demands which may have to be met, nor impose any limitations on them. They offer themselves to their partner by constantly asking what they can "do," provided that it doesn't involve their personal commitment. Through his illness, the patient places a definite load on his partner, deeply disturbing him and robbing him of his peace of mind. On the one hand the patient feels very guilty, for he has been taught since childhood not to expect anything from anybody. But on the other hand his illness has taken on a character of revenge, directed towards his partner. "I'm so sorry, dear, that my illness forces you to offer me help against my will." The patient puts his partner in a double bind in that verbally he behaves in accordance with the partner's expectations: "Don't worry about me and my illness, go skiing, find yourself a girlfriend, get on with your job. . . ." But if the partner follows those suggestions, which do fulfil his own intentions, he will be plagued by a guilty conscience and any possible pleasure he might have enjoyed by leaving the patient will be destroyed. Should the partner drop his initial approach of not caring and begin to look after the patient, he will feel angry and resentful for surrendering to the client's illness. Thus while his partner walks into a trap the patient seems above reproach, consciously and verbally rejecting any secondary gains from illness and denying making any attempt to obtain them. The therapist too may fail to develop a rapport with this type of patient. He tends to be obscure in his statements and undermines treatment, for example by pointing out the therapist's faults in order to frustrate and belittle him and prove him incapable of giving help. All the patient's behavior is focused on maintaining his psychosomatic defense, and he will reject secondary gains from illness by pathologically disguising his refusal of help. In treatment, all therapeutic efforts will concentrate initially on helping the patient to recognize himself as a sick person and to accept himself in this state. The personal history to his predicament is an extreme form of helplessness. He is often depressive, has low self-esteem and may feel acutely guilty about his own lack of responsibility and tendency to be self-destructive.

Case 28:
     An academic, married for thirty years, had always expected his wife to fall in with the routine of his work, to allow him all possible freedom and make no demands on him whatsoever. Nevertheless, the basic conflict of their marriage arose because the wife, although she followed his demands, wanted to be informed about everything he was doing and thinking and thus participate in it. The man considered this tendency of hers an intolerable encroachment and insisted

that she stop. For several years the woman had been troubled by chronic primary polyarthritis, which at present seriously impairs her movements. She has to walk with sticks and can barely go upstairs. She continually expresses her feeling of guilt at the inconvenience which her illness must cause her husband, and tries to make herself independent of him. Whatever she says, however, she cannot help but be hurt by his lack of sympathy for her condition, although she hides her need for protection and dependence and stresses her autonomy somewhat provocatively. The man, on the other hand, feels confined by her illness and would rather lead his own life. Occasionally he goes away to participate in a sport or take holidays by himself, but his bad conscience about his wife destroys any enjoyment which these moments of solitude might bring. When he does help her he becomes upset and annoyed easily, as nothing really pleases her. They torment each other over the illness, denying the existence of their anger or guilt. More specifically, the wife denies that she would actually love to be taken care of by her husband, while the husband refuses to admit that he feels confined and overburdened by the weight of her illness. The wife tells him, "Take a trip somewhere, it will do you good," fantasizing all the while, "If only he would stay with me." When she is left alone in the house, she has attacks of anxiety. Her husband secretly cherishes the idea of a divorce or separation after which he would put his wife in a home for the disabled; all of which he vigorously refuses to admit in her presence. His spouse is apprehensive about this very prospect. Because entering a home is unthinkable to her she emphasizes even more strongly her independence. Thus they can neither leave nor come closer to each other.

Case 29:

A 39-year-old woman entered in-patient psychotherapy because of functional leg paralysis and migraine attacks. Nine years ago she had married a Swiss with whom she has been living in Africa. The man was a successful engineer and a keen sportsman. Their life-style was completely within the neocolonial and feudal microcosm. The man's employer, a large company, provided them with an apartment, transportation and generally completely defined their existence. The man enjoyed the social life and was a keen party-goer. The marriage came about allegedly for practical reasons. At the beginning of their relationship, the woman lacked the courage to make any demands of her husband. She subordinated herself to him and was anxious to make his life as comfortable and attractive as possible. He, on the other hand, showed little interest in his relationship with his wife and completely immersed himself in his sporting and social exploits. Marital tension was not brought out into the open and both had a true aversion to major confrontations. For twenty years, the patient has suffered from migraine attacks, two a week on average, during which she retreats to her bed. These attacks frequently seem to have coincided with her husband's frustrations, at which point she would immediately withdraw to her room. The patient never dared bother her husband with any problems and in fact kept all her marital frustrations to herself. Instead nearly every year she would go to Switzerland for months at a time for one illness or another. Once she broke a bone during a sporting trip with her husband, another time her thyroid gland needed to be operated on, or a suspected duodenal ulcer examined, etc. Recently, she had six months of treatment in Africa for some obscure fever and received injections of Vitamin B12 for overall strengthening. Coughs and bronchitis followed and were treated with antibiotics and further vitamin injections. When she began to have headaches as well doctors suspected malaria and, although diagnosis was never confirmed, she was treated with quinine. Then she suddenly began to suffer from parasthesia and tingling and weakness in her legs, which gave reason to suspect inflammation of the nerves, possibly as a result of a quinine overdose. Finally, the woman was transferred to a clinic in Zurich where no organic factor in her illness was proven.

Thus the patient came to our psychotherapy clinic. The treatment encountered difficulties because of her low awareness of conflict. She appeared to be well-adjusted in her external behavior, always friendly with everybody, considerate, helpful, grateful and undemanding. Because of weakness in her knees she could only take walks when accompanied, a situation which she tried to avoid in accordance with her desire to be independent. Most importantly, she strove to conceal any trace of her marital problems. Her migraine attacks tended to occur first of all during therapeutic interviews on the marriage. Because of her symptoms, the patient was able to transform her temporary visit to Switzerland into a permanent return. She bought her own house and wrote to her husband to tell him that the African climate made it impossible for her to return. Making use of her illness, she forced her husband to yield and resettle in Switzerland.

Noteworthy in this case is that the patient managed to convince a number of doctors of the existence of somatic malfunctions, without their ever reaching a definite somatic diagnosis.

Forms of Psychosomatic Illness of the Couple

According to *Mitscherlich* (1967), in a somewhat simplified approach, three kinds of psychosomatic symptoms can be distinguished:

1. *conversion symptoms*, where the body becomes a medium which symbolically represents an otherwise inexpressible conflict;

2. *affective equivalents*, where the body becomes a medium for acting out strong affective feelings;

3. *stress correlatives*, where the body shows signs of decompensation as a result of strong inner tension.

These three types of symptoms may be combined in specific cases, with different emphasis being placed on one or the other.

1. *Conversion symptoms*

Conversion symptoms are symbolic expressions of an uncontrollable conflict. Shown in movements or expressed in 'organic language,' the organic symptom is in this case a form of behavior consciously ignored by the subject. The ill subject's behavior may be humble, but occasionally be seen to be strikingly impassive. The dynamics of conversion symptoms are a mode of communication established for the sake of a specific conflict with a specific partner. The symptom-carrier addresses through his unconscious the unconscious of his partner. The symptom often serves as a means to reach a compromise of the partners' divergent claims. "I cannot keep my eyes open," says a husband suffering from blepharospasm, a spasmodic closure of the eyelids. He maintains a secret liaison and is afraid "to look his wife in the eye." He cannot approach his own situation with open eyes either.

A girl collapses at the front door of a house with hysterical leg paralysis and so causes a young man living on the ground floor, with whom she is secretly in love, to carry her in his arms to her own apartment on the third floor. "My feet are so weak that without your helping hand I cannot go on in life."

Which symptoms of illness can or cannot be classified as conversion symptoms has been a subject of discussion among psychiatrists, who are far from arriving at any standard formula. It seems to me that the question of nosographic classification is less important than the psychodynamic meaning of the concept of conversion symptoms as unconscious behavioral language. This will be shown in the following case of cardiac neurosis, an ailment which, incidentally, *G. Engel* considers a typical conversion symptom operation.

Case 30:

A 28-year-old man had grown up as an only child in overprotective surroundings. During his first trip abroad, while in Paris, he met his future wife and the first girlfriend he had ever had. She too was an only child. Soon after their honeymoon, a protracted struggle broke out between them about the location of their future home. The man urged her to come back to Zurich while his wife insisted on staying in Paris. At about this time the man became bad tempered and nervous and began to suffer from an irritated colon. He caught flu two months after they were married, and this was followed by acute cardiac neurosis with sensations of pressure and piercing pain in the cardiac region and a panic-like fear of heart attack. All these symptoms were without any objective cardiac disorder. The doctor, called in an emergency, tried to console the man's fears about his physical condition but suggested he return to Switzerland where the mountains and winter sports might be conducive to his health. His wife had to accept the doctor's recommendations and the couple moved to Zurich where they initially shared a house with his parents. After three years the wife had still not learned a word of German, and so was never able to go shopping or talk to the neighbors. She spent the day by herself waiting for her husband to come home in the evening, when he had to do all the things she had omitted because of her language problem. The woman was deeply unhappy; she continually talked of returning to Paris and refused to become settled in Zurich. She did her best to undermine her husband's professional career and particularly his chances of getting a post in the diplomatic service, which might have meant irregular working hours and coming home late. Thus after temporary progress coinciding with their return to Zurich, the symptoms of cardiac neurosis reappeared: fear of being alone, agoraphobia and fear of helplessness. The

limitation of the sphere of his active life and a subsequent inability to work also became apparent. This is how the man
found his way to in-patient psychotherapy.

With his hospitalization, the marriage situation underwent a profound upheaval. The wife became extremely upset
and insisted that her husband come home immediately. When
he refused she ran away to her parents, refusing to return until he was released. She was opposed to his therapist and tried
to disrupt the therapeutic process. Later we learned that she
herself had developed anxiety neurosis symptoms such as a
fear of being alone and anxiety attacks at night.

An important step in achieving progress in the client's
treatment was to win his wife's sympathy towards therapy.
She was made aware that the more she imposed limitations
on her husband, the more she would force him to retain his
symptoms and thus decrease her chances of returning to
Paris. She had to realize that the man would only be able to
muster enough courage to move to Paris if he could acquire
self-confidence and regain his health. To enable him to do so
she would have to allow him more living space, but this pre-
supposed her becoming adjusted to Zurich, learning the
language and becoming independent. The development of
symptoms of cardiac neurosis evidently helped the couple
avoid the conflict of deciding on the location of their future
home. The husband was unable to express his desire to return
to Zurich in any direct way. It was his symptoms which then
appealed to the partner: "My heart is here, I am sure to die
unless I go back to my hometown. It isn't me, it's my heart
that forces me. . . ." The man could thus disclaim any responsibility for the choice of location. It was not he expressing his wish but the all-powerful heart speaking to the
woman's heart. Her interpretation of his symptoms was:
"My husband has a heart problem. He should come straight
home in the evenings and rest with me. He should be careful
and not go out by himself. When a man has a heart problem
like his, he should never be alone. No-one can tell when he
might have an attack." The message she managed to transmit
to her husband was that he should follow her unquestioning-
ly and never take a step outside his circle of sorrow. The
symptom thus enabled the woman to keep her husband in
total dependence; it neutralized the marital tension and
helped to integrate the demands of both partners in a state of
acceptable compromise.

2. *Affective equivalents*

We consider an affective equivalent to be the parallel organic manifestation of strong affective feelings. The somatic symptom can become a medium for emotional release although the accompanying fantasies need not necessarily enter into consciouness or be recognized as such by the subject. The development of symptoms may be instantaneous (paroxysmal) and acute. The symptom, serving as an outlet for unbearable affective stress, brings the symptom-carrier and the people around him to a point of high agitation. Examples of affective equivalents are asthmatic attacks, migraines, certain forms of epilepsy, hysterical blackouts, paroxysmal hysterical excitation, hyperventilation, tetany, phobic cardiac panic states, etc. A state of calm follows this type of dramatic explosion, as after a cleansing storm.

Case 31: *An example of paroxysmal hysterical excitation.*

An unstable young man has become settled under the motherly influence of his wife. He seems to be aware that his wife's strict control is necessary, but also feels overly dominated by her. The following interaction occurs repeatedly. The tension builds up hour by hour and day by day until it triggers off an hysterical fit of rage in the man. In this state of confused awareness he hurls curses and abuse at his wife. She is speechless and stupefied at first, but then screams at him, "It's not you. It's the devil speaking through you!" Obscene swearing continues for a few minutes and then the man, stricken with weakness, is no longer able to support himself and collapses on the floor at his wife's feet, saying nothing. The woman is now full of compassion and concern. She drags him to bed, undresses him and cares for him until he wakes; whereupon they both relax.

The tension between 'master' and 'slave' in this anal collusion unfolds like a ritual. The man first behaves like an enraged braggart, frightening his wife and swearing at her. In this strange state he appears to be out of his mind. But his performance is then transformed into its opposite and he falls at his wife's feet, totally submitting to her. This releases the tension between the two, after which there is a state of peace and reconciliation until the next attack of aggression. The conflict never becomes verbalized and is always expressed in this paroxysmal form.

In any specific case more than one type of symptom may appear. In the above example the symptom is obviously characteristic of affective equivalence, although there is also an element of conversion in the transformation from self-assertive fits of rage to helpless collapse.

3. *Stress correlatives*

Strong mental tension may predispose organic processes towards participating in the trials of the mind, notably by impairing the vegetative and endocrine functions, which may result in actual organic dysfunctions.

However, in a given conflict, it is a matter of controversy to what extent any psychosomatic illness exhibiting organic dysfunction can be interpreted as a specific expression of a definite personality structure. Organic susceptibility to stress has also been a subject of discussion. There is no doubt that mental stress can be detrimental to the general condition and resistance of an organism and thereby precipitate the development of all kinds of illness.

Patients with psychosomatic-organic illnesses often appear to behave quite differently from patients with conversion symptoms and affective equivalents. These others are verbally inhibited, but frequently very expressive physically, and characteristically gesticulate and mimic enthusiastically. When they speak their tension emerges in nervous finger twisting, sweating, blushing, etc.; whereas patients with psychosomatic-organic illnesses behave in an overcontrolled manner, are always friendly, restrained in their gestures and make few accompanying movements. The neutralizing of the conflict is less perceptible in psychosomatic-organic cases as the partners usually refuse to admit that any couple conflict exists at all.

Stress correlatives often arise as the result of somatic decompensation, a situation in which a fuse blows, as it were, and the capacity for mental activity is exhausted. Typical psychosomatic stress correlatives are stomach ulcers, ulcerative colitis, chronic primary polyarthritis, etc.

Case 32:
A 44-year-old warehouse worker had lived what might be called a reckless life. He would quit his job at the slightest disagreement with his co-workers; he had been a hobo for a time and a heavy drinker; and he had served a number of sentences for brawling and theft. After meeting his future wife, whom he married fourteen years ago, his conduct underwent a profound transformation. He stopped drinking and smoking, stopped mixing with his former associates, and stayed at home in the evenings to watch television. In the last fourteen years he has changed his job only once and was

regarded by his previous employer as a disciplined and willing worker. However, his interpersonal behavior had become limited. He would now sit morosely at home saying little. He provoked his wife into giving him instructions, such as on how to dress for example, and once she did so would angrily retort that she just ordered him around all the time and that he couldn't stand it any more. In the ensuing rage he would beat both his wife and himself. She finally sought advice from a marriage counselor. Six months before beginning therapy with us, she took a holiday at an unknown location with their daughter, who was particularly dear to her father. The client was very distressed and frustrated, and felt abandoned. Soon afterwards he began to experience severe stomach problems. He had to be hospitalized and an ulcer was diagnosed and operated on. The ulcer continued recurring and the patient steadily lost weight. Other operations followed for jejunal peptic ulcer and an abcess in the small intestine, all of which led to his overall emaciation. When he entered our psychotherapy clinic, he had already been hospitalized for six months. He was clearly a difficult patient, especially for the nurses, from whom he demanded an impossible amount of care and attention while complaining about their negligence and indifference. It was obvious that he transferred his resentment towards his wife onto the nurses. He was unresponsive to psychotherapeutic discussion as he failed to see any conflict with his wife and described their relationship as problem-free. His bad temper had its outlet in stomach and intestinal ailments. The smallest frustration would cause him unbearable pain, which would then subside when suitable medication was applied. The marital conflict was thus displaced into a conflict with the hospital staff. Our psychotherapy with his problem was a failure. Because of his ulcers the client had to be transferred to a surgical ward, from which he wished never to return to us.

Psychosomatic Collusion in the Doctor-Patient Relationship

As already mentioned, the development of psychosomatic symptoms is often accompanied by an apparent normalization of social behavior. In his interests and fantasies, the psychosomatically-ill person becomes confined to his somatic dysfunctions. He has been described as an "emotional illiterate" in that he is unable to perceive his feelings and mental processes; instead he registers physical states with great accuracy.

This type of person therefore behaves as most biologically-oriented doctors would like their ideal patient to behave. He can provide a detailed account of his somatic processes as he is indeed very capable of perceiving them adequately. Moreover, he trusts authority, he has confidence in every medical instruction, allows all kinds of examinations to be performed on him, remains passive and tends to exaggerate and idolize the physician's power. Most significantly, he represses any psychological observations about himself. He is content to remain within the area delineated by all the optimistic medical stock formulas that he repeats internally to himself or would like to hear repeated over and over again by his doctor. "Keep your chin up! Have courage! Relax, don't take everything so seriously. You should let go, mix with people, take some exercise, buy yourself something healthy like vitamins, salads, organically-grown vegetables. Pull yourself together. Get some sun. Sleep a lot. Get some fresh air and above all don't think too much, and keep smiling. All's well; if you think it's not, either you've eaten something bad or the weather is no good. Damn this weather!"

Doctors with a strictly scientific approach will always welcome this type of patient. Under pressure of time they need individuals who fit easily into scientific explanations and accept them, and do not tend to complicate matters with psychological intrusions. This is yet another collusion born of our times, a collusion between biologically-oriented members of the medical profession and their psychosomatically-ill patients who so conveniently repress any trace of psychological disorder! Thus the patient believes that if he visits his doctor, it is only to indicate to him his somatic illness. Similarly, the doctor makes it a point of medical policy that the patient should not expect anything from him other than the diagnosis of his physical condition. He rejects the idea of discussing the patient's mental state and sees it as an intolerable infringement of the patient's privacy.

This particular type of partner choice is followed, however, by a stage of partner conflict. Something doesn't look quite right, for the patient's complaint is not confirmed by physical examination or, worse still, there may not be any such confirmation at all. In spite of this, the somatic doctor-patient collusion is often maintained. The slightest physical ailment or any suspicion pulled out of the air may provide justification for obtaining a prescription for some useless drug. The patient loses confidence in the doctor who fails to diagnose his complaint, while the doctor feels dismayed by his own ignorance and the patient's lack of trust in him. So, to avoid the impending threat, he directs his patient to another specialist, who will in all probability repeat the same procedure from the beginning.

The question then is, to what extent do the doctors themselves cause psychosomatic illness. The widespread resistance amongst doctors to psychosomatic medicine has been maintained for such a long time because the great majority of patients and their relatives are in agreement despite the fact that this adds to their present deep mistrust of the medical profession.

10

CHANGING THERAPEUTIC
PERSPECTIVES

Difficulties for the Psychoanalyst in Couples Therapy

The Effect of Individual Psychoanalysis
on Partner Conflict

The Therapist in Collusion with his Client—
as Analogy to the Client's Marriage

Goals of Joint Therapy

Applying the Concept of Collusion to Marriage Therapy

Difficulties for the Psychoanalyst
in Couples Therapy

Forty to sixty percent of those coming to psychotherapy for the first
time do so because of problems they encounter with their partners. It
would therefore seem logical to assume that joint therapy is one of the
most strongly-developed areas in psychotherapy. In reality, the contrary
appears to be true. Although there has been rapid growth of interest in
couple conflict in the last decade, few fully qualified psychotherapists
can be said to be specialists in couples therapy.

The reason for the current situation is historical. Since Freud, psychoanalytic theory has continually incorporated new material, neces-
sitating readjustment, changes in emphasis and reformulation; and it has

become such an intricate body of knowledge that most analysts can no longer tell the forest from the trees. For some, the very complexity itself is a disconcerting factor. Others have expended vast amounts of mental energy on assimilating the wealth of psychoanalytic thought. When a human being is examined as if under a microscope specific areas are brought more sharply into focus, but as magnification increases, a sense of the whole is eventually lost. Indeed, the psychoanalytic approach often fails to make sufficient allowance for what can be seen with the naked eye once the magnifying glass has been removed.

A number of analysts with whom I have raised this problem suggested that analytical theory would be too complex for it to be applied simultaneously to two individuals. A therapeutic relationship with one individual at a time would give them greater security. The essence of the neurotic disturbance in relationship, they argue, manifests itself after all, in the client's transference onto the analyst, and this can be observed more clearly with a direct approach. However, what often seems to receive insufficient attention is the way in which the client's disturbances in relationship first emerge during interaction with an actual partner and how they originate from the interdependence of two interacting personalities. These disturbances can be resolved through therapy only to the extent that it is possible within the structure as a whole of the relationship with the actual partner.

Whenever marital conflict is the subject of psychotherapy, attention must be given to the client's partner at least in order to distinguish their actual behavior from the client's description of it.

A further objection raised by analysts is that the therapist can hardly act as a savior of the marriage union or function as an ally if he concentrates on the client's neurotic choices. The individual who comes to us for help, they argue, expects to find guidance in our consulting room for his self-development. Clashes between his self-development and his marriage cannot be avoided and, from the client's point of view, priority must be given to the therapeutic process. This approach very clearly reflects the value judgment that (a) marriage is an entity and, (b) the marriage partner is secondary to the individual being treated. The individual is not expected to give precedence to the welfare of his marriage and of his partner. The underlying assumption, which emphasizes the individual's needs—and which dates back to the turn of this century—is by no means as widely accepted in other cultures. The individualistic approach needs to be re-evaluated, especially in relation to the interdependence of partners.

Given a certain degree of courage, the analyst will question whether he is not facing an emotional block in himself when he comes to terms with marriage therapy. For although he may not question its general purpose, he may feel somewhat apprehensive when embarking upon joint therapy ventures. Under these circumstances the territory is left open to parish clergy and marriage counselors; people whose fate it often is to be shunned as amateurs. The gap which has resulted from this psychotherapeutic aloofness has given rise to the growth of whole new areas of business. Therapeutic marital lore spreads itself thick and fast through the pages of women's magazines and best sellers, flooding the planet with often quite fantastic pair experiments and marital self-therapies. Occasionally a psychotherapist questions me in confidence: "How did you actually end up there, practicing marriage therapy?", suggesting with a knowing wink, "I bet you did it because you were in a fix in your own marriage, weren't you?" An analyst myself, I reply: "What on earth happened to you that you didn't go into marriage therapy yourself?" My firm impression is that there is many an analyst who has maintained a safe distance from couples therapy because of the need to cover up his own marital problems.

A successful analyst has a high degree of empathy and insight. He is able to hold his client's emotions and inner experiences in juxtaposition to his own affective reactions, his own counter-transference. He is capable of temporary affective identification with his client and subsequent detachment from him (*Kemper*, 1952). It is possible for him to evoke and re-evoke manifold feelings in himself as vehicle of the therapeutic process. This ability to empathize can also be observed in a sophisticated form in the narcissistic or schizoid personality (cf. *Kohut*). The therapeutic setting often serves the analyst as a vehicle for his own personal growth, for it is within the therapeutic framework that his personality structure does indeed find its richest social nourishment. And yet this very vehicle may fail to function in an extra-therapeutic relationship. In the context of a specific couple relationship, the analyst cannot be a mirror or a projection screen. In this situation, it is not enough to perceive the affections of one's partner in love and to try to understand them better and better. In his professional capacity the analyst is responsible for verbal interpretation rather than social 'acting out,' which is just the opposite of what should happen in a marital relationship. Here the analyst must be able to dispense with his analytical procedure and assume a role of his own. Here he has to 'perform' in the strict sense of the word, more than by merely interpreting his partner's behavior.

Indeed, because of their personalities, most analysts find it difficult to give up their introspective and interpretative approach in a close, non-therapeutic relationship. Their marriage partner may feel initial satisfaction at being offered a little psychological insight into themselves, but they will ultimately find the relationship one-sided and will be curious to know their analytical partner as a real person in flesh and blood. However, the more they urge the analyst to show his hand, the more carefully the latter will shield himself, in a very similar way to the case of narcissistic collusion described earlier. In choosing his profession, the analyst's motivation may have been to find a socially-acceptable defense system for his own problems of relationship, a system in which he could hopefully satisfy his clients as much as himself. But in the marital context, the non-analytical partner may at some stage feel humiliated by the analytically-developed partner. Consequently, he attempts to come to terms with the characteristic analytical approach and devotes himself to psychoanalysis. But then the teacher-pupil relationship makes itself felt even more strongly. The pupil probably feels that they are only entitled to pick up a few analytic crumbs from the master's table, an attitude which clearly undermines the principle of equal-worth between partners. Quite often the marriage partner becomes hostile towards further analyzing and crosses over to the opposite camp, that is direct social 'acting out' where action is a form of reaction to the system of concepts devalued by the analyst's interpretative approach. This is the form of behavior which makes many an analyst feel redundant. The analyst is likely to retreat if a client happens to scream at him, start an argument with him or make a fool of him in front of others. He consoles himself with the thought that 'acting out' is taken by many analysts as an indication of primitive reaction. Therefore, it is inappropriate to place himself on such a direct, uncontrolled level with his partner. The more the analyst relies on interpretation, the more strongly the partner tends to 'act out,' and the more the partner acts out, the more tenaciously the analyst clings to his interpretative routine. A relationship syndrome, which I have described as hysterical marriage, results. Confronted with the problem of partner choice, an analyst tends to play the role of savior and healer to an apparently weak and helpless woman. By helping her through her misfortunes, he satisfies his need for narcissistic self-esteem. Indeed, the oral and narcissistic character of such a relationship cannot be denied: on one side an idealized helper, a woman's protector giving himself to her with warmth and understanding; on the other, a delicate, fragile but grateful and precious female. In the opposite enactment of the same syndrome, the man takes no counter-action, despite the increasingly regressive and demanding behavior of his wife, and repentently retreats into a corner. Through this type of avoidance behavior he tries to provoke his wife to even more violent screaming. As an hysterophile, the analyst will experience this type of outburst as disagreeable but fascinating, since he discovers in it a substitute for his own lost spontaneity.

Many analysts see the failures of their own marriages as painful and unhealthy, which may explain why they feel unqualified for marriage therapy. It is because of their emotional ambivalence that they advise marriage therapy in those cases which they expect will lead to therapeutic failure.

The Effect of Individual Psychoanalysis on Partner Conflict

Counter-transference Onto the Untreated Partner

A serious objection which has been raised against couples therapy is that the free development of analytical transference is obstructed when dissonant partners are involved in the same analytical process for any length of time. Moreover, it has been suggested that any neurotic deviation in the client's marriage will enter his relationship with the therapist and will receive better treatment in the security of the therapist's couch than in any other setting. Conversely, the analyst has been accused of viewing the partner's presence as an agent limiting his therapeutic territory. To be sure, involvement in an intense and intimate relationship with the client, the unfolding of the client's idealized transference, the therapist's counter-transference reactions, his empathetic approach and partial identification with the client are all facets of the fascinating and deeply-rewarding side of the analytical process. In fact, from a more objective perspective, this may provide a motive for choosing psychoanalysis rather than anything else as one's profession. All these opportunities seem to be denied to the analyst when the client's partner also participates in therapy. They tend to accuse the analyst of being biased or insist on sharing in the process of identification and empathy. Psychoanalysis and the entire classical psychoanalytical line of thought thus finds it impossible to reconcile itself to couple treatment.

Indeed, as long as we remain within an analytical frame of reference, there is a complete range of arguments against couples therapy available to us and we are well-equipped to counter any temptation to drift into active marriage therapy. Only when we are willing to take a look over the analytical garden wall do we begin to have doubts about the individualistic approach. The basic question which preoccupies us then is: What effect does an analytical relationship have upon the non-analytical interaction of the partners? To answer this question, I shall investigate the therapist-client-partner triangle.

The fact that one of the marriage partners enters an exclusive relationship with the therapist places a heavy pressure upon the dyad. The
situation violates nearly every principle described earlier for maintaining
the marriage union. It implies a biased opening of dyadic boundaries
and the emergence of a two-against-one system in which the therapist
and the client, interacting with each other, are viewed by the other partner as united against him. The other partner inevitably feels doomed to
be excluded from affecting the outcome of the analysis, regardless of
whether or not this is to the advantage of anyone involved in the process. Moreover, it undermines the principle of equal-worth in that the
client attains personal growth through the therapist's support, a gain obviously inaccessible to the other partner.

Communications and systems theory have demonstrated that it is
not possible to change one component of a relationship set without causing changes in all its constituent parts. It follows therefore that any
deeper therapeutic treatment of a married client cannot take place without alienating their partner. In an unfavorable outcome, the partner will
reinforce his complementary behavior (i.e. his negative feedback) in
order to neutralize all his partner's efforts towards self-transformation.
If the outcome is successful, the partner will attain personal growth with
the client (i.e. positive feedback: see *Watzlawick, Beavin & Jackson*),
and the relationship as a whole thus undergoes transformation. However, if we abide by the principle of *primum nihil nocere*, the highest
tenet of therapeutic treatment, we should seriously consider the adverse
effects which individual therapy has upon the client's family, rather than
continue to shrug our shoulders whenever such evidence is presented to
us.

Let us try to place ourselves in the position of the partner who remains outside treatment. If he happens to have an oral fixation he will
be jealous of the client who appears to be receiving so much attention
from the therapist, or he may try to compete with the therapist for the
protective role. The anal character will be concerned that the therapist
might take the partner away from him, deprive him of his control over
the partner or form an alliance with the partner that excludes him. The
phallic character will fear having his position with the partner undermined by the therapist.

I would like to develop the discussion of the client-partner-therapist
set further by reference to a married couple with anxiety neurosis, a disturbance which often appears to me to be a negative side-effect of individual therapy. Perhaps the woman suffers from agoraphobia which
occurs in connection with her husband's infidelity. It is revealed during
individual therapy that the woman is disturbed by sexual desires and extramarital fantasies which she represses (as she fears divorce) and pro-

jects onto her husband. In this marriage the man behaves like a king and claims every freedom and form of autonomy for himself, against which his wife jealously protests. Individual therapy has had a beneficial effect on the woman as far as her agoraphobia is concerned. She has ceased nagging the man and gradually, if somewhat timidly, begun to admit her own sexual fantasies. However, the woman suddenly tells us that her husband has not only ended his affair but that he himself shows signs of jealousy, has become argumentative at home, behaves like an autocrat and crushes every independent initiative she takes. The wife, and unfortunately the therapist as well, feel a reluctant satisfaction, for it now seems obvious that this self-assured man was only able to keep the position of the stronger partner because his wife played the role of the jealous weakling.

The man is obviously apprehensive about the prospect of his wife's leaving him or becoming liberated. At this stage he seeks contact with the therapist, who, however, refuses to counsel him as he believes it might pose a threat to his therapeutic program. At best, he finds the time for one interview with the man. The way the husband approaches the therapist is very different from the way in which patients usually ask for assistance. At the interview he appears arrogant, demanding and confident, and not at all a pitiful, sympathy-seeking and miserable fellow. Alternatively, he may try to present himself as a co-therapist ready to investigate with the therapist his wife's weird behavior. Either directly or indirectly, he will make it clear that he has been annoyed at the course which the therapy has taken and now has no choice but to intervene. His attitude towards the therapist is ambivalent. On the one hand, he feels a need to put himself under the wing of a confidant whom he can trust and on whom he can totally rely. On the other hand, he rejects the role of patient and feels responsible for the functioning of the dyad, as someone who is still able to play his social roles under very difficult circumstances. He seeks reassurance that his behavior is absolutely correct from a therapeutic point of view. There is little doubt that unless we want to create an overcompensating weakling, as therapists we ought to aid this narcissistically-insecure man. In fact, there is a danger that he will become ill and perhaps even more ill than his wife. It is in this situation that the concept of collusion may prove most valuable in that it helps both partners to see the interdependence of their behavior.

In reference to the client's husband, or addressing him directly, the therapist might say:

It is easy to imagine what a heavy load my client places on her husband because of her problem; nevertheless the fact remains that he rather than she should be held solely responsible for the social functioning of their marriage and family for some time. In this particular case, the greatest danger is that my client's husband might be reluctant to recognize his own fears and weaknesses. My experience suggests that refusal to recognize these states for a longer period is unnatural for anybody: even the strongest of men occasionally need help and guidance. The goal of my therapy would therefore be that both he and his wife abandon their extreme roles. The wife should learn to assume independent responsibility for herself despite her fears and sense of weakness, and the husband, in order to best serve the purpose of therapy, should help her achieve emancipation. This may not be easy for him to do because his wife may have to go through a stage of emphasizing her independence somewhat provocatively. However, this is a transition stage and one that commonly occurs. Nevertheless, it is not unusual for him to find it difficult to overcome his own anxiety and weaknesses, especially when his partner is provoking him. It may also seem that the therapist is inciting and agitating his client in order to estrange him from his partner. This is not the goal of my treatment, however. My goal is rather that both partners evolve within their relationship so that each has the same amount of freedom and loyalty, and each is equally responsible for the marriage and the family.

The therapist frequently finds that his work is jeopardized by the intervention of the client's partner. He suspects that the visitor arrives only to claim his rights of ownership and to draw the woman back into his sphere of influence. The therapist fears that the man will destroy his client's budding efforts to gain autonomy. Therefore, in order to protect his client, he exacts a certain amount of self-sacrifice from the partner. Should the partner be unwilling to compromise, the therapist will feel justified in excluding him from any involvement in the process. He may flatly reject him or just deter him by saying that he, too, qualifies for therapeutic treatment. At this stage, a power struggle between the therapist and the marriage partner for the possession of the client is likely to occur. Each suspects the other of trying to gain favor with the client and tries therefore to keep the client within his own sphere of influence. The therapist encourages his client to be autonomous and thus becomes involved in a three-way collusion around the theme 'fear of divorce *versus* desire for independence.'

1. Through her close relationship with the therapist, the client overcomes her anxiety about separation. Treatment, together with the positive expectations of the therapist, have provided her with an incentive for emancipation. She seeks the therapist's approval by stressing her detachment and independence from her husband. Through her provocations she incites her husband to oppose the therapist and thus attempts to vicariously experience her own resistance to therapy through this channel.

2. The husband begins increasingly to fear divorce and no longer

emphasizes his own demands for independence. Now that his wife is increasing her distance from him, he tries to undermine her therapy and thus subjugate her once again.

3. The therapist is undecided as to whether or not he should help his client gain her independence regardless of all the possible negative reactions of her husband. However, he does support the client's efforts to achieve independence.

For the majority of therapists, the outcome of treatment conducted in this way might read as follows: "With an initially dependent, anxious and noticeably neurotic patient, highly-promising progress has been evidenced during therapy. She has become essentially independent and mature. This is shown particularly by the fact that she managed to shake off her deviant relationship with her seriously-disturbed husband and endure, without a single relapse, the ensuing divorce suit. Her husband, an abnormally-jealous man, tried to cut short her therapy, using various tactics to obstruct her autonomous development. Several attempts were made to confront the man with his exaggerated weaknesses and fears. Unfortunately he was persistent in refusing any aid, as a result of which divorce was the only choice open to the client."

What has really happened? Perhaps nothing in a therapeutic sense, or perhaps the system has been rearranged so that instead of being dependent on her husband, the woman has now become dependent on her therapist. She may now try to avoid separation from the therapist by devoting herself to a therapeutic profession to become a faithful follower of her new master! By using the collusion model, the therapist might have become aware of the mutual problems that the partners shared, although it may prove difficult at times to see that they do share problems at all. However, when the therapist concentrates on counter-transference onto his client and, instead of controlling his aggressive and negative feelings, projects them onto the client's family and relatives, a major therapeutic opportunity is wasted. The therapist's control over his counter-transference onto the relatives should be recognized as more important, even though more difficult, than his counter-transference onto the patient. It is all too easy to turn relatives into scapegoats for the failure of treatment and brand them as psychopaths or paranoids. By attempting to avoid having anything to do with them, one frustrates and provokes them from the outset, and it is not then surprising that they reject therapy and refuse to accept observations about their marriage. Indeed, family members are treated as counter-transference outlaws: the best thing to do would be to shoot them. For the therapist, it is gratifying to feel superior, courageous, strong and successful, even if it means that in this triangular relationship he is seeking revenge for his own oedipal wound.

The Therapist in Collusion With His Client—
As Analogy to the Client's Marriage

As with any dyadic relationship, a long-term therapeutic process may become collusive; it is a specific collusion entangling the therapist and his client. Therapist and client threaten to fall into a certain pattern of interaction, which is characterized by common blind spots. Over a period of time, the client learns how to draw the therapist's interest and can usually predict how and when he will intervene. The longer therapy lasts, the more they will iron out the differences between them and the greater will be the danger of the therapy degenerating into a specific *modus vivendi*.

From its beginnings, psychoanalysis was aware of this danger. By completing training analysis and allowing control analysts to participate in the therapeutic process, it should be possible for the therapist to avoid an unconscious personal bias. The fact that collusion occurs in spite of all these measures suggests how difficult it is not to stray onto the collusive path.

An example of narcissistic therapist-client collusion is given by directors of therapeutic institutions who offer themselves as identification figures to their trainees, often former patients. These trainees borrow from their 'godfathers' certain ideals of personal growth through which they try to elevate their own self-image, thus establishing a narcissistic collusion. It may also be an oral collusion, as when the therapist offers himself as a bountiful mother, taking the client under his wings as a child substitute, or offers himself as a vehicle to carry the client through to 'the other side' in anticipation of receiving their gratitude and recognition. If it is a case of anal collusion, the therapist will enjoy the power and control he has over his totally dependent patients. Finally, in phallic collusion he builds his masculine self-esteem when he can make all his female clients fall in love with him. It is to the advantage of the therapist's art if he is able to recognize any of these collusive urges in himself. Unfortunately, training and control analysts are frequently not sufficiently aware of these tendencies. As *D. Beckman* (1974) writes, the psychoanalyst may display uncontrolled affective traits which are due to a neurotic transference, the so-called residual neurosis. Apart from the counter-transference within his conscious grasp, the psychoanalyst may reveal another counter-transference of which he is unaware, causing resistance in himself. On the other hand, the client, apart from his transference onto the analyst, can maintain a counter-transference onto him as well in that he may register in himself emotional responses to the analyst's persistent neurotic fears and impulses. For example, Beckman has pointed out that the stronger the phallic and genital components the diagnostician determines in the fluid test (*Giessen Test*), the less likely he himself is to be assigned the same components by anyone else; and the more clients he diagnoses as depressive, the more often he is declared by others to be subject to phallic and genital urges. One analyst's interpretation may describe a client as showing prevailing oral fears and desires while another's assessment may reveal phallic and genital impulses. Complete openness of the analyst towards his patient is a valid yet utopian ideal. In selecting his patients, the analyst, according to *Beckman*, follows rules very similar to those determining marital partner selection.

The nature of the collusion between the therapist and his client seems therefore to be similar to that of the collusion between the client and his marriage partner. The partner and the therapist have complementary positions in relation to the client. Like the poles of a magnet, they are attracted to the client, but like true magnetic poles they repel each other. The analyst and the partner, if he is in a progressive position, both feel stronger and healthier when they relate to the client than when they do not relate to them. The analyst and the partner enter into a symmetrical relationship which contains a seed of escalation and rivalry. One of the reasons why the relationship of the therapist to the client's relatives appears to be so difficult is that the therapist recognizes in them all that he so carefully rejects in himself; in particular, he suspects them of struggling to become stable and strong at the expense of the helpless client. The client's relatives function as a projection or substitute for the therapist's negative identity. The therapist feels that the client's relatives try to establish themselves as helpers, leaders and mothers by making the patient weak, dependent and ill. We therapists do not do this but, deep down, wouldn't we really like to?

I believe that the concept of collusion can be highly productive for therapists in enabling them to achieve an adequate overview of the individual disclosures of patients. With couple dynamics in mind, it is easier for them to approach the pair as a unit without the danger of identifying with the more agreeable partner and also without the phobic counterreaction of having to devote special attention to the one who is not as charming and friendly. During joint therapy, the therapist would feel freer to pay special attention to one partner for a time if he knew that he could approach the other when necessary and thus restore equilibrium. More importantly, he might be able to reach a better understanding of the problem of his counter-transference upon the client's relatives.

Goals of Joint Therapy

In agreement with the majority of therapists, I do not see that the aim of joint therapy is to save the marriage at all costs. I see it rather as helping a couple out of the stagnation of their collusion so that they can again be capable of free interaction, and of making independent decisions and therefore, of also initiating divorce. Marriage therapy ought to lead to a clarification of the relationship. Divorce may therefore be the successful outcome of marriage therapy. Short-term joint treatment can break through marital stalemate, and much more quickly than psychoanalysis which may drag on for years. The following letter from a woman was written to me a year after a four-week intensive course in joint marriage therapy. Both she and her husband had a history of several years of individual psychoanalysis.

> Dear Mr. Willi,
>
> You told us last year that you would like to be kept informed about our lives. Six months ago I separated from Freddy and moved with the children to a four-room apartment in a new housing development. The separation was peaceful and our last Christmas together was pleasant and friendly. For both of us separation seemed to be the best and only honest way out. The children, whom we had told about our problem, also found separation to be the best solution. Freddy lives alone in the house and our daily help, whom we share, looks after him.
>
> Meanwhile, I have settled down quite well. The children go to school nearby. They have kept the same friends they had before, seem happy and accept the step we've taken. They often go and have dinner with Freddy and they stayed with him when I went on a holiday. Freddy puts a lot of heart into looking after the children and they are full of admiration for their father, who is changing so much. We both meet together in a restaurant from time to time or Freddy comes to see me at home to discuss any problems which may have come up.
>
> The divorce proceedings are being handled with great understanding and fairness . . . now it is left to the lawyers to divorce us, most probably towards the end of June. Freddy and I will do everything to remain good friends, despite the distance between us. I would like to add that I have no plans of remarriage in the near future.
>
> To be sure, our separation does pose some problems,

but Freddy and I both believe that we have done the necessary and right thing. I would like to thank you for all you
have done for us. Although it wasn't possible for us to go on
living together, we can nevertheless speak to each other and
solve our problems honestly and with understanding.

With best regards,
Yours,
A.B.

In my opinion, the purpose of treating marital collusion lies in
attaining three goals:

—*the first is that the client gains self-knowledge.* At the termination
of therapy, each partner should have gained some insight into his deep
personal motives for clinging tenaciously to one specific external mode
of behavior. He should be able to say which ideals have prompted him
to graft this deviant behavior onto himself and which fears, guilt feelings
and weaknesses he has tried to conceal in doing so. He should become
intimate with those elements of his personality which he tried to project
onto his partner and integrate them within himself. To be able to do
this, he should achieve greater flexibility in relation to both his progressive and regressive roles.

—*the second is that the client gains a greater understanding of his*
partner; that he has an insight into those deeper personal problems that
prevent his partner from breaking free of their deviant behavior.
Through a better understanding of his partner, he should be able to accept them as they are, and not as he, the client, would like them to be.

—*the third is the client's cognition of dyadic dynamics*; as it emerges
out of their commonly-shared activities, particularly in terms of the hin-
drance to their relationship by the escalation of provocation on both
sides.

Defining the common basic themes existing in the dynamics of the
couple is, I believe, the most crucial and usually for the partners the least
expected experience during therapy. Having pictured themselves in their
polarized roles as having nothing to do with each other any longer, they
are suddenly amazed to realize that they are sitting in the same boat.
What they formerly experienced as a barrier now appears to be a force
for unification.

The objective of marriage therapy is not so much to reverse collusive
themes as to generate a state of free and flexible equilibrium. The dy-
namics of the dyad can only develop when partners maintain a balanced
relationship over a longer period of time. However, this state of balance
can deviate from a free-flowing, steady interaction into a state of hostili-

ty in which both partners adopt rigid extreme roles. To recapture the healthy balanced state, basic collusion themes can be used as vehicles of mutual and individual growth. This would imply:
> *narcissistic theme—recognition of the partner's ego-boundaries;*
> *oral theme—free interchange of give and take;*
> *anal and sadistic theme—unity without repression;*
> *phallic theme—complementarity while preserving sexual identity.*

Before proceeding further, I would like to consider the *problem of insight*. Communications and behavioral therapists occasionally pass scornful remarks about analytical introspective counseling, which they say may produce a stimulating experience but has no real effect upon behavior. I cannot share this point of view. Admittedly the partner's behavior can be modified to only a limited degree in marriage therapy. However, most partners can reach increased mutual tolerance fairly easily through a better understanding of themselves, of each other and their relationship. An understanding of each other may fail to be reached through direct exercises in openness or clarity of communication because both partners are insufficiently aware of all the contradictory and ambivalent forms which their needs and behavioral patterns may take. To gain an understanding of each other and to treat each other as true partners, accepting the partner in all his weaknesses and limited possibilities of relating, appears to be the most important aim not only of marriage therapy but also of marriage as a whole.

Applying the Concept of Collusion to Marriage Therapy

It may be disappointing to some readers that so little has been said in this book about the therapeutic techniques that the concept of collusion can provide. I have devoted a separate study to the subject of marriage therapy as collusion therapy (*Willi*, 1978). In this book, I am concerned with collusion in terms of dyadic dynamics, a subject going beyond the scope of a strictly therapeutic perspective. The concept of collusion is a means to an overview of conflicts in the life of the couple rather than a therapeutic technique in its own right. It can be a useful tool in every form of marriage counseling, be it classical psychoanalysis; analytical joint therapy; role-playing; behavioral, communications or systems therapy.

Marriage therapists find it difficult to focus on both partners at the same time while searching for the causes and background to their marital conflict. They must treat each of them with equal dedication and identify with the welfare of the pair rather than with only one of the partners. There is a modern trend to talk about couple and marital conflicts as communication problems. Practically speaking, there are unfortunately few therapists who are able to see a marital conflict as a two-way conflict rather than as a failure of one of the partners alone. Of course, using the concept of collusion will not mean that the therapist must rigidly confine himself to the cognition of the common unconscious of the couple. He should rather attempt to see one partner in the context of the perceptions, feelings, fears and needs of the other and thus restore a balance to his approach, as well as to his perceptions, interpretations and impulses to identify. Thus, during joint therapy, he will not allow himself to see one partner as ill, weak or guilty and allow the other to relate to him as a co-therapist. Should this be difficult, he might repeatedly question why this partner, now functioning as co-therapist, selected this 'ill' person as his mate and allowed them to develop a specific form of deviant behavior. On the other hand, it is necessary that he control his counter-transference and question why he perceives only failure in one partner and only positiveness in the other. I believe that the concept of collusion could be of particular use to psychoanalysts in helping them overcome their aversion to joint marriage therapy.

The concept of collusion can also be of fundamental importance to every couple seeking treatment, or at least encourage them in it. Usually, only one partner takes the initiative in marriage therapy. He may then either introduce himself as a sufferer of symptoms which occur during marital stress or come directly to the therapist complaining, usually because his partner is breaking up their marriage. His partner will be reluctant to submit to treatment for fear of being cornered by the therapist as a scapegoat, which is unfortunately validated by all those therapists who give preference to one partner. However, the couple's fear of bias will be eliminated if the therapist makes it absolutely clear during the first interview that he starts from the working hypothesis that both parties are 50% responsible for any marital conflict and that, on purely theoretical grounds, it is unlikely that more blame can be laid on one partner than on the other. An even more important step would be to then point out to the couple that although they appear to be polar opposites, they are in reality deeply connected, indeed bound to each other through their common unconscious. That this unconscious link exists can be demonstrated to the couple even during the first therapeutic session.

An important question to resolve is whether a given marital conflict is best suited to joint therapy or whether it can also be treated through individual therapy. Certainly one component of the marriage unit cannot be modified without influencing the marriage as a whole. However, it does not follow that individual therapy to treat a client with a marital disturbance is doomed to failure. Admittedly, in order to achieve restoration of their self-esteem and a gradual strengthening of their self-confidence, most clients do need the shield of individual therapy. The actual presence of their partner may be felt as a handicap. In presenting my view of psychoanalysis and individual therapy, I do not wish to imply that I am against these methods *per se*, but I am against the way in which therapists apply individual therapy. Of greater importance than the question of technique, in both joint and individual therapy, is the attitude and motivation of the therapist himself. Therefore I believe that often marriage therapy can only be conducted as individual therapy if the therapist never loses sight of a collusion specific to a given marriage. He will then be able to recognize statements the client makes about his partner, and to allow for the partner's complementary behavior. More importantly, he will control his counter-transference onto the marriage partner at least to the same extent as onto the client. He will be constantly aware that the partner who remains outside treatment is handicapped by the other's therapy, and will strive to make his client understand his partner's reactions rather than allow himself to be provoked into uniting with the client against the partner. When the partner approaches him, the therapist will offer him sympathetic understanding rather than use him as a narcissistic prop by turning him into a client and putting him on the couch. On the contrary, he will attempt to explain to the partner the nature of the impact of individual therapy upon the marriage, allowing of course for the partner's reactions. He may also wish to speak with the partner about the possibility of conducting parallel individual therapy for him or about the merits and disadvantages of joint therapy. When these conditions exist, the marriage as a unit may also be ready for psychoanalytical treatment.

Classical psychoanalysis, in its basic formulation, does not allow for joint therapy being conducted by one and the same therapist. On the other hand, joint therapy conducted with another therapist is, in my experience, not only permissible but also offers a unique therapeutic opportunity. Still, the method generally used is analytically-oriented psychotherapy or analytical focal therapy, both of which provide the therapist with a wider sphere of control. All the possible variations of individual and joint treatment are available—by one or two different therapists at the same time. Joint treatment contains within it a number of therapeutic possibilities which are not accessible to the individual therapist, however, and these should be a part of the repertoire of every advanced psychotherapist.

Although I have expressed criticism of psychoanalytical method on several occasions, the analytical method comes closest to my ideas in its aim, its concept of man and therapeutic procedure. However, in the field of marriage and family therapies, various communication and systems techniques appear to be gaining prominence over analytical thought and method. To me the debate between systems and communication therapies on the one side and psychoanalysis on the other is of little importance, as I think that both concepts complement rather than exclude each other! This is not the place to dwell on the details of the differences between these approaches. It seems to me that most couple conflicts reach a state of crisis because they are not capable of taking a more objective view of their problem, which is a necessary requirement for analytical therapy. I can imagine that communication and interaction programs, if systematically applied, can bring about therapeutic change more easily than an unstructured analytical interview. When such exercises create real experiences, they may pave the way for restoring mutual confidence and a deeper therapeutic exchange.

The same is true of specific sexual disturbances which are so inaccessible to conscious reflection that virtually no real change can be achieved merely by using introspection. Practical training programs, such as those developed by *Masters* and *Johnson*, can prove effective shortcuts. The shortcomings of the analytical method can be seen in excessive concentration on the origins and motivations of deviant behavior at the expense of direct involvement in the here and now.

The analytic method may also rely too heavily on the client's capacity to change his behavior as a result of induced introspection. The shortcomings of systems and communication therapies may be that they make almost no allowance for unconscious dyadic dynamics or transference and counter-transference processes. While psychoanalysts can be criticized for being conservative, some communication therapists appear to me to be aggressive and manipulative. They also place too much emphasis on restructuring two-person systems, at any cost and without questioning in greater depth how far their own compulsive need to modify behavior is related to personal tensions springing from their unconscious. Psychoanalysis has shown that one form of defense consists in the client's defenseless adaptation to the expectations of the therapist.

In joint therapy, the danger of adaptation to the therapist's expectations is considerable because the partners compete with each other to earn the therapist's approval and try to separate themselves by being amenable. The couples most difficult to treat are those who have acquired a certain style of communication from previous partnership trainings, which they have perfected only to avoid any real confrontation between each other. Ultimately, their behavior proves ill-adapted to the values and purpose of communication therapies and to the dynamics of group sub-cultures. For any deeper understanding of the marriage rela-

ABILITY TO TRUE PERSPECTIVE OF THE OTHER — RECOGNIZE SEPARATION

✳

tionship, the ability to understand and differentiate between the partner's personality and one's own personality is of essential importance. I see the therapist's purpose not so much in precipitating the highest degree of openness, freedom, intimacy or mutual positive reinforcement as in promoting a form of relationship which satisfies the inclinations and impulses of the partners to a realistic degree; a form of relationship in which the partners can accept themselves in spite of all their limited behavioral alternatives not only in order to gain real freedom but also a sense of responsibility to, and solidarity with, their partner, family and social milieu.

APPENDIX

A CASE MODEL:
Ingmar Bergman's *Scenes from a Marriage*

In the case histories presented earlier, those aspects which were not directly related to the specific points under discussion were omitted for the sake of brevity. Some readers may therefore find it difficult, on reaching the end of this book, to clearly see how collusion works in a concrete situation. To these readers, I would recommend Ingmar Bergman's *Scenes from a Marriage*, a film in which marital crisis is depicted with unparalleled veracity and honesty, enabling the reader to partake emotionally at a most intimate level. Those who missed the film can read the English translation of Bergman's scenario by Alan Blair, published by Calder & Boyars Ltd.

Let us imagine that the characters, Johan and Marianne, come to me for marriage therapy. By approaching me, they would immediately place our relationship on a specific level, as it would be a typical liaison encountered in professional life. To undertake this particular case, I would have to determine the conditions and aims of treatment and, according to my experience, assess costs and benefits acceptable both to clients and myself. As to the theoretical ideas presented in this book, I would certainly seek to put them into practice when treating the couple. But I would at the same time remind myself that theories assign a certain level of abstraction to this marital conflict and in the process of reducing issues to their smallest denominator there is a risk of losing sight of the very essence at hand. Indeed, I must be alert and not recoil in the face of fresh and puzzling or obscure details of this specific case and never identify with any concept so much that I adjust reality to my preconceptions, however dear to me they may be. More importantly, because I would encounter these people in the context of my work, my attitude to their marital problem would be fundamentally different from that which I might adopt towards a couple of friends, or towards my own marriage partner. By adhering to a specific theoretical concept, the psychotherapist always runs the risk of losing sight of the complexity of the human dilemma confronting him. Yet his preconception is an important tool in his work since it enables him to isolate relevant aspects in a therapeutic situation, and to determine their interrelation. Which aspects are relevant will be dependent upon the therapist's point of view, his understanding of marriage and his personality (cf. Chapter 4). A marital problem can be psychologically interpreted in numerous ways and thus while any interpretation may contain valid insights, it cannot claim to be all-embracing.

Turning to the therapeutic interpretation of *Scenes from a Marriage*, three aspects appear to be relevant:

1 the crisis in marriage as a social and cultural institution;
2 mid-life crisis;
3 the collusion.

1   Crisis in Marriage as a Social Institution

Bergman's work took many couples by storm, making them aware of crises in their own relationships which they had either avoided seeing or been unable to see. Marianne and Johan married around 1962 when there was little questioning of the institution of marriage. Since then, the social attitude to marriage has drastically changed. This profound social transformation bred anxiety and defensiveness. People who had repressed their doubts about marriage now became aware of their true feelings and marital break-down seemed inevitable.

Bergman writes of his film:

> *Sixth scene*: My idea now is that two new people begin to emerge from all this devastation. Maybe that is a little too optimistic but I can't help it, that's how it turned out. Both Johan and Marianne have walked through the vale of tears and made it rich in springs. They are beginning to acquire a new knowledge of themselves, in a manner of speaking. This is not just a matter of resignation, but concerns love too. For the first time, Marianne sits down and listens to her troublesome mother. Johan looks at his own situation with forgiveness and is good to Marianne in a new and adult way. Everything is still in confusion and nothing is any better. All relations are muddled and their lives are incontestably based on a heap of wretched compromises. But somehow they are

now citizens of the world of reality in quite a different way from before. At least I think so. There's no solution at hand, anyway, so there's no happy ending.

Most critics have perceived the following scene as a criticism of middle-class marriage, and this may in fact have been *Bergman*'s intention. Marianne says to Johan in the divorce scene:

"To say something reasonable, you should be glad I've made myself free and that I want to live my own life. I think you should do exactly the same. You should free yourself from the past, every bit of it. And start afresh under completely different conditions. At this very moment you have a marvelous chance."

Their marriage crisis is therefore an expression of a reappraisal of marriage as a social institution, an aspect I could not deal with in detail as it fell beyond my thematic framework. However, in therapy I would pay considerable attention to both the social and cultural aspects.

2   Mid-Life Crisis

At the onset of their crisis, Johan is 43 and Marianne, 35. They have been married for 10 years and have become fully established. Johan is an Associate Professor at the Psychotechnical Institute and Marianne is a divorce lawyer. They have two children, live in a beautiful family house and own a weekend cottage. In every respect they appear to have completed the foundation and creativity period of their marriage. The mid-life crisis seems to hold sway over them. Johan says during the divorce scene:

"I'll be forty-five this summer. I can reasonably expect to live for another thirty years. But viewed objectively I'm already a corpse. For the next twenty years I'll go around embittering my own life and other people's merely by existing. I am regarded as an expensive, unproductive unit which by rights should be got rid of by rationalization. And this is supposed to be the prime of life, when you really make yourself useful, when you've gained a little experience. Shit, no. Throw the bugger out. Or let him creep around until he rots. I'm so goddamn tired, Marianne. If I had the guts I'd make a clean break and move to the country or ask for a job as

teacher in a small town. Sometimes I wish I could
. . . .(*Drinks*) Well, that's my sad story.''

Johan is appalled by the utter emptiness of their routine life. He is
fed up with conventions and social pressures; he would like to leave
everything behind and be free.

> "All this fucking harping on what we're supposed to do,
> what we must do, what we must take into consideration.
> What your mother will think. What the children will say.
> How we had best arrange that dinner party and shouldn't we
> invite my father after all. We must go to the west coast. We
> must go to the mountains. We must go to St. Moritz. We
> must celebrate Christmas, Easter, Whitsun, birthdays, name-
> days, the whole fucking lot. I know I'm being unfair. I know
> what I'm saying now is all goddamn nonsense. I know that
> we've had a good life. And actually I think I still love you. In
> fact, in one way I love you *more* now since I met Paula. But
> can you understand this bitterness?

And later, in the same conversation he says:

> "Both you and I have escaped into a state of existence
> that has been hermetically sealed. Everything has been neatly
> arranged, all cracks have been stopped up, it has all gone like
> clockwork. We have died from lack of oxygen.
> . . . I don't have much self-knowledge and I understand
> very little of reality in spite of having read a lot of books. But
> something tells me that this catastrophe is a chance in a
> million for both you and me."

Johan hopes to start a new life with his mistress. He briefs Marianne on
his relationship with Paula:

> "We lived it up in the evenings and behaved like pigs.
> We got mixed up in drunken brawls and were kicked out of
> the hotel. You remember I told you I had changed my hotel
> because the traffic was so noisy. We ended up in a squalid lit-
> tle place on a back street, and suddenly we clicked and made
> love day and night. She said that it had never been so good
> for her before. I felt terrifically high, of course."

In a later scene, after his break-up with Paula, he says to Marianne:

"To be quite frank, I'm pretty tired of her. I suppose you think it's disloyal of me to sit here running Paula down. But she forfeited my loyalty long ago. I'm fed up with her. With her emotional storms and scenes and tears and hysterics, then making it all up and saying how much she loves me. (*Checking himself*) I'll tell you this, Marianne. The best thing about Paula was that she taught me to shout and brawl. It was even permissible to strike her. I wasn't aware that I had any feelings at all. If I were to tell you . . . you'd think I was lying. Sometimes I thought I was mixed up in a grotesque play, in which I was both actor and audience. Our fights used to go on for days and nights on end, until we collapsed from sheer exhaustion."

Thus first Johan, and then Marianne, undergo the identity crisis of middle-age and try to break out of life's deadening routine. Rather than turn into statues, they would prefer to step down from their pedestals and experience change and movement. Breaking away is not so easy. Johann actually fails to give up his past and begin everything anew. He carries his past with him, although he strives to destroy it, and so finds himself drifting back to Marianne over and over again. For it is Marianne who knows his scar; she knows that in opening herself to him she would only force him to explode even further, hurting himself in a way she could not bear. Thus, though separated and divorced, they remain connected to each other, and very closely. There is a warm chagrin, quiet resignation and self-pity about their relationship which is so common for the middle-aged. Johan and Marianne personify the complexities experienced at this time of life. In a very real sense, they have ruined their lives. This is particularly true of Johan. He has failed professionally, his grandiose ambitions failed to materialize, he drives a worn-out, second-hand car and yet his life is richer and more genuine because of his crisis.

In the final scene, five years after their divorce and twenty years after their wedding when he is 53 and she 45, they tell each other:

Marianne: You're much more handsome than before. And you look so gentle and kind. You always had such a tense look before, sort of anxious and on your guard.
Johan: Oh, really?
Marianne: Are people beastly to you?
Johan: (*Smiling*) I don't really know. I think perhaps I've stopped defending myself. Someone said

I'd grown slack and gave in too easily. That I diminished myself. It's not true. If anything, I think I've found my right proportions. And that I've accepted my limitations with a certain humility. That makes me kind and a bit mournful.

Marianne: (*Tenderly*) And you with your great expectations.

Johan: . . .It was my father who had the great expectations, not I. But I wanted desperately to please Daddy, so I tried all the time to live up to *his* expectations. Not mine. When I was little I had very modest and pleasant ideas as to what I would do when I grew up.

Marianne: (*Smiling*) What were they?

Johan: Have I never told you?

Marianne: If so I've forgotten.

Johan: Yes, of course. (*Pause*) Well, you see, I had an old uncle. He had a little store at Sigtuna that sold books and toys and stationery. I was often allowed to go and see him, as I was a sickly child and in need of quiet and fresh air. Sometimes he and Aunt Emma let me help them in the store. I liked that more than anything. My dream was to own a store like that. There you have my ambitions.

Marianne: Yes, we should have had a little store. (*Smiles*) How content we'd have been. We'd have grown fat and comfortable and had a lot of children, and slept well and been respected and have joined some local society and never quarreled.

Johan: How strange, talking about all that never was. Anyway, you'd never have settled down in some sleepy little place in the country.

Marianne: No, that's true. (*Serious*) I used to dream of pleading the cause of the oppressed. There were no limits to my ambitions. And then I became a divorce lawyer.

Johan has matured. His emancipation is now more than a mere attempt to rid himself of the naïve identities of adolescence and follow a path opposite to the one he trod before. He has discovered his real self, is faithful to his discovery and regards himself as a survivor. He sees his former existence as being the necessary preparation for a more fully-integrated life ascended to through crisis. In a similar sense, Marianne also achieves deep reconciliation in that she feels they are closer to each other, despite external separation.

3   The Collusion

In what way do this couple manifest their collusion, the term we have used to describe the unconscious interplay of partners resulting from a similar type of fixation upon traumatic childhood experiences? Neither Marianne nor Johan appears to suffer, in a more specific sense, from any neurotic interpersonal disturbance. However, both seem to have been strongly affected by their respective inadequate up-bringings, and each suffers quite severely from irrational ontological fears and guilt. These are all conditions conducive to the emergence of collusion, as described earlier in this book.

Their conflict can then quite clearly be shown to be an anal-sadistic collusion with a prevailing jealousy-infidelity syndrome. Initially, the partners inhabit a suffocating world of security, order and self-restraint, held together by artificial and self-imposed duties, a world in which anything that threatens their interdependence is immediately suppressed. Their crisis is triggered off by the sado-masochistic power struggle between Katarina and Peter. For Johan and Marianne it is terrifying to see this struggle and yet the sight of the love-hate ambivalence in all its violence comes as a lasting shock, making them recognize their own aggressive and libidinal drives. The anal-sadistic collusion between Katarina and Peter arouses the anal-sadistic collusion between Marianne and Johan, and their jealousy-infidelity syndrome about separation. Despite. their formal separation, they stay together for hours on end, and later, although living in other relationships, they still maintain the bond between them. When they meet again after Johan's trip with Paula, Johan is already becoming jealous of Marianne's lover. The jealousy-infidelity collusion is revealed in the divorce scene, where it is Marianne who wants freedom while Johan now experiences anxiety about separation.

Marianne:	I'm not responsible for you. I live my own life and I'm capable of looking after myself and the children. Do you suppose I don't grasp what you've been sitting here saying all evening. *You don't want a divorce!*
Johan:	(*Caught*) I never heard anything so absurd!
Marianne:	If it's so absurd then you can prove the opposite by signing the papers here and now.

Johan:	All right.
Marianne:	Johan! Be honest now! Look at me! Look at me, Johan. You've changed your mind? You don't want us to divorce, do you? You thought we might pick up our marriage again. You were going to suggest something of the kind this evening. Go on, admit it.
Johan:	Well, suppose I did have thoughts in that direction. Is it a crime? I confess I'm beaten. Is *that* what you want to hear? I'm tired of Paula. I'm homesick. Oh, I know, Marianne. You needn't put on that smile. I'm a failure and I'm going downhill and I'm tired and homeless. This isn't the right moment to ask you to go on with the marriage. I know what you're going to say. But you asked me. And I'm giving you a straight answer. I was bound to you in a different and deeper way than I realized. I was dependent on all those things that are called home and family and regular life and quiet everyday routine. I'm tired of living alone.

As soon as Marianne takes the emancipated role, Johan is forced into a dependent position. Yet their love-hate relationship holds them close together, each striving to overcome the other and destroy their relationship in order to protect him or herself from further frustration. It is a case of unintentional divorce, an outcome which neither one intended but which nevertheless occurs as a result of compulsive escalation.

The battle between Marianne and Johan never culminates in a full-scale outburst of sado-masochistic collusion as shown in its classical form by Katarina and Peter; rather it has within it a deeper existential dimension of narcissistic collusion with the conflict syndrome of love as ego-confirmation. The opening scene shows this theme clearly:

"How would you describe yourself in a few words?" asks the interviewer, Mrs. Palm.

Johan:	That's not an easy one.
Mrs. Palm:	Not so difficult either, surely?
Johan:	I mean, there's a risk of misunderstanding.
Mrs. Palm:	Do you think so?
Johan:	Yes. It might sound conceited if I described myself as extremely intelligent, successful, youthful, well-balanced, and sexy. A man

with a world conscience, cultivated, well-read, popular, and a good mixer. Let me see, what else can I think of . . . friendly. Friendly in a nice way even to people who are worse off. I like sports. I'm a good family man. A good son. I have no debts and I pay my taxes. I respect our government whatever it does, and I love our royal family. I've left the state church. Is this enough or do you want more details? I'm a splendid lover. Aren't I, Marianne?

Mrs. Palm: (*With a smile*) Perhaps we can return to the question. How about you, Marianne? What do you have to say?

Marianne: Hmm, what can I say. . . . I'm married to Johan and have two daughters.

Mrs. Palm: Yes. . . .

Marianne: That's all I can think of for the moment.

Mrs. Palm: There must be something. . . .

Marianne: I think Johan is rather nice.

Johan: Kind of you, I'm sure.

Marianne: We've been married for ten years.

Johan: I just renewed the contract.

Marianne: I doubt if I have the same natural appreciation of my own excellence as Johan. But to tell the truth, I'm glad I can live the life I do. It's a good life, if you know what I mean. Well, what else can I say. . . .Oh dear, this is difficult!

Obviously Marianne cannot answer the question alone and uses Johan as a substitute for herself. I do not exist, she seems to suggest; I exist only in relation to Johan. Her complementary altruistic narcissism is clearly demonstrated later during a psychotherapy session when she can observe herself more clearly. She reads to Johan from her diary:

"Suddenly I turned around and looked at the old picture of my school class when I was ten. I seemed to be aware of something that had been lying in readiness for a long time but beyond my grasp. To my surpise I have to admit that *I don't know who I am*. I haven't the vaguest idea. I have always done what people told me. As far back as I can remember I've been obedient, adaptable, almost meek. Now that I think about it, I had one or two violent outbursts of

self-assertion as a little girl. But I remember also that Mother
punished all such lapses from convention with exemplary severity. For my sisters and me our entire upbringing was aimed at being *agreeable*. I was rather ugly and clumsy and was
constantly informed of the fact. By degrees I found that if I
kept my thoughts to myself and was ingratiating and far-
sighted, such behavior brought its rewards. The really big deception, however, occurred during puberty. All my thoughts,
feelings, and actions revolved around sex. I didn't let on
about this to my parents, or to anyone else for that matter.
Then it became second nature to be deceitful, surreptitious,
and secretive. My father wanted me to be a lawyer like
himself. I once hinted that I'd prefer to be an actress. Or at
any rate to have *something* to do with the theater. I remember they just laughed at me. So it has gone on and on. In my
relations with other people. In my relations with men. The
same perpetual dissimulation. The same desperate attempts
to please everybody. I have never thought: What do *I* want?
But always: What does *he* want me to want? It's not unself-
ishness as I used to think, but sheer cowardice, and what's
worse—utter ignorance of who I am. I have never lived a
dramatic life, I have no gift for that sort of thing. But for the
first time I feel intensely excited at the thought of finding out
exactly what I want to do with myself. In the snug little world
where both Johan and I have lived so unconsciously, taking
everything for granted, there is a cruelty and brutality im-
plied which frightens me more and more when I think back
on it. Outward security demands a high price: the acceptance
of a continuous destruction of the personality. (I think this
applies especially to women; men have somewhat wider
margins.) It is easy right at the outset to deform a little
child's cautious attempts at self-assertion. It was done in my
case with injections of a poison which is one hundred percent
effective: *bad conscience*. First toward Mother, then toward
those around me, and, last but not least, toward Jesus and
God. I see in a flash what kind of person I would have been
had I not allowed myself to be brainwashed. And I wonder
now whether I am hopelessly lost. Whether all the potential
for joy—joy for myself and others—that was innate in me is
dead or whether it's just asleep and can be awakened. I
wonder what kind of wife or woman I would have become if
I'd been able to use my resources as they were intended.
Would Johan and I have got married at all in that case? Yes,
I'm sure we would, because now that I think about it, we

were genuinely in love with each other in a devoted and passionate way. Our mistake was that we didn't break out of the family circle and escape far away and create something worthwhile on our own terms."

During the divorce scene, she tells Johan how she let him influence her thoughts and feelings:

"I've considered you far too much during our married life. I think consideration killed off love. Has it struck you that we never quarreled? I think we even thought it was vulgar to quarrel. No, we sat down and talked so sensibly to each other. And you, having studied more and knowing more about the mind, told me what I *really* thought. What I felt *deep down*. I never understood what you were talking about. I merely felt a heavy weight like a sorrow. Had I allowed myself not to react with a bad conscience, I'd have known that everything we said and did to each other was wrong."

Marianne's upbringing was designed to make her self-effacing, submissive and kind. It eradicated any tendencies towards self-assertion and self-awareness. Sex had to be repressed for it was seen as a threat to her dependence on her parents and a threat to her security. All her efforts were directed towards conforming her behavior, her thoughts and her feelings to society's expectations.

The conflict between her own feelings and efforts and the expectations of others led her to inhibit her growth neurotically to adopt an attitude of *regressive-narcissistic self-denial*.

But Johan also appears to have undergone such a conflict; which may serve as an example of the progressive (i.e. overcompensating) role in narcissistic collusion. He says:

"It was my father who had the great expectations, not I. But I wanted so desperately to please Daddy, so I tried all the time to live up to *his* expectations. Not mine. . . ."

And in the same dialogue, Marianne says of Johan:

"First it was your mother who adored you and thought you were a genius. And then the whole succession of women who have behaved in exactly the same way as your mother. Including me. I wonder what it is in you that sabotages all natural maturity."

Johan also failed to develop a self of his own, having sought instead to fulfil the internalized expectations of his parents and obediently function as an auxiliary of his ideal self. Marianne's function was to help him to meet his parents' expectations.

The socio-cultural aspect appears to determine the collusion in that neither partner is able to develop an autonomous self, but instead allows a false self to be imposed upon them—especially by their parents. The key to their marriage is therefore self-denial as this allows them to create an idealized symbiosis. The couple have thus violated the *demarcation principle*; in their external relationships they have failed to become independent from their parents, so they try to merge with each other to become whole. Marianne lives only through Johan and feels that she is indispensable to him, as she tells him after his trip with Paula:

> "I can't see how you're going to cope without me. Sometimes I feel quite desperate and think: *I must look after Johan*. He's my responsibility. It's up to me to see that Johan is all right. Only in that way will my life have a worthwhile meaning. One can't live alone and strong. One must have someone's hand to hold."

For Johan this is intolerable. He feels that through her self-denial Marianne is manipulating him and pushing him towards annihilation. So he tries to rid himself of her, to destroy her in order to gain his final freedom and be able to live independently. He tries, as a first step, to move to America with Paula. He does not succeed. Then, when discussing the divorce, he explodes in an outburst of hatred towards Marianne and attacks her. Throwing Marianne to the floor and treading on her with his foot, he breaks into a convulsive scream, "I'll kill you! I'll kill you! I'll kill you!" He does his utmost to destroy both their illusions of ever attaining symbiosis and security in love. He says to Marianne:

> "Do you know what my security looks like? I'll tell you. I think this way: Loneliness is absolute. It's an illusion to imagine anything else. Be aware of it. And try to act accordingly. Don't expect anything but trouble. If something nice happens, all the better. Don't think that you can ever do away with loneliness. It is absolute. You can invent fellowship on different levels, but it will only be a fiction about religion, politics, love, art, and so on. The loneliness is nonetheless complete. What's so treacherous is that sometime you may be struck by an idea of fellowship. Bear in mind that it's an illusion. Then you won't be disappointed afterwards, when

everything goes back to normal. You must live with the realization of absolute loneliness.''

If at first Marianne opposed Johan's emancipation and tried her utmost to restore their marital symbiosis, she now turns towards a genuine quest for her own development. She too has to draw a clearer boundary line between Johan and herself, uprooting him in order to make closer contact with herself. She tells Johan about her psychotherapy:

> . . . .I'm trying hard to learn to talk. Oh yes, and I got rid of your furniture and moved into your study. If you only knew what a bad conscience I had!—while at the same time feeling awfully daring.''

In both a literal and a figurative sense, she takes possession of their house and fills it with her own self, after throwing out all the keepsakes she had received from him. The demarcation is highly precarious, however, for she still finds she is deeply affected when he tries to resume their relationship after his trip with Paula.

> Marianne: But I'm bound to you. I can't think why. Maybe I'm a perverted masochist or else I'm just the faithful type who forms only one attachment in life. I don't know. It's so difficult, Johan. I don't want to live with anyone else. Other men bore me. I'm not saying this to give you a bad conscience or to blackmail you emotionally. I'm only telling you how it is. That's why I just can't bear it if you start kissing me and making love to me. Because then all my defenses break down. I can't explain it in any other way. And then it's so lonely again after you've gone.

As she says on the occasion of the divorce, she is still uncertain about whether or not she could manage to live on her own. She has to defend herself desperately against reuniting with Johan.

> Marianne: After a week or two we'd slip back into the old groove, our old nagging, our old aggressions. All our good resolutions would be forgotten. We wouldn't have learned anything. Everything would be the same as before. Or worse. It would be a mistake.

Marianne is also ready to destroy Johan in order to separate herself from him. For the first time she seems to realize how soft and vulnerable Johan really is and how much she has idealized him. When she realizes this, her reaction is one of disappointment and anger.

> Marianne: Do you suppose that I've gone through all I have and come out on the other side and started a life of my own which every day I'm thankful for, just to take charge of you and see that you don't go to the dogs because you're so weak and full of self-pity? If I didn't think you were so deplorable I'd laugh at you. When I think of what you've done to me during the last few years, I feel sick with fury. Go on, look at me. I'm proof against that gaze of yours. I've hardened myself. If you knew how many times I've dreamt I battered you to death, that I murdered you, that I stabbed you, that I kicked you. If you only knew what a goddamn relief it is to say all this to you at last.

The first years of their marriage correspond to narcissistic partner choice. The woman, in the position of complementary narcissist, gives herself to her husband, living for him and through him alone, while the man flourishes and grows in self-esteem because of his spouse's idealization of him. However, the crisis starts when the man begins to feel conditioned by her idealization and tries to rid himself of it. He does so by trying to destroy her, but this fills him with guilt.

His wife feels hurt and frustrated. However, this couple does not simply become trapped in a collusion, for the woman soon realizes that she should develop personally rather than let her husband be responsible for her. Because she is capable of doing this, she cannot be categorized as a neurotic narcissist. It is mainly as a result of her initiative that divorce proceedings are instituted. The divorce decree establishes an external boundary that protects and separates the partners from each other. However, internally they continue to be 'married at a distance.' This type of relationship enables both partners to reach the optimum interaction possible between them.

> Johan: I can only answer for myself. And I think I love you in my imperfect and rather selfish way. And at times I think you love me in your stormy, emotional way. In fact, I think that you and I

love one another. In an earthly and imperfect
way.

Neither places restrictive expectations on the other any longer.
Neither needs to keep the other at a distance by hurting or humiliating
them. Both achieve a high measure of true understanding for each other,
and an openness and sincerity in their love. They begin to find freedom
in their relationship and break out of the collusive pattern. Where the
woman had once done everything at home to care for the man, almost
suffocating him with attention, she now is able to just sit and watch
while he prepares a fire in the weekend cottage.

Would Marriage Therapy Help?

I shall ask a difficult and obviously hypothetical question. How could a
marriage therapist help this couple? Firstly, the practical question arises
as to whether or not both partners would be motivated by the idea of
changing themselves and their marital situation to undertake marriage
therapy. Despite their suffering, many couples cope with their difficulties and disturbances in order to avoid going through the pain of
therapy, choosing instead to be reconciled to a *status quo*. Marianne had
a little psychotherapy behind her and I have the impression that she ultimately coped better with the whole crisis than Johan did. Johan obviously has a low opinion of psychotherapy and does not seem willing to
start working on their crisis.

Johan:	(*Continuing*) And for that reason I never grew up. Why should I? It would mean that I was forced to manage on my own. I might even have to accept responsibility.
Marianne:	What an awful anticlimax, Johan dear.
Johan:	I don't *want* to mature, you see. That's why An- na is a good wife.

This would seem to show that they would not be equally willing to undergo psychotherapeutic treatment of their problem.

Still, let us assume that they would both genuinely desire therapeutic treatment of their marital entanglement. Would the outcome then
have been different and better? Viewed from the outside, their marriage
has broken down. From within, Marianne and Johan celebrate the twen-
tieth anniversary of their marriage in the final scene:

Marianne:	We're celebrating our twentieth anniversary. We got married in August twenty years ago.
Johan:	So we did. Twenty years.
Marianne:	A whole life. We've lived through a whole grown-up life with each other. How strange to think of it. (*Weeps suddenly*)
Johan:	(*Gently*) Dearest. Dearest heart.

Bergman seems to be suggesting that the only way this couple could achieve inner maturity was through external dissolution of their bond. Once the external bond was no more, the woman could achieve autonomous personal growth; Marianne could become Marianne and Johan could become Johan. The separation and demarcation, now externally secured, enabled the partners to come closer inwardly without the threat of symbiotic fusion.

Should I undertake to treat this couple, I would try to help them reach inner intimacy not through external separation but through *inner separation and demarcation!* I believe that for both partners the process of individual growth would have assumed different dimensions had they trodden this path together, recognizing clearly not only the unconscious interplay through which they immobilized each other, but also the related unconscious elements which could help them on their difficult path to maturity. And the way of therapy would certainly lead through the vale of tears; it is a difficult and painful journey. The psychological state of their relationship at the end of the film, when Marianne meets Johan seven years after their divorce, is depicted in the dream from which she awakes at Johan's side, crying in fear.

| Johan: | Don't you remember what frightened you? |
| Marianne: | We have to go along a dangerous road or something. I want you to take my hands so that we can hold onto each other. (*Frightened*) But it's no good. I no longer have any hands. I have only a couple of stumps that end at the elbows. At that moment I am slithering in soft sand. I can't get hold of you. You're all standing up there on the road and I can't reach you. |

The emancipation of Marianne, as the dream suggests, does not consist in liberation but, unfortunately, amputation. True, she is standing there on her own feet, yet the ground she is standing on is not firm but of shifting sand. She would like to give Johan her hand so that they can hold each other firmly. But her hands are gone, only her upper arms are left. She despairs when she is not able to reach him. The film ends with an air of fear and confusion; with the impression that it has all gone from bad to worse, with no apparent answer in sight. The couple confess their love to each other, a subtle but fragile love strengthened by doubts which prevent them from trusting each other.

I would not see the purpose of therapy as trading the autonomy and self-realization of the partners for the amputation of the potential in their relationship. Rather it should enable them to find a dialectical equilibrium between the need to develop their own personalities and the yearning for a way of life together, as a balance between 'self-realization within marriage' and 'self-realization through marriage.'

BRIEF GLOSSARY OF TERMS

Ambivalence (E. BLEULER): concurrence of opposite emotions, e.g. repulsion-attraction.

Anal-sadistic stage (FREUD): developmental stage between the ages of two and four, comprising the establishment of basic ego-functions (speech, self-assertion), independent fully-developed mobility (running, climbing, mastering one's environment), and control of sphincter muscles (toilet-training) (see page 59). Fixation on this phase in maturity engenders anal-retentive character traits (see page 98), such as excessive possessiveness, orderliness, penny-pinching, or the opposite of anal desire such as messiness or squandering. The sadistic character trait manifests itself in the desire to govern, and the masochistic trait in the desire for submission and passive abandon.

Autonomy: self-determination, independence.

Claustrophobia: irrational, neurotic fear of confined spaces.

Collusion: (lat. colludere = play together) in this book, a concealed, often unconscious game between partners played over a period of time as a defense enabling them to cope with the fears and guilt feelings they share unconsciously, and as a result of which each considers himself to be inseparable from the other (see page 166).

Compensation (ADLER): levelling up. *Decompensation*: refusal to make mental efforts towards levelling up; loss of mental balance and functional ability. *Overcompensation*: exaggerated striving towards the preservation or restoration of mental balance, or the equalization of low self-esteem.

Complementary: designed to complete.

Counter-transference: analyst's emotional reaction to the client's transference onto him, often strongly influenced by the analyst's personal conflict bias.

Dyad: two-person group. *Intradyadic*: within the pair; *extradyadic*: outside the pair.

Identity: sameness, the perception of oneself as an integral, continuous and meaningful entity.

Inadequate: unable to cope with a situation.

Interindividual: between several individuals.

Internalize: identify oneself internally with the concepts, expectations, words and ideas of another.

Intraindividual: within the same individual.

Libido: (lat. desire, love) according to Freud, sexual energy as the principal vehicle of mental development.

Narcissism (FREUD): self-love. In psychoanalysis, a state in which the libido governs the ego and turns it into a sexual object (see pp 59, 61).

Oedipus complex (FREUD): according to ancient Greek legend, Oedipus murdered his father and married his mother, unaware of their relationship to him. Psychoanalysis adopted the legend to describe the erotic attachment of the son to his mother, and his rivalry with his father. Fear of the father (or mother) leads to *castration anxiety*. Especially active in the phallic-oedipal stage between the ages of four and seven years (see pp 59, 123). A close, though inexact, counterpart in the daughter's attachment to her father is described as *Electra complex* (c. g. jung).

Oral: (lat. os = mouth), referring to the mouth. *Oral stage* (FREUD): developmental stage from birth until the end of the first year (see pp 59, 80). *Oral character*: greedy, unsatisfied, desirous of care, tenderness and protection (see page 85).

Progressive: directed forward. In this book, compulsory drive towards tough, controlled, 'mature and adult' behavior. *Regressive*: reversion to an earlier developmental stage. In this book, helpless, child-like, dependent and irresponsible behavior.

Transference: in psychoanalysis, generally a redirection of emotional conflicts with any person, particularly one's parents, towards a therapist.

BIBLIOGRAPHY

Abraham, K. "Äusserungsformen des weiblichen Kastrationskomplexes." *Int. Ztschr. Psa.* VII (1921):422–452.

Argelander, H. *Gruppenprozesse. Wege zur Anwendung der Psychoanalyse in Behandlung, Lehre und Forschung.* Reinbek: Rowohlt, 1972.

Argyle, M. *The Psychology of Interpersonal Behaviour.* London: Pelican, 1967.

Arieti, S. *Interpretation of Schizophrenia.* New York: Brunner, 1955.

Bach, G. R. & Wyden, P. *Intimate Enemy: How to Fight Fair in Love and Marriage.* New York: Morrow, 1969.

Baker Miller, J. *Psychoanalysis and Women.* New York: Penguin Books, 1973.

Balint, M. *Thrills and Regressions.* New York: Intnl. Univs. Pr., 1959.
Primary Love and Psychoanalytic Technique. London: The Hogarth Press, 1965.

Bannister, K. & Pincus, L. *Shared Fantasy in Marital Problems: Therapy in a Four Person Relationship.* London: The Tavistock Institute of Human Relations, 1971.

Bateson, G., Jackson, D. D., Haley, J. & Weakland, J. W. "Towards a Theory of Schizophrenia." In *Schizophrenia and the Family,* edited by Theodore Lidz et al. New York: Intnl. Univs. Pr., 1967.

Beckmann, D. *Der Analytiker und sein Patient.* Bern: Huber, 1974.
"Paardynamik und Gesundheitsverhalten." In *Familie und seelische Krankheit,* edited by H. E. Richter, H. Strotzka, J. Willi, pp. 123–130. Reinbek: Rowohlt, 1976.
"Selbst- und Fremdbild der Frau." *Familiendynamik* 2 (1977):35– 49.

Beckmann, D., Braehler, E., and Richter, H. E. *Neustandardisierung des Giessen-Tests (GT).* Unpublished manuscript, 1977.

Bergman, I. *Scenes from a Marriage.* Translated from the Swedish by Alan Blair. London: Calder & Boyers, 1974.

Bion, W. R. *Experiences in Groups.* London: Tavistock Publications, 1961.

Boszormenyi-Nagy, I. & Spark, G. *Invisible Loyalties.* Hagerstown, MD: Harper & Row, 1973.

Bowen, M. "Family and Family Group Therapy." In *Comprehensive Group Psychotherapy,* edited by Harold I. Kaplan & Benjamin J. Saddock. Baltimore: Williams & Wilkins, 1971.
"On the Differentiation of Self." In *Family Interaction: A Dialogue between Family Researchers and Family Therapists,* edited by James Framo et al. New York: Springer Publishing, 1972.

Caruso, I. A. *Soziale Aspekte der Psychoanalyse*. Stuttgart: Klett, 1962.
 Die Trennung der Liebenden. Eine Phänomenologie des Todes. Bern: Huber, 1968.
Collins, V., Kreitman, N., Nelson, B. & Troop, J. "Neurosis and Marital Interaction. III. Family Roles and Functions." *Brit. J. Psychiat.* 119 (1971): 233–242.
D'Eaubonne, F. *Feminismus oder Tod*. Munich: Frauenoffensive, 1975.
Deutsch, H. "Kasuistik zum 'induzierten Irresein'." *Wien. Klin. Wschr.* 31 (1918): 809–812.
Dicks, H. *Marital Tensions: Clinical Studies Towards a Psychological Theory of Interaction*. New York: Basic Books, 1967.
Duss-von Werdt, J. *Die Junge Kleinfamilie*. Forthcoming.
Engel, G. L. *Psychological Development in Health and Disease*. Philadelphia: W. B. Saunders, 1962.
Erikson, E. H. *Childhood and Society*. (revised edition). St. Albans: Triad/Paladin, 1977.
 "The Problem of Ego-Identity." *J. Amer. Psa. Assoc.* 4:56–121.
Ezriel, H. "A Psychoanalytic Approach to Group Treatment." *Brit J. Med. Psychol.* 23 (1950):59–74.
Fairbairn, W. R. *Psychoanalytic Studies of the Personality*. London: Tavistock Publications, 1952.
Freud, S. *Psychoneuroses*. New York: Johnson Reprint, 1909.
 "Three Contributions to the Theory of Sex." In *The Basic Writings of Sigmund Freud*. New York: The Modern Library, 1938.
 Totem and Taboo. New York: W. W. Norton, 1952.
Fuller, F. F. "Influence of Sex of Counselor and of Client on Client Expressions of Feeling." *J. Counsel. Psychol.* 10 (1963):34–40.
Gastager, H. *Die Fassadenfamilie*. Munich: Kindler, 1973.
Grinberg, L., Langer, M. & Rodriqué, E. *Psicoterapie del Grupo; su Enfoque Psico-Analitico*. Buenos Aires, 1957.
Grotjahn, M. *Psychoanalysis and the Family Neurosis*. New York: W. W. Norton, 1960.
Haley, J. *Strategies of Psychotherapy*. New York: Grune & Stratton, 1963.
Heider, F. *The Psychology of Interpersonal Relations*. New York: John Wiley, 1958.
Heigl-Evers, A. *Konzepte der analytischen Gruppenpsychotherapie*. Gottingen: Vandenhoek & Ruprecht, 1972.
Jung, C. G. *Psychological Types*. Collected Works, vol. 6. Princeton: Princeton U. P., 1979.
Kemper, W. "Die Gegenübertragung." *Psyche* 7 (1952):593.
Klein, M. *Das Seelenleben des Kleinkindes und andere Beiträge zur Psychoanalyse*. Stuttgart: Klett, 1962.
Kohut, H. *Analysis of Self: A Systematic Approach to the Psychoanalytic Treatment of Narcissistic Personality Disorders*. New York: Intnl. Univs. Pr., 1971.
Kreitman, N. "The Patient's Spouse." *Brit. J. Psychiat.* 110 (1964):159–173.
 "Married Couples admitted to Mental Hospitals." *Brit. J. Psychiat.* 114 (1968):699–718.
Kreitman, N., Collins, Y., Nelson, B. & Troop, J. "Neurosis and Marital Interaction. IV. Manifest Psychological Interaction." *Brit. J. Psychiat.* 119 (1971):243–252.

Kuiper, P. C. *Die seelischen Krankheit des Menschen*. Bern / Stuttgart: Huber / Klett, 1968.

Laing, R. D. *The Divided Self*. New York: Pantheon, 1969. *The Self and Others*. London: Penguin, 1972.

Laplanche, J. & Pontalis, J.-B. *The Language of Psycho-Analysis*. Translated from the French by Donald Micholson-Smith. New York: W. W. Norton, 1974.

Lemaire, J.-G. *Ehekonflikte. Ursachen und Hilfe*. (Translated from the French). Gottingen: Vandenhoek & Ruprecht, 1968.

Lidz, T. *The Person: His Development Throughout the Life Cycle*. New York: Basic Books, 1968.

Locke, H. J. *Predicting Adjustment in Marriage: A Comparison of a Divorced and a Happily Married Group*. Westport: Greenwood, 1968.

Macoby, E. E. & Jacklin, C. N. *The Psychology of Sex Differences*. Stanford: Stanford U. Pr., 1974.

Mainprice, J. *Marital Interaction and some Illnesses in Children*. London: The Tavistock Institute of Human Relations (Institute of Marital Studies), 1974.

Mandel, A., Mandel, K. H., Stadter, E. & Zimmer, D. *Einübing in Partnerschaft durch Kommunikationstherapie und Verhaltenstherapie*. Munich: Pfeiffer, 1971.

Manika, C. "Sind Frauen 'fraulicher' und Männer 'männlicher,' wenn sie in der Paarsituation aufeinander bezogen sind? Untersuchung mit dem Individuellen und Gemeinsamen Rorschach-Versuch. *Familiendynamik* 3 (1978).

Masters, W. H. & Johnson, V. E. *Human Sexual Inadequacy*. Harpers Ferry: Little Brown, 1970.

McCall, G. J. & Simmons, J. L. *Identities and Interactions*. New York: Free Press, 1966.

Mead, M. *Male and Female*. New York: Wm. Morrow, 1975.

Meerwein, F. *Die Grundlagen des ärztlichen Gesprachs*. Bern: Huber, 1969.

Minuchin, S. *Families and Family Therapy*. Cambridge, MA: Harvard U. Pr., 1974.

Mitscherlich, A. *Krankheit als Konflikt*. Studien zur psychosomatischen Medizin, 2. Frankfurt: Suhrkamp, 1967.

Mittelmann, B. "Complementary Neurotic Reactions in Intimate Relationships." *Psychoanalyt. Quart.* 13 (1944):479-483.

Nelson, B., Collins, Y., Kreitman, N. & Troop, J. "Neurosis and Marital Interaction. II. Time Sharing and Social Activity." *Brit. J. Psychiat.* 117 (1970): 47-58.

Newcomb, T. M. *The Acquaintance Process*. New York: Irvington, 1961.

Nielson, J. "Mental Disorders in Married Couples (Assortative Mating)." *Brit. J. Psychiat.* 110 (1964):683-697.

Ovenstone, I. M. K. "The Development of Neurosis in the Wives of Neurotic Men. Part I. Symptomatology and Personality." *Brit. J. Psychiat.* 122 (1973):35-45.

Parkes, C. M., Benjamin, B. & Fitzgerald, R. G. "Broken Heart: A Statistical Study of Increased Mortality among Widowers." *Brit. Med. J.* 1 (1969): 740-743.

Penrose, L. "Mental Illness in Husband and Wife." *Psychiat. Quart. Suppl.* 18 (1944).

Pulver, S. E. & Brunt, M. Y. "Deflection of hostility in folie à deux." *Arch. Gen. Psychiat.* 5 (1961):257-265.

Richter, H. E. *Eltern, Kind und Neurose.* Reinbek: Rowohlt, 1967.
   *The Family as Patient. The Origin, Nature and Treatment of Marital and
   Family Conflicts.* Translated from the German by Denver and Helen
   Lindley. New York: Farrar, Strauss & Giroux, 1973.
   Die Gruppe. Reinbek: Rowohlt, 1972.
   Lernziel Solidarität. Reinbek: Rowohlt, 1974.
Richter, H. E. & Beckmann, D. *Herzneurose.* Stuttgart: Thieme, 1969.
Scharfetter, C. *Symbiontische Psychosen.* Baltimore: Williams & Wilkins, 1970.
Schenda, R. *Das Eland der alten Leute.* Dusseldorf: Patmos, 1972.
Scheu, U. *Wir werden nicht als Mädchen geboren—wir werden dazu gemacht.*
   Frankfurt: Fischer, 1977.
Schindler, R. "Grundprinzipien der Psychodynamik in der Gruppe." *Psyche* 11
   (1957 / 58):308.
   "Über den wechselseitigen Einfluss von Gesprächsinhalt, Gruppenposition
   und Ich-Gestalt in der analytischen Gruppenpsychotherapie." *Psyche* 14
   (1960 / 61):382.
Schur, M. *Comments on the Metapsychology of Somatization.* The Psycho-
   analytic Study of the Child, edited by Ruth S. Eissler et al, vol. 10. New
   York: Intnl. Univs. Pr., 1945.
Schwäbisch, L. & Siems, M. *Anleitung zum sozialen Lernen für Paare, Gruppen
   und Erzieher.* Reinbek: Rowohlt, 1974.
Searles, H. F. "The Effort to Drive the Other Person Crazy—an Element in the
   Aetiology and Psychotherapy of Schizophrenia." In *Schizophrenia and the
   Family,* edited by Theodore Lidz et al. New York: Intnl. Univs. Pr., 1967.
Slater, E. & Woodside, M. *Patterns of Marriage.* London: Cassell, 1951.
Spitz, R. A. & Cobliner, W. G. *The First Year of Life.* New York: Intnl. Univs.
   Pr., 1966.
Stierlin, H. *Das Tun des Einen ist das Tun des Anderen.* Frankfurt: Suhrkamp,
   1971.
   "Trennungskonflikte bei Jugendlichen." *Psyche* 28 (1974):719–746.
   Eltern und Kinder im Prozess der Ablösung. Frankfurt: Suhrkamp, 1975.
   Von der Psychoanalyse zur Familientherapie. Stuttgart: Klett, 1975.
   "Familiendynamische Aspekte der Übertragen und Gegenübertragung."
   Familiendynamik 2 (1977):182–197.
Stock-Whitaker, D. & Lieberman, A. *Psychotherapy through the Group Pro-
   cess.* London: Tavistock Publications, 1965.
Stuart, R. B. "Operant—Interpersonal Treatment for Marital Discord." *Journal
   of Consulting and Clinical Psychology* 33 (1969):675–682.
Straus, M. A. "Cultural and Social Organizational Influences on Violence be-
   tween Family Members." In *Configurations: Biological and Sexual Factors
   in Sexual and Family Life,* edited by R. Price & D. Barrier, Lexington, MA:
   Lexington Books, 1974.
Watzlawick, P., Beavin, J. H. & Jackson, D. D. *Pragmatics of Human Com-
   munication.* New York: W. W. Norton, 1967.
Wickler, W. *Sind wir Sünder? Naturgesetze der Ehe.* Munich: Knaur, 1969.
Wienold, W. H. *Kontakt, Einfühlung und Attraktion. Zur Entwicklung von
   Paarbeziehungen.* Stuttgart: Enke, 1972.
Willi, J. "Die Schizophrenie in ihrer Auswirkung auf die Eltern." *Schweiz.
   Arch. Neurol., Neurochir., Psychiat.* 89 (1962):426–463.
   "Der Gemeinsame Rorschach-Versuch, ein Mittel zum Studium von Part-
   nerbeziehungen." *Psychother. Psychosom.* 16 (1968a):375–384.

"Der Gemeinsame Rorschach-Versuch, ein diagnostisches Hilfsmittel in der Eheberatung." *Ehe* 5 (1968b):163–175.

"Joint Rorschach testing of partner relationships." *Family Process* 8 (1969):64–78.

"Zur Psychopathologie der Hysterischen Ehe." *Nervenarzt* 41 (1970):157–165.

"Die psychologische Beziehung zwischen Partnerwahl und Ehekonflikt." *Neue Zürcher Zeitung* Nos. 65 and 89, 1971.

"Die hysterische Ehe." *Psyche* 24 (1972a):326–356.

"Die angstneurotische Ehe." *Nervenarzt* 43 (1972b):399–408.

Die Kollusion als Grundbegriff für die Ehepsychologie und Ehetherapie. Sonderheft Gruppenpsychotherapie und Gruppendynamik. Gottingen: Vandenhoek & Ruprecht, 1972c.

"Ehekonflikt und Partnerwahl." In *Almanach*, pp. 95–112. Stuttgart: Stuttg. Akad. Tiefenpsycholog. und analyt. Psychother. e. V., 1973.

"Zur Psychodynamik und Therapie ehelicher Dreiecksbeziehungen." *Psychosomatische Medizin* 4 (1973):193–198.

Der Gemeinsame Rorschach-Versuch. Bern: Hans Huber, 1973.

"The Hysterical Marriage." In *Contemporary Marriage, Structure, Dynamics and Therapy*, edited by Henry Grunebaum and Jacob Christ, pp. 435–456. Boston: Little Brown, 1976.

Therapie der Zweierbeziehung. Reinbek: Rowohlt, 1978.

Willi, J. & Rotach, M. "Über die spezifische Struktur und Dynamik der Ehepaar-Therapiegruppe." *Ehe* 4 (1970):165.

Winch, R. F. *Mate Selection: A Study of Complementary Needs.* New York: Harper & Row, 1958.

INDEX

Adjustment, mutual, 35, 157, 160
Affective equivalence, 214
Alliance, 172, 176
Anal sadistic, character, 99
    collusion, 95, 102
    jealousy-infidelity collusion, 115
    parent-child collusion, 97
    power-struggle, 110
    stage of development, 96
Anorexia nervosa, 87, 172
Argelander, H., 168
Argyle, M., 159

Balance, individual, 120, 124
    inter-individual, 122, 124
    of autonomy and dependence, 10, 29
    of debit and credit, 205
    of self-esteem, 24
    therapeutic, 232-236
Balint, M., 22, 112
Battle of the sexes, 12
Beckmann, D., 3, 4, 9, 13, 202, 228
Behavioral counselling, 139
Bergman, I., 237-253
Biases, common unconscious, 147, 167
Bion, W. R., 168
Boszormenyi-Nagy, I. et al, 6, 176, 187, 205
Boundaries of the dyadic system, 18
Bowen, M., 26

Childhood and marital conflict, 23, 48
Children, 173, 187
    in collusion with parents, 83, 97, 190
    role in marital conflict, 41

Choice of partner, 32, 125, 133
    heterogamy, 158
    homogamy, 158
    mutual adjustment, 159-162
    not a key-in-lock phenomenon, 158
Collusion, anal-sadistic, 95
    between physician and patient, 216
    between therapist and patient, 229
    bibliographical references, 167
    choice of partner, 158
    concept, 52, 55
    definition, 55, 162, 164
    destructive arrangement, 152
    in group processes, 167
    narcissistic, 60
    neurotic conflict as, 162, 163
    of family, 191
    oral, 80
    patterns, 57
    phallic-oedipal, 120
    psychosomatic, 193-218
    similar basic disturbances, 55, 147
Communication, psychosomatic, 202
    theory, 48, 50, 51, 193, 235
Conjoint therapy, 233
Conversion symptoms, 211
Coping mechanisms, 124, 171, 174
Counter transference, 221-225, 235
Couple formation, 32
Crisis, in phases of marriage, 31-43
    marriage as an institution, 11, 19

Defense syndrome, as progressive and
    regressive behavior, 21-24, 141-155
    psychosomatic illness, 199

Demarcation principle, 18, 176
Denfield, 20
Dicks, H., 45, 166–168
Differentiation of self, 26
Divorce, 11, 38, 230
Duss-von Werdt, J., 3
Dyad, balance in, 144, 146
    dynamic principles of, 17–29
    extra-dyadic boundaries, 18
    intra-dyadic boundaries, 18
Dynamic principles of partner
    relationships, 17

Engel, G. L., 80, 81, 212
Equal self-esteem, 24
Erikson, E. H., 32, 69, 81, 83
Extramarital relations, 19, 38, 115, 178
Ezriel, H., 168

Fairbairn, W. R., 166
Family therapy, 20, 50, 187
Fear of marriage, 72
Formation of stable couple, 32
Freud, S., 69, 200
Fuller, F. F., 3

Goals of therapy, 20, 230–236
Grinberg, L. et al, 168

Heider, F., 160
Heigl-Evers, A., 168

Illness behavior, help rejection, 207
    of partner, 193–218
    of psychosomatic patient, 193–218
Individualistic approach to marital
    therapy, 46–48, 223, 233
Infidelity-jealousy collusion, 115
Insight, 232
Interaction personality, 9, 159

Jealousy-infidelity collusion, 115
Joint Rorschach procedure (Willi), 9, 159

Kemper, W., 221
Klein, M., 166
Kohut, H., 62, 221
Kreitman, N., 158, 159

Laing, R. D., 159, 160, 165, 166
Lidz, T., 35

Macoby, E. & Jacklin, C., 9
Mainprice, J., 168
Marriage, contract, 19, 20
    institution, 19
    fear of, 72
    phases of, 31
Masochistic character, 107
Midlife crisis, 37
Miller, Jean Baker, 9, 10
Minuchin, S., 17, 20
Mitscherlich, A., 200, 211

Narcissistic, character, 61
    collusion, 61, 67–80
    complementary character, 70
    partner relationship, 67
Neutralization of conflict, 193

Old age, marriage in, 43
Oral, character, 80, 85
    collusion, 80, 83, 88–95
    mother-child collusion, 83
    stage of development, 80

Phases of marriage, 31
Possessiveness, 96–97, 179
Power struggle, 110
Procreation, 35
Progressive defense behavior, 23
Projection, 123
Psychoanalysis, and couples therapy, 219
    and marital conflicts, 45
Psychosomatic illnesses of couples, 193

Reaction formation, 23
Regressive defense behavior, 23
Richter, H., 3, 10, 120, 121, 190, 202
Role differentiation, 125
Rorschach tests *cf Joint Rorschach*

Sadistic character, 107
Sado-masochistic collusion, 107
Scheu, U., 9
Schur, M., 201
Secondary gain from illness, 205

Self, individual, 148
  mutual, 39, 148, 150
Slater, E. & Woodside, M., 159
Stages of marriage, 31
Stierlin, H., 7, 9, 187
Stock-Whitaker, D. & Lieberman, A., 168
Straus, M. A., 5
Stress, correlatives, 215
  couples in, 145

Therapy of marital conflict, individual, 223
  conjoint, 233
Triangulation of couple conflict, 171–191

Watzlawick, P. et al, 25, 51, 110, 160, 194, 202, 224
Wienold, W. H., 160
Willi, J., 25, 126, 232